Ikka Boyd grew up in Finland during the War. Her mother's family, who were farmers, used to send them extra rations. Ikka and her little playmates soon turned the butter and honey into toffee. In these childhood games, Ikka always liked to play the cook, never the princess!

Ikka grew up, went to University and eventually married an English lawyer. They started touring France on holidays, what a new world of food and wine they found.

When Ikka's two children were small, she and a friend started an outside catering company, 'Victoria Cooks', which thrived for 10 years in London.

Now she and her family live in Herefordshire where Ikka often writes about food in the local paper and loves cooking for the family, village functions and for the Herefordshire branch of International Wine and Food Society, which she originally started.

RECIPES FOR MY DAUGHTER

Ikka Boyd

Recipes for
My Daughter

Vanguard Press

VANGUARD PAPERBACK

© Copyright 2002
Ikka Boyd

A CIP catalogue record for this title is
available from the British Library
ISBN 1 903489 58 X

Photographs by the courtesy of Ronald Wilkins

Vanguard Press is an imprint of
Pegasus Elliot MacKenzie Publishers Ltd.
www.pegasuspublishers.com

First Published in 2002

Vanguard Press
Sheraton House Castle Park
Cambridge England

Printed & Bound in Great Britain

Dedication

This book is dedicated with love to my daughter, Karin, my husband, John, and my son, Roderick, without whom this book would never have been written.

Foreword

Ikka Boyd's delightful book is the result of a lifetime's interest in food, natural greed (her own admission) and the courage to try new dishes then attempting to make them herself.

Her initial interest was probably based on the good cooking she had at home in Finland. Her mother was a natural cook who had some training but learnt a lot at home on the farm. After Ikka's mother married, she started a business which gave her the chance to stay in top-flight hotels where she found classical French and other European dishes which she then reproduced at home. It was in this environment that, as a child, Ikka was encouraged to make culinary experiments.

She married an Englishman, settled in this country and learnt about English food and cooking. Later on, when the family acquired a cottage in France, Ikka was bowled over with the refinement of French cuisine. By the 70s, she had become a fully-fledged 'foodie' inspired by the recipes of Robert Carrier and Elizabeth David.

A friend urged Ikka to join her in a catering venture in London, so enabling her to develop her great interest into a business. She and her late partner ran 'Victoria's Cooks' successfully for 10 years, building up a clientele which included The Good Food Guide, The International Wine and Food Society, the Finnish Embassy plus many business firms – and brought up two children at the same time.

Though she has retired now, she still loves to spend time in her kitchen as a recreation, entertaining friends and members of the Herefordshire Branch of The International Wine and Food Society which she founded.

And so, the circle has joined. The main reason for writing this book, which includes many of the recipes from around the world that Ikka has cooked over the years, planning hassle-free dinner parties and so much more culinary wisdom, was to satisfy the pleading of her newly-married daughter for advice and to ensure that these favourite recipes, some of her own childhood, would not be lost – maybe to be carried over for another generation.

Margaret Drake
Editor, Food & Wine Newsletter
The International Wine & Food Society

Articles

Recipes

STARTERS

Asparagus & Egg Mousse	114
Asparagus with Sauce Ravigote	119
Aubergine Pâté	82
Avocado Mousse	76
Avocado Purée (Guacamole)	79
Brussels Soup	98
Buckwheat Pancakes with Smoked Salmon	93
Ceviche (Raw Marinated Fish)	120
Chicken & Avocado Soup	90
Cold Apple & Parsnip Soup	89
Crab Gumbo	99
Crab Mousse	78
Crème Vichyssoise (Leek & Potato Soup)	105
Cucumber Mousse	71
Egg Mayonnaise	96
Egg Mousse	74
Fennel Baked with Cheese	94
Finnish Fish Soup	70
Finnish Summer Soup	106
Finnish Yoghurt (Viili)	73
French Fish Soup	84
Garlic Mushrooms	122
Gazpacho – Iced Soup	113
Herring Eye	81
Jansson's Temptation	83
Leeks Provençale	80
Marinaded Kippers	107
Melitzanes – Tomato & Aubergine Bake	108
Melba Toast	101
Mushrooms à la Grèque	118
Mussels Gratinée – Façon Marianne	111
Onion Quiche	102
Onion Tomato & Basil Flan	115
Red Pepper Mousse	100
Rillettes (Potted Pork)	87
Risotto with Sprue Asparagus	103
Simple Danish Pâté	95
Smoked Haddock in Cream & Spring Onion Sauce	69
Smoked Haddock Mousse	117
Smoked Mackerel Pâté	116
Smoked Salmon Pâté	112
Smoked Trout Pâté	104
Soup of Jerusalem Artichokes	92
Spare Ribs of Pork – Chinese Style	121

MAIN COURSE DISHES

Baked Plaice or Sole	146
Beef Nasi Goreng	179
Beef Olives	186
Beef Stew with Red Wine	131
Beef Stroganoff	142
Butterfly Chicken	167
Cabbage Parcels (Dolmas)	169
Casseroled Pheasant or Pigeon	173
Chicken Breast Stuffed with Herb Cheese	135
Chicken Liver Pilau	194
Chicken with a Wine & Mustard Sauce	183
Christmas Ham	172
Curried Meat Balls	163
Fillet Steak with Béarnaise Sauce	157
Finnish Meat Balls with Piquant Sauce	191
Finnish Steak with Onion	158
Fish in Dill Sauce	137
Fish Pie	134
Grilled Fresh Mackerel with Mustard	161
Haddock & Sweetcorn Bake	198
Ham in Jelly – Jambon Persillé	139
Hamburgers à la Lindström	197
Hot Madras Curry	165
Jellied Beef	141
Kedgeree	175
Lamb Rogan Gosh	178
Lemon Chicken	185
Meat Galantine	140
Mini Smörgåsbord	195
Minute Steak	160
Moroccan Lamb	189
Moussaka	143
Pasta with Blue Cheese Sauce	193
Poached Chicken with Pepper Mayonnaise	150
Pork Goulash – Hungarian	196
Pork Steaks with Paprika Sauce	170
Pork with Prunes	145
Prawn & Fetta Ragout	127
Quick Seafood Pilau	154
Rich Venison Pie	204
Roast Duck with Apple & Celery Stuffing	181
Roast Goose Dinner	176
Roast Hake	138
Roast Lamb with Crust	155

ACCOMPANIMENTS
AND OTHER DISHES

SAUCES, DRESSINGS & SALADS

Apple Sauce	252
Béarnaise Sauce	251
Blue Cheese Dressing	258
Cold Herb Sauce for Salmon	248
Cold Piquant Sauce	255
Cold Sauce Sabayon	256
French Dressing	258
French Dressing with Olive Oil	261
Hollandaise Sauce	249
Hot Piquant Sauce with Tomatoes	254
Mustard Dressing for Smoked Salmon	262
Onion Sauce	253
Oriental Dressing	261
Parisian Dressing	259
Remoulade Sauce	250
Sauce for Cold Turkey	260
Sour Cream Dressing for Salmon	263
Swedish Sauce	247
Tomato Sauce for Pasta or Pizza	257

Salads

Aubergine Salad	272
Bean Salad	247
Easy Lentil Salad	275
Ham with Grape Salad	267
Herring Salad with Beetroot Dressing	269
Kalamares Salad	271
Mixed Bean Salad	276
Seafood Salad	273
Westcoast Salad	268

PUDDING DISHES

BAKING RECIPES

DRINKS PARTY SNACKS & DIPS

Karin's Plea

"Mum, when are you going to finish that cookery book? I need it NOW!"

Some years later: "All right, I know there will be no cookery book: just give me the recipes on bits of paper so I can use them."

Later still: "You promised to do it when you moved down to the country, but you have not even started yet!"

This has been the story of my book, which I have been longing to write as I know it is there, just ready to get onto the typewriter. I planned to produce a book in which I would collect together all I had learnt about cooking over the years though, of course, one goes on learning all the time. The book would be something useful, something of myself. Perhaps my family would pass it on to the grandchildren one day.

Some of my hesitancy is, perhaps, because I am not trained in cooking. I just love pottering in the kitchen and sharing the good things that come out of it with my family and friends. Perhaps I have some natural talent for it as even at school I always got top marks in cooking, which amazed me as I never tried particularly hard.

I remember, from my school days, all those lessons when I never seemed to get the sponge cake mixture quite right, however long I whipped it. We also had to do some very dreary dishes. The worst I remember was called 'False meat soup'. It may have been a war-time recipe. It consisted mostly of bones, a few root vegetables and oats to add bulk. The recipe I found most impressive was a millefeuille; a wonderful gateau made of about 6 layers of the thinnest pastry, interleaved with strawberries and cream. I have never dared to make it since!

Like most cooks, I have collected boxes of recipes and newspaper cuttings since my discovery, in the sixties, of the food articles of Robert Carrier in The Sunday Times, and the cookery books of Elizabeth David. This coincided with a period of our starting to go on holiday to France, where we eventually bought a small holiday home, an old barn now converted to a cottage.

Today I use few cookery books, but read them avidly and dip into my old files when I need some ideas.

I have heard many say, and I agree with them, that as one gets older one's preference is more for simple food cooked really well. The homelier dishes appeal more than the very rich, elaborate ones. My mother was a very good cook. She came from farming stock and could cook traditional farm fare, but also some rather elegant food. She had actually been to cookery school for a month or two, and her job had taken her to many good hotels where she had sampled fine food.

As I come from Finland, you may wonder how good the food there really is. In fact it can be pretty good, especially in first class restaurants. There the chefs have been classically trained in French 'haute cuisine'. One thing about the Finns; they are eager to learn and copy where they see real excellence.

Ethnic cooking, the simple peasant dishes that involve making something delicious out of almost nothing, or at least from very humble ingredients, appeals to me. This sort of cooking takes some time and may not be easy. Try making cabbage dolmas or apple strudel! However, these dishes are worth the effort and can often be made in big batches and eaten over several meals. Good party food, too.

I am thinking particularly of the wonderful Finnish feasts you always get at country celebrations, weddings and funerals. Apart from the marinaded fish dishes and freshly smoked fish, home cured ham, local cheeses and traditional salads, etc. you are offered at least 4 traditional vegetable dishes, baked in the oven, and several casseroles containing meat and game. All these things keep well and improve with re-heating.

There are so many different types of cooking. Nowadays we tend to prefer the quick grills, pasta dishes and stir-fries to save time. I prefer the slow roast and slowly cooked stews, where the flavours develop and create an amazing harmony. Just think of the odd ingredients we may put in a dish: cubes of bacon, onion, bits of carrots, some mushrooms, a few herbs, perhaps some garlic, a glass of wine and a piece of meat or chicken. A few hours later the heat has worked its magic and turned these scraps of food into an aromatic and delicious feast! It never fails to amaze me.

It is not wise to include dishes for parties that need last minute attention. You do not want to appear at the dining table with a shining red face, your hair all over the place and your nerves probably shattered, too. My advice is, cook these dishes for just a few friends and stick to the more traditional slow cooked dishes for more formal parties.

This book is going to reflect my background and the places where I have learnt about good food, Scandinavia, where I come from, England where there are so many good ingredients and France with its great culinary tradition.,

My own repertoire was greatly widened by my 10 years in outside catering in London. I still shudder at this description of my activities as a caterer. It always seemed to be more accurately described as a party planner with food as a vital part. So often clients came to us having no idea what they wanted and what would be acceptable to their guests. I and my partners had to draw on our own experience of what we would like ourselves on a similar occasion. It gave me a great deal of satisfaction if the party got really going, if people chatted and had fun. I think we played a real part in relaxing people and most people always cheer up when they see food, especially journalists!

We cooked everything fresh in my kitchen or in my partners' home. Nothing was frozen, before or after cooking. we devised our own menus and often had to choose the wines for the meal. The prices we charged were reasonable. Our service was efficient, but friendly and informal. I did not have to look far for ideas. I cooked dishes I knew well. I remember putting down the first fifteen menus with 3-course meals in bed one Sunday morning and thinking to myself, perhaps I do know more that I thought!

But the experience while working with Victoria Cooks, as our firm was called, is another story, so no more about that here. Those years certainly improved my cooking skills. We had to find out how to cook for great numbers (you cannot just double up the ingredients), and how some recipes just did not work. You have to listen to criticism with great respect as you learn more from that than from a shower of compliments.

Karin, my darling daughter, has just got engaged and now it is high time I passed my knowledge of cooking tips on to her. She and her fiancé love food and wine and entertaining their friends. I hope this book will be of some help and remind her of the parties we have had at home. I wonder if I could get the book out in time for her wedding?

A year after the wedding!

I am still working on the book and Karin hasn't even mentioned it lately as she must have given up on me!

It is not easy for me to put down recipes if you are a little bit slap-dash, as I am, and like to improvise. After all these years my cooking is done rather quickly and ingredients added as the mood takes me, so it is quite hard to make the recipes precise.

Good food does take some time to prepare. For a special dish you have to make sure you have all the right ingredients to hand. My cupboard used to be full of exotic spices vinegars and honeys until I started catering commercially. Then I found that it was more important to have plenty of the ordinary ingredients in a fresh condition, than a cupboard full of exotic sauces and vinegars. I eventually had to throw away jars of strange pickles, spices and expensive odds and ends that I never used, such as frilly cutlet collars and plastic icing sets, etc., that once seemed a good idea.

A good kitchen layout is important. Avoid keeping things you use often below waist level. Make sure you have plenty of work surfaces and ideally a large kitchen table. I sit at this table and do most of my preparation work by it. It is also a table at which I entertain most of my friends who pop in, and at weekends, guests also seem to gravitate towards the kitchen. A large fridge is most useful, and a cooker which has more than four rings, and more than one oven would be ideal.

A friend of mine had her kitchen specially extended to allow for a little socialising while she was cooking. She told me that recently her daughter, who was going through a difficult divorce, found the kitchen the best place to talk in. The homely surroundings and the intimacy of a kitchen makes it easier.

Have you noticed that the people who have the latest, vast kitchen with every gadget, are the people who hardly ever cook? A kitchen should not look all clinical. It should look a little bit like your sittingroom with some flowers and comfortable chairs and your cookery books on hand. As regards the fashion in kitchens, don't change your old kitchen just for the sake of changing the colour scheme. If the units are still in good working order one can give the kitchen a more superficial make-over with new tops and doors for the units, etc. without spending a whole lot of money on renewing everything. One sometimes finds that a new kitchen that has been put in by the vendor, specifically to attract a buyer, is then likely to be changed as soon as the buyer moves in. People like to put their own 'stamp' on kitchens.

About equipment. Get a few, quality basics in durable materials, plain and solid, meant for the kind of fuel you use: electricity, gas or Aga. Personally I am not so fond of cast iron pans because they are so heavy, especially when full. Remember to buy a few really large pots for party cooking, and store these somewhere out of the way, as they are not often used. Sometimes you can buy large saucepans in junk and antique shops or at car boot sales, for cooking hams or large pies.

I would invest in cheaper china for everyday use, which you don't mind if you chip or break, but a good set of china with at least 12 place settings for best. Plain white is a good choice. Ask friends and relatives to give you special serving dishes as presents, for example, soup tureens, casseroles, gratin dishes, tea and coffee pots, etc. Food looks so much more appetising when it is served on an appropriate dish. I love my Portuguese fish dishes, my scallop shells from the fishmonger for seafood starters and my large, papier maché shell for crisps. Plain white ovenware is also best as food looks good in it.

Now you are ready to cook – what shall we cook?

The food should suit the occasion. There are times when sausage and mash or macaroni cheese is more welcome than more exotic dishes. If you are cooking for other people, take into account their likes and dislikes, age and appetite. Older people seem to like simple food, not too rich, but well cooked. Children like familiar things, but on young 'foodies' you can experiment.

When I was young I used to adore rich, elaborate dishes, with sauces and garnishes and creamy desserts. However, one's tastes change. André Simon, the great gourmet and wine connoisseur, said his favourite meal was a nice omelette with herbs to start with and a grilled Sole for his main course. Incidentally, he also said, if you find a good restaurant, stick to it as you will always get a warm welcome and be well looked after.

What about cookery books, how many do you need?

I would suggest get a good basic English cookery book and a large, comprehensive compendium such as 'The Joy of Cooking' by Irma S. Rombauer and Marion Rombauer Becker, which explains how to deal with every kind of raw material in the kitchen, their season and ways of cooking them. I have now stopped buying cookery books, I must have hundreds already, and I dip into them from time to time to get inspiration. I never resent the price of a cookery book if there is one recipe in that book that I keep using time and again. Among my favourite cookery books are those by Elizabeth David, for instance 'French provincial cooking', Robert Carrier's 'Great dishes of the World', the 'Consumer Association's Dinner Party Book' and Claudia Roden's 'Middle Eastern Food'. Sainsbury's small cookery books are excellent for the beginner and my latest discovery is a book called 'Goose fat and garlic' (Country recipes from South West France) by Jeanne Strang.

Poor cookery books have recipes that do not work or do not taste good. There are quite a few current recipes that combine very strange and unusual ingredients, spices and herbs, thereby trying to add a little extra 'value' or 'mystique' to the dish. If it works, fine, but often such dishes are not the kind one would enjoy regularly. Superfluous decorations, such as redcurrants and mint leaves with everything, don't add anything to the taste of the dish.

Elizabeth David said that her heart sank if she went to dinner and there was not bread and butter on the table. I agree with her. Whatever the dinner is like you can always comfort yourself with some good, fresh bread and butter. Bread can offset some of the richness of the food.

So you have got friends coming to dinner – how do you entertain them? With love and generosity!

Offer the best you can afford. If your purse does not stretch to wine, offer them cider. Give of your time and take trouble. You can use humble ingredients and still give a feast.

Finished at last!

After several attempts over the years, this book has finally been written. It is a collection of recipes I have used time and again over the years and of which I have not tired. The aim of the book is to help my daughter, now newly married, to cook and entertain. Hopefully the book will also be useful to other young people.

The recipes reflect my background, living in Finland for the first 25 years of my life, spending a lot of time in France in our cottage there, touring round Europe and of course learning about English food here in Britain, where so many excellent raw materials can be obtained. I am particularly pleased to introduce you to some Scandinavian dishes which have generally been appreciated by my English guests. It is a cuisine that needs to be discovered.

My interest in food started in about 1964 with cookery articles in the Sunday papers and the books of Robert Carrier and Elizabeth David. Incidentally, the latter wrote her French Provincial Cooking at our local hotel here in Ross-on-Wye. Since then my eyes have been opened to the variety of interesting dishes that I have been able to sample abroad. My husband says I remembered places by the meals we enjoyed there. I also catered professionally in London for 10 years which was an excellent learning experience. I learnt so much from the Good Food Guide and the International Wine and Food Society, who were among my clients.

I am very much indebted to my late Mother whose cooking at home was always of the honest, old-fashioned kind, and to the authors of so many cookery books that have inspired me with recipes I have used over the years and adapted in my own way. Some recipes have been given to me by friends, others I have put together myself. With this book I hope to perpetuate their use, at least within my own family. The book is dedicated to my daughter and through her to all the young brides who are starting married life and the work of cooking for their families. I hope more husbands will be inspired to help them in this daily task. I am also very much indebted to my son and husband who have appreciated my culinary efforts over the years. My very special thanks to my husband who not only supported the creation of this book financially, encouraged me to cook, but also to write. And finally a warm thank you to my friend Meg McNair who toiled over the book, typing it, and inspiring me.

Karin, my darling daughter – you have asked me to write this book for so long. Here it is at last. I hope it will be of help.

Helpful Hints

- **Oven temperature**. Once upon a time we used to cook on old, cast iron stoves or open fires, and nobody knew what temperature they reached. Broadly speaking, one was only able to tell whether the temperature was hot, medium or cool. One knew that in a hot oven food cooked more quickly than in a cool oven, but eventually the food cooked in both types of oven. This is why you should not worry too much if you cannot tell at what temperature your dish should be cooked, because you can tell by looking at it and testing the dish with a skewer. With baking, you have to take more care with the oven temperatures. Fruit cakes require lower temperatures, egg custards and meringues very low temperatures.
- When making a **cheese sauce** cook sauce well _before_ adding the cheese. If you add cheese to a gratin dish in the oven, do not cook it for too long. A teaspoon of mustard is a good addition to a cheese sauce.
- **Clear meat soups, or bouillon**. Bring the meat to the boil starting with _cold_ water and remove the scum that appears when the broth is about to boil before adding any herbs, peppercorns or vegetables.
- **Garlic** can be obtained as white, stripy or purple. The last kind is the most expensive and keeps best. Persillade is a mixture of chopped parsley and garlic which is a good addition to a soup or a salad, added at the last moment. Garlic, once it is cooked, does not make the breath smell the way it does if eaten raw.
- **How to skin tomatoes and peaches**. Score tomatoes or peaches around the 'waist' with a sharp knife. Pour boiling water over them to cover them. Leave for 2 to 3 minutes and then peel them. The skin comes off easily where you have scored them. For many dishes you also remove the seeds from the tomatoes before chopping them. In the case of peaches you need to halve them and remove the stone. The peaches can then be stuffed with an almond and sugar paste and baked, or sliced into a fruit salad.
- For a **caramel or syrup**, dissolve sugar in the water without boiling or stirring. Then simmer to thicken syrup.
- To dissolve **gelatine**, add it to a small quantity of cold water. Heat gently but do not boil. Shake the pan at intervals but do not stir. Gelatine does not set well if dissolved in too little water. Too much water does not matter provided you do not exceed the total amount of liquid recommended for the recipe. Add gelatine when the rest of your mixture is ready. Do not add new ingredients _after_ you have added the gelatine unless they are whipped cream or whipped egg whites.
- If a **sauce** is _lumpy_ there is not enough fat in it. The fat to flour ratio must be correct:- (1 tbs. fat to 1 tbs. flour.) If the sauce has gone lumpy you can strain it to improve the texture or try putting it in a blender for a few minutes.
  If a **sauce** is _greasy_ you need to either skim off the fat or add some starch. The starch absorbs the fat. A roux (mixture of fat and flour) made of 2 tbs. flour to 2 oz butter will thicken 1 pint of sauce such as béchamel.
- If a **sauce made with eggs and butter or oil** has curdled, put it in a blender and it may come together again.

- Four eggs will set 1 pint of liquid such as milk for a baked egg custard, or in quiches.
- For **meringues**, use 1 egg white per 2 oz caster sugar.
- **Egg yolks whipped with sugar** for a cake are 'sufficiently beaten' if a spoon dipped in it leaves a trail.
- **Liaison** means a thickening agent such as flour, cornflour, egg and cream. To make a roux to thicken a sauce you use 2 tbs. flour to 2 oz fat. Fry these gently together until brown for a brown sauce. For a white sauce do not allow the ingredients to brown. Add the stock or milk for your sauce, gradually, whisking all the time. Flour needs to cook for 2 or 3 minutes to loose its raw flavour.
- Cut **vegetables** in pieces of about equal size if you wish them to all be cooked at the same time. (e.g. do not cook large potatoes with small ones but cut the large ones to match the size of the small ones.)
- The **curry paste** used, for instance, for coronation chicken, can be prepared in advance and keeps in the fridge for about a month.
- Wet the baking tray with water before placing **puff pastry** on it as it will rise better.
- **French dressing**. I use a ratio of 4 tbs. of oil to 1tbs. of vinegar in my dressings. Elizabeth David goes as far as to say that 8 tbs. of oil to 1 tbs. vinegar is preferable. The French pay as much attention to the quality of the vinegar as to that of the oil. Olive oil has a thicker texture than vegetable oils and so sticks more to the salad leaves. A tip given to me by a French woman was to use some olive oil with ordinary vegetable oil. In this way the dressing will still taste of olive oil, but will not be so heavy. I always crush a clove of garlic into my dressing which I keep in a jam jar, but _not_ in the fridge. Olive oil and garlic are not used in traditional Scandinavian dishes.
- I find most food **coated in mayonnaise** keeps well, such as coronation chicken and potato salad. If cooked **beetroot** looks 'glossy' you can be pretty sure it has 'gone off'.
- Do not keep **cooked meat, poultry or rice** in closed containers in the fridge where they go off more quickly. Cover them loosely with foil. _Do the safety test_! If it smells odd, DON'T eat it! A slightly sour smell is often a sign that the dish has gone off.
- **A little mould on bread or cheese or jam** is not very dangerous, you can just cut it off or spoon it off and still eat the rest without coming to any harm. If the taste is right, don't worry. (Be careful about unpasteurized cheese.)
- **Always cool dishes completely** (leave lid off), before putting them in the fridge. You can cover the dish once it is cold enough to go into the fridge. A cooked dish can start fermenting if the lid is on firmly on a hot day.
- If **raw fish** smells unpleasant it is not worth eating, but cooked fish can keep quite well in the fridge.
- **Raw shellfish** should either be _very_ fresh or used _immediately_ after de-frosting. Cooked shellfish such as lobster and prawns keeps quite a long time in the fridge, especially in a French dressing.

Definitions:
- **A Mousse** has more yolks than whites. (Yolks thicken things.)

- **A Soufflé** has more whites than yolks. (Whites lighten the mixture.)
- **To brown meat or chicken** use a mixture of butter and oil. Oil reaches a higher temperature before it burns than butter, so stops the dish burning. Butter burns easily, but gives the flavour. Fry the food on a high heat and _leave_ the pieces for a while before turning them over to give them a chance to brown. Constant turning while frying delays the browning. When you are trying to fry, for instance cubed pork, and the pork doesn't brown because juices come out of the meat, pour off the juices, add a little more oil and continue frying. You can add the juices later to the dish.
- Brush the bottom of a **pastry tart** with hot apricot jam to prevent it from getting soggy from, say, the juices of the fruit to be cooked in the tart. It is a good idea to pre-bake tart bases and quiche bases to make sure the pastry is cooked through.
- To **glaze** tarts heat apricot jam and lemon juice in a little water and brush it over the tart before baking.
- **Nuts** and **sugar** burn easily on high heat, say under a hot grill.
- Whip **cream** lightly for mixing into soufflés, but harder if you use the cream for piping. Over-whipped cream can curdle. Do not whip sour cream, it gets thinner if you do so.
- An easy way of **decorating** baked vegetable purées, iced cakes or shortbread is by drawing the back of a fork over the surface, thereby creating lines.
- **Potatoes** do not fall apart so quickly when you boil them if you only keep the lid partly on the saucepan. Use floury potatoes for dishes which require soft textures such as for mashing or baking in cream in the oven. Waxy or new potatoes are better for potato salads and to fry after boiling.
- **Omelettes** should be cooked quickly on high heat. A famous chef made his apprentices fry omelettes on the back ring of a gas cooker with the front ring alight. If the apprentice burnt his arm, he had taken too long over the job. It was a lesson he didn't easily forget!
  Remember to leave the omelette a bit runny before folding it, it will continue cooking in its own heat. Make sure your filling is prepared before you start cooking the omelette and is at the right temperature.
- **Scrambled eggs** should be taken off the heat while still runny and creamy. They should not be dry and grainy.
- To present **fish** nicely to be served poached, roll the filleted fish up loosely, leaving the ends underneath.
- When making **tuiles** – very thin biscuits the shape of pantiles – make sure the biscuits are evenly brown, not white in the middle, then place them on an oiled rolling pin and leave to cool before removing.
- **Chocolate ganache** (filling) for cakes. Melt 2½ oz plain chocolate with ¾ oz butter and 4 tbs. cream. Leave to cool before using.
- **Pancake batter** should, if possible, be left for up to an hour for the flour to expand before frying.
- **Roasting meat**. Test if the meat is cooked by inserting a skewer in the thickest part. If the juice that comes out is pink or bloody the meat is medium or rare. If the liquid comes out clear the meat is well done. It is _important_ to cook chicken and pork until well done for health reasons.

Food texture

Texture is very important. A meal that just consists of soft, wet courses seems less attractive than when crisp and soft-textured dishes alternate.

Personally, I really have a problem eating some slimy, soft textured food such as oysters or mushrooms like cèpes. Slimy texture combined with richness is just too much for me. Even in salads one should combine soft and hard textures. Carrots, unless they are grated and celery can be too hard, unless combined with tomatoes or lettuce. Florets of raw cauliflower, slices of raw courgette, nuts and seeds are welcome, not just for their flavour but also for their texture.

For this reason, one prefers toast or crusty bread with a soft paté because the two textures compliment each other. Neither would one serve a vegetable in purée form (except perhaps mashed potatoes) with a stew type dish. In this case the vegetables should be kept whole or in chunks.

Sauces are sensitive to texture. Sometimes just a little thickening can enhance a gravy or a curry. Too much thickening can ruin them. Making a sauce with flour and butter (a roux) is always going to produce a better flavoured sauce than one just thickened with cornflour and water. Rich thickening agents are not necessary if the sauce or soup is already full flavoured. Fish soups do not need thickening at all.

If you wish to prepare several sweets for a large dinner party, it is a good idea to serve some soft textured sweets, (such as mousses), but also some with a pastry base, such as tarts. I find men tend to go for the pastry desserts whereas ladies prefer the soufflé type.

The ups and downs of cooking

What is it that makes a good cook? Surely, if you have been trained in cooking, everything that you cook must always turn out well. Not necessarily. Many times a dish goes slightly wrong, but generally there are ways of putting these faults right. Often it is a question that the dish did not turn out as you had expected: The risotto is bland, the fishcakes are too heavy, the meat loaf too hard. One asks oneself, "What did I do wrong?" An experienced cook may work out a solution. For instance, you cook a sauce for a little longer to concentrate the flavour. You add a little more milk to make the soup less salty, or you put some breadcrumbs into meat balls to lighten them.

Why do I not succeed first time? asks the novice cook. Sometimes we have ourselves to blame. We haven't read the recipe properly or perhaps we have poor technique. However, recipes can also be poor, and sometimes it is impossible to create a good result if you follow them. An experienced cook can spot a poor recipe, but the novice often blames him/herself for failing and decides cooking is just not for him/her.

Gradually we learn to improvise a little. We add some herbs for flavour or we crumble a little bit of a stock cube into the gravy, a little wine or lemon juice may be worth trying too.

It is interesting how a dish which has been re-heated often tastes better than the first time around. The flavours have had time to develop and to concentrate by evaporation. Also, when re-heating you may be adding a little stock or milk to enrich the dish and correct the consistency. It is a good idea to taste what you have cooked while the dish is hot, but also when it is cold. Then the true flavours of the dish show up. If it tastes good when it is cold the dish was well done, this especially applies to meat stews and soups.

How exciting it is to have a new food experience! To try a new ingredient or a new way of cooking it. This often happens abroad. I have a very good memory for food I have eaten and can recall quite vividly some dishes I tasted for the first time, such as the soft seductive gnocchi we had in Germany by Lake Constance. When I came home I tried to make these but I never managed to create them successfully.

I try to use new ingredients, such as shark or fresh tuna or squid to see if we can include them in the family repertoire. The first attempt is not always successful. I remember membranes in the monkfish once ruining a beautiful fish stew and the shark steaks and the conger eel that were very tough. It is a pity that the shops that sell these things don't teach us how to cook them. Then we might come back for more.

The dinner party

You have probably often entertained your friends to a meal without calling it a dinner party, but if you want to put on a slightly more formal affair, there are many things to be taken into consideration if you wish for a smoothly run event and the most important of this is timing. Plan it all like a military operation. Don't start cooking as the guests arrive, with the shopping still in the bags. Here are a few hints.

1. Plan the Menu days in advance, Use recipes that you know well, or have confidence in. It is unwise to try a new recipe unless you are an experienced cook. Don't choose dishes that require last minute attention. Cook a little more than you think you need for the numbers coming, to allow for second helpings. Allow time for shopping, the flowers, cocktail bits, candles, napkins, etc.

2. Shop one or two days before. With supermarket goods you don't have to worry too much about the raw materials going 'off', but fish should be bought on the same day, if possible, unless its smoked or vacuum packed.

3. Cook some dishes beforehand, especially starters and sweets, if possible. These can be decorated on the day. Even the main course can be cooked in advance and perhaps frozen, say if it is a goulash or a stew, but remember to bake pastry from raw if you are using it, and do not try to re-heat. It is possible to re-heat pastry successfully in an oven but you cannot do it in a microwave.

4. Arrange your flowers and perhaps lay the table the night before. Take out china and any serving dishes you may need.

5. On the day you now just have to cook the main course, or perhaps finish it and the starter and the puddings. Prepare the vegetables, chill the wines, and prepare the nibbles that you serve with drinks. Tidy the kitchen so that the sink isn't full of dirty pans.

Now you really have done well, so have a little drink while you are dressing for dinner. It helps to settle the nerves.

How to tackle the washing up

There are many schools of thought about this subject. Some people insist on washing everything by hand immediately after the dinner party. Some people leave it all to the next day. But these are my conclusions:-

1. <u>Get a dishwasher</u>. It is worth it even just for two people, as you can store the dirty dishes away from sight until the end of the day or when the machine is full. There is no drying up to do. However, take care of your antique cut glass. They can go cloudy in the dishwashers. Don't put in bone handled knives as the glue holding the handles may dissolve in the heat of the dishwasher.

2. <u>After the party, do not wash up if you feel very tired</u>. It is all so much easier in the morning when you are fresh and have had a cup of tea or two. Before you go to bed put the pots and pans to soak. They will then clean up much more easily.

3. <u>Try to avoid drying up</u>. Leave the dishes to drain by themselves. In Scandinavia, tea cloths and Jay cloths are now 'out', not considered hygienic, but if this is going a little too far, I think a good idea would be to invest in a drying cupboard. This is a cupboard above the sink, where you put your washed dishes to drip and dry out of sight, a bit like the plate drying racks of old. Wet saucepans dry quickly on top of an Aga.

4. <u>Get a good husband or partner to share the job with you</u>. I have a superb washer up in my husband, he actually likes the job. He says it's 'therapeutic' and he even loves wiping the kitchen surfaces with disinfectant. Marvellous!!

The drinks party

Once or twice a year it is nice to have a larger, more formal drinks party to which you invite a full house of friends and others you have met and would like to know better: Perhaps, also, duty guests such as your boss or relatives and associates that you do not normally see very often or in a social setting.

The purpose of a drinks party is often to meet new friends to see if you get on and like each other's lifestyles. If you do, next time you may invite them to a dinner party.

I used to feel very awkward and a bit annoyed at having to attend quite a few drinks parties when I was new in England. We do not have drinks parties in Scandinavia, except in embassies or on very formal occasions. We hardly knew some of the people who asked us and it was only afterwards that I realised how kind they had been to us. At these parties you often meet somebody new and interesting, get the feel of your neighbourhood and how people live. All very useful especially to a stranger. Good friendships can begin at these parties, so do go if you get invited. Very soon you will get the hang of it and enjoy it too.

Here is some helpful advice.

1. Invite at least 25% more guests than you expect to come as you will find that many people are too busy to accept your invitation. Make sure you include the time and date and place of the party on your invitation. Include your telephone number. State the date by which you hope for a reply. As a guest it is helpful to reply promptly, especially if you can't attend so that the hostess can ask some other people in your place.
2. Send out, preferably, written invitations, a postcard will do, with all the information on it. These should be sent out about 4 weeks before the party. Include RSVP on the card, which means 'reply please'.
3. Invite a mix of people, old and young, old friends and new. The older guests oil the wheels of a party because they do know how to cope, and the young add the glamour and excitement.
4. Well before the party, plan the drinks, the wines and the food you are going to serve. You may be able to pick up some bargains at wine wholesalers or from your favourite supermarket. Allow half a bottle a head. Also, serve some gin and sherry if people cannot take wine and have plenty of soft drinks including sparkling water for those who have to drive home. A nice fruit punch would be a pleasant, non-alcoholic alternative. If you know that some of your guests prefer beer and cider make sure that you have some on hand.
5. To make it easy for yourself, you might only serve white and red wine, or Bucks Fizz, which is a mixture of half sparkling white wine and half orange juice. Another good mix is sparkling wine with a little blackcurrant liqueur, called a

'Kir'.

6. Two days before the party tidy the house and shop for flowers and food. Arrange the flowers.

7. The day before, make all the food preparations you can, such as hard-boiled eggs, trout Pâté, sausage rolls, mayonnaise, and dips, etc. Allow about six canapés per person with a good variety, including some suitable for vegetarians.

8. On the day, prepare and finish your canapés and get out your serving dishes. Also, arrange the bar with the glasses and the drinks. Do not put the bar in a narrow doorway because people always tend to congregate near the drinks. Cheese straws are always popular. Prepare the food, say 4 cold nibbles and one or two hot ones. **The cold** ones may include simple things like cubes of tasty cheese, salami and radishes, Pâté on crusty baguette slices, stuffed eggs, triangles of smoked salmon on brown bread and parma ham with melon on wooden cocktail sticks. Don't make too many complicated dishes. **The hot** ones, small cocktail sausages are always popular and so are small sausage rolls which you can buy frozen and just bake on the day. If you are a keen cook you might prepare little meat balls that you serve hot with a piquant sauce, or your own pizzas that you cut into strips but make sure they have plenty of topping.

9. Just before the guests arrive, check that there are some crisps and nuts out, ash trays and small serviettes. Before the party you will have prepared trays of your cold eats, a few varieties on each, ready to whisk out from the kitchen at the right moment. To start with guests will not be interested in the food, but will welcome it later on. Heat the hot snacks half way through the party as its arrival will keep the party going.

10. Make use of your relatives and friends to help you serve the drinks but keep a close eye that guests always have a drink in their hand. Encourage guests to help themselves from the bar. Notice if any of your guests are on their own, or look uncomfortable and try to bring them into a group or introduce them to new people. A good way to get them involved is to ask them to take a tray of food or a bottle round. A good party lasts about 2 to 3 hours. Don't mind if people leave early. They may have another engagement afterwards.

When the party is over sit down with your family and have a drink yourself and relish the thoughts of having given a good party. As regards the financial side, these parties do not work out very expensive and should not tax anybody's budget or cooking abilities too much.

Kitchen equipment
I hardly ever use

Gravy boat that separates fat from juice. I skim the fat off before straining.

Mandolin for slicing vegetables. I only use it for cucumber when I have to do large quantities such as for a Danish salad.

Deep fat fryer. As I use it so rarely I have to fill it up with fresh oil each time.

A separate oil and vinegar set. I like to mix my own dressing which I keep in a screw-top jar. It does not have to be left in the fridge, in fact the cold congeals the oil.

Poultry scissors. I cut off chicken and duck joints after cooking, when it is easier, with a heavy knife.

Icing set. (The ones with thin nozzles and various star nozzles) My faithful icing bag and 2 nozzles suffice for my cake decorations, both with cream and names on birthday cakes.

Sandwich toaster. Filling always seems to stick to the inside and burns.

Roasting pan with lid. I seldom use this for roasting as I can control the browning better with just some loose foil over the meat.

Kitchen equipment
I would not do without

1. **Magimix**. Blender/food processor, but cannot whip.

2. **Electric whisk**, to complement above.

3. **Electric carving knife** for cutting neat slices of meat, hot or cold.

4. **Cafétière** for making small quantities of coffee. For large quantities for parties the old saucepan is best with the coffee strained into thermoses.

5. Good **vegetable/fruit peeler**
   Vegetable knives – serrated and plain
   Sharp meat knife – un-serrated
   Large bread knife – serrated

6. Lots of **mixing bowls** of various sizes: some plastic some heavy china.

7. **Hand whisks** – a balloon whisk and a flat-coiled whisk.

8. Many **wooden spoons**, especially for thick sauces.

9. **Meat and sugar thermometers**.

10. **Garlic press**.

11. **Sieves**, small and large to strain gravy, take lumps out of flour or icing sugar.

12. **Colander** for rice, vegetables etc.

13. **Pans**. Non-stick milk pan, small
    3 medium non-stick pans
    2 large saucepans for soup and to boil chicken
    1 double boiler for making sauces
    1 oblong salmon cooking pan
    1 very large pan to hold a turkey, or jam, or a ham for boiling whole, (a large, deep jam kettle will do)
    2 medium non-stick frying pans
    1 large sauté pan, (diameter 15" x 1½" high sides,) with a lid

14. Non-stick **cake tins**. (some loose bottomed and some firm bottomed).

15. Glass **lemon squeezer**. (the plastic ones are not so comfortable to use).

16. **Grater** for cheese or lemon peel.

17. **Room in the fridge for vegetables**. They deteriorate at room temperature. They need to be loosely wrapped, not exposed to air. (The same applies to food in the fridge: always wrap as it deteriorates from dehydration.)

The reluctant cook

In the case of the very busy or reluctant hostess, I would suggest that you develop a repertoire of half a dozen main courses that you can cook with confidence, and buy in the starter and the puddings for your dinner parties. I have met so many professional women who dread cooking never having learnt how to do it. For them it is worth just learning a few dishes and feeling comfortable about making them. You do not have to serve cold food just because you want to prepare things in advance. Most of the dishes I suggest below are served hot after re-heating and do not loose their flavour or character by being cooked twice.

List of dishes you can prepare the day before:

Chicken Dijonnaise
Beef stew with red wine
Beef olives
Pork Goulash
Spring lamb
Venison pie
Chicken in paprika sauce
Prawn and fetta ragout
Lamb kofta curry
Salmon Coulibiac
Kedgeree

Cold dishes:

Coronation chicken
Beef in jelly
Cold salmon steaks with rémoulade or avocado sauce

Note:

All these dishes can be served with just rice and a salad, but the <u>Salmon Coulibiac</u> should have boiled potatoes in stead of rice with it and the <u>Kedgeree</u> only a salad.

Planning for Christmas

Christmas can be a very busy and stressful time, especially if you have family coming and you have a full-time job. For working wives, I suggest they cheat a little and take the easy option. Do not try to make everything yourself. You can get excellent Christmas puddings, cakes and mince pies, ready-made these days, so buy them, or ask one of your guests to provide some items.

There is also much delicious food obtainable by post. Last Christmas we feasted on some oak-roasted salmon from the Black Mountain Smokery at Crickhowell in Wales. That was a splendid starter for which I only had to make a sour cream and chive sauce. Scottish salmon and various patés are very useful for starters and Scottish venison for a casserole you might prepare beforehand.

Start early and make up *lists*; tick items off when they are taken care of. Space out the work so that everything does not get left to the last minute.

In November:

- Buy your presents and wrapping paper and write your Christmas letter if you usually do one. Buy stamps for the Christmas cards.
- Overseas presents will have to be dispatched by the end of the month at which time you can also buy charity Christmas cards.
- Order your tree, (especially if you want a tall one), fresh turkey, ham or piece of gammon.
- Order your wines from the wine merchants. It is generally too late in December.
- Make the Christmas cake and pudding, or buy them when they appear in the shops.
- Stock up with fruit juices, mixers and mineral water.

In December:

- Buy your cake and pudding if you have not made one yourself. (The shops can run out of them.)
- Mail your cards and letters, especially for overseas.
- Check over your wardrobe and make hairdressing appointments.
- Buy chocolates, nuts and cocktail nibbles. Buy Christmas crackers.

Christmas week:

- Collect the tree or have it delivered. Leave it outside until you need it.
- Buy holly, mistletoe and flowers for the house. Flowering pot plants such as hyacinths and poinsettias last well.

- Make a list of the meals for the next 5 days.

Five days before Christmas:

- Prepare the bedrooms for guests.
- Soak ham overnight.
- Check staple goods in your store cupboard, such as tea, coffee, butter, cheese, pickles, etc.
- Make mince pies or buy them. Buy cranberry sauce.
- Make a casserole and a special dessert and put them in the freezer.
- Make brandy butter.

Four days before Christmas:

- Shop for the groceries that you have found you will need.
- Buy last minute presents.
- Wrap all presents.
- Decorate the house.
- Boil the ham and allow it to cool in its liquid.

Three days before Christmas:

- Buy the fresh vegetables such as potatoes, sprouts, coleslaw ingredients, salads and fruit that you will need.
- Finish the ham (taking off the skin and preparing the crust and baking the ham).
- Decorate the tree.

Two days before Christmas:

- Prepare stockings for the children or those adults who still have them!
- Decorate the dining table in a festive way, preparing the candles, making sure you have the right cloths and napkins, etc.
- Make stuffing for the turkey.
- Collect turkey from the butcher.
- Prepare any sauces such as bread sauce or piquant sauce for turkey leftovers.
- Check on cream, milk and bread supplies.

Christmas Eve:

- Prepare turkey and stuff it.
- Prepare bacon rolls.
- Prepare sprouts.

Christmas morning:

- Set out the last Christmas cards.

- Prepare the potatoes.
- Place presents under the tree.
- Put turkey on to roast (allow 3½ hours at 200° C for a 15 lb. turkey. Cover loosely with foil).
- Start steaming the pudding (2-3 hours), or use microwave 10-15 minutes, see wrapper.
- Take brandy butter out of the fridge.
- Roast potatoes and bacon rolls.

NOW:

- Sit down and have a nice glass of wine while everything is cooking!
- We like to go to church in the morning and have some Madeira and Christmas cake when we get back. Sometimes we even open the Christmas presents before lunch as we cannot wait any longer.
- P.S. Remember to ring some of your family members or special friends.

HAPPY CHRISTMAS!

The Smörgåsbord

The Scandinavian cold table

This large array of dishes served at a single meal is often synonymous with Scandinavian food. It was served on any important occasion when great numbers were expected such as weddings, funerals, and special birthdays.

A cold table may have originated from the simple food found in the farmer's larder that was served to any visitor who turned up unexpectedly and needed some refreshment. The wife went into her larder and brought out some marinaded herring, a common winter food, some ham and cheese, pickles and some home-made bread and butter. The meal was often accompanied by schnapps, a drink of distilled alcohol, to warm the traveller and washed down with some home-made beer.

This simple repast grew and grew, salads of various kinds were added and also hot dishes, meat and fish stews and potatoes followed by a rather plain pudding or two. In the hands of the good cook, who had the means, it turned into a feast with something for everybody.

Today you can still find a fully fledged smörgåsbord if you look for it. Some large hotels specialise in it and it is common on luxurious ferries where people have plenty of time to eat.

Here is some advice on how to eat a smörgåsbord, which incidentally is Swedish and means 'the sandwich table'. You always start with the tastiest morsels, that is herrings pickled in various ways, in marinades of dill, tomato, sherry, mustard or spices, which you eat with potatoes and some bread and butter. By the way, you change your plate for every different type of food you eat.

Then you go on to the fish proper, smoked salmon or eel, if you are lucky, or poached, cold white fish perhaps served with a mayonnaise sauce. Take time to enjoy the unpeeled, freshly cooked prawns which go very well with some white wine.

Now you have a little pause and cut yourself a slice of cheese with which to clean your palate after all that fish. But soon you are ready again to tuck into the cold meats, the ham, tongue and other charcuterie and patés with some salads, not forgetting all the pickles such as beetroot, gherkins and onions.

Then you have a little rest after which you turn up again, with a fresh plate, to have something hot and tasty, perhaps meatballs, which are the Scandinavian's favourite dish. Perhaps you may have a casserole of various meats, or just a slice of the beef joint with a little gravy and some glazed onions. The Scandinavians eat potatoes with everything; rice and pasta have only recently become widely used.

The hot dishes also include fish dishes such as fried plaice with rémoulade sauce or fresh salmon baked in a savoury custard.

The cheese board is still beckoning you with its many varieties of mainly hard and blue cheeses, but nowadays also soft cheeses such as camembert. These are served with many different types of bread, especially ryebread and crispbread and butter of course.

You must not forget the puddings. You say you cannot possibly eat another thing but soon you feel that a little blancmange or fresh fruit would not do you any harm. A cup of excellent, clear black coffee and perhaps a brandy is the perfect ending to such a repast.

What do you drink with such a meal? You normally have schnapps or beer or both with your herring, a glass of white wine with your fish and a glass of red with your meatballs.

You have eaten too much and still you have only been able to taste a small proportion of the dishes offered to you, but I urge you not to skip the herring course as most people find it quite delicious.
Eating such a meal on a ferry, looking out over the calm sea with the beautiful islands gliding past is a memorable experience and should be savoured over several hours. In the Nordic summer the sun hardly sets at all.

If the party is enjoyed at home it is a tradition to toast each other frequently and also to sing some schnapps songs with each glass of akvavit. These songs are very short and humorous and people brought up on them vie with each other to introduce a song. We do this at home. My children are now grown up but they are teaching the Scandinavian schnapps songs to their young friends with all the ceremonies that go with this tradition.
1.   One can now get a schnapps song on the Nokia mobile phone while you wait to be connected.
2.   The heads of the EU gathered recently at a large banquet in Stockholm, and there too, schnapps songs were sung to the consternation of the foreign delegates!

How to thicken soups and sauces

There are many ways to thicken soup and gravy. The first one is my favourite because it does not add too many calories to a dish, but neither does it add much flavour. It is simply there to alter the consistency so that it is more 'velvety'.

1. **Cornflour**. A teaspoon or two of cornflour, mixed with cold water, added to sauces, soups or curries can greatly improve the way they taste and feel, simply by their texture. Remember always to put cornflour into water, not the other way around and stir well until smooth and silky before adding to the dish. Cornflour cooks in about a minute.
2. **Flour**. Flour needs to be mixed with fat, and the liquid added gradually while whisking. **a**. Melt one tablespoon of butter in a saucepan. Add one tbs. flour. Mix until butter has been absorbed into flour. Then add liquid, whether soup or gravy. Be careful to cook the dish another 10 minutes for the flour to swell and lose its raw flavour. Stir to break up any lumps. **b**. Flour kneaded into butter can be dropped into a soup, where it will dissolve and thicken it. **c**. Flour can be fried in butter until it is a nutty brown, when it will be suitable to thicken a brown gravy (but not a sauce that should be white or pale).
3. **Egg yolks**. Egg yolks can be used to thicken soups. Mix them well before adding, and make sure you whisk the soup vigorously while you add them. Be careful not to allow the soup to boil after adding the eggs as they will curdle. The eggs will improve the flavour and consistency of the soup considerably. The famous Chicken Broth of Greece (Avlogomeno), is greatly improved by the egg yolks.
4. **Rice and Pasta**. A little rice and pasta can be added to soups to give them a slightly cloudy appearance, and a little more texture.
5. **Puréed Vegetables**. Puréed vegetables are very good for thickening soup. Say you have a meat broth, with many different kinds of vegetable in it, you may prefer to puree some of them, such as the potatoes, to give the soup a fuller texture. An example is the leek and potato soup called 'Vichyssoise', in which the vegetables are cooked in chunks first and then pureed to give a smooth thick soup.
   Cream and eggs. Adding cream to a sauce tends to thicken it and also make it taste blander, so don't swamp a tasty sauce with cream because you will spoil its flavour. If you mix cream with egg yolks it will thicken a sauce beautifully, but be careful not to boil the sauce afterwards, just heat it gently while stirring. This thickening method is excellent poured over fruit tarts before baking because the egg and cream mixture will mop up the juices from the fruit and set them, allowing you then to cut up the tart much more easily.

A personal view of
three different eating traditions

France, UK and Scandinavia

In France

The way people in France approach eating and appreciate food may seem a little strange to us in the UK. To start with, they only seem to have one kind of breakfast, with fresh bread, jam, croissants and coffee. Every day!

They also seem to eat vegetables in quite a different way from our own. They serve them as a starter or *after* the main course. However, they do value every kind of food very much and want to savour that particular food on its own, prepared in the best way to bring out the flavour, not merely as an accompaniment to other dishes. They are very imaginative in making something delicious out of almost nothing.

The main meal of the day is midday, so everything stops and people go home, even quite a long way, to have their proper meal and a rest. This takes at least two hours. The modern office workers eating in canteens in town obviously cannot indulge themselves like this.

The evening meals can be perfunctory, just soup and a bit of cheese perhaps. It is a chance to weed the garden and to chat with the neighbours, perhaps over a glass of something.

The other difference is that at formal meals the cheese is always eaten before the dessert. I have been told this is because one wants to finish the red wine with the cheese. Salad is often served as a course on its own after the main meat dish, but rarely contains anything but lettuce and a nice vinaigrette dressing. The pudding is not very elaborate. They seem to like their apple tarts and ice creams. The starters are more interesting than the puddings.

Bread is eaten with every meal. You buy it twice a day to get it fresh and there is not much choice, often just the baguettes in different sizes. In the country people do buy huge round loaves with a hard crust. They are useful if the people live far from the bakery as they can last a week and the stale stuff can be added to the soup to thicken it. The French never waste anything.

In UK

Meals in the UK are rather different. We start with a breakfast which can be as small and as slimming as cereal and yoghurt, but also a real feast. The real English breakfast includes bacon, sausages, eggs and many other things and so it ends up as a meal that can carry you through most of the day. This kind of breakfast is still available in hotels (where it can cost the same as a light lunch!) and enjoyed at home, perhaps at weekends. At 11 o'clock the British drink coffee which to the continentals is a strange time, as they drink coffee in the afternoon. Lunch is at 1 o'clock, later than in many countries abroad. Food is pretty plain, meat fish and vegetables cooked very simply. However there are some lovely puddings to discover; the tarts and pies, suet puddings and trifles are coming back and always popular. Three or four different kinds of vegetables are often served up with main meals and they and the puddings are probably meant to fill up any gaps if there was not much meat to go round. Gravy is not taken very seriously, but there is generally much of it.

In the UK we are now greatly influenced by foreign food and eat enormous quantities of pizzas and curries so people obviously have a taste for the exotic. Curry apparently has overtaken fish and chips as our most popular meal. Both can be glorious if cooked with care.

Cheese normally finishes the meal. It's a good bet that we do not need it after our nice dessert. People tend to stick to the familiar cheddar and stilton, which can be excellent, but there must be a taste for foreign cheeses too, judging by the huge choice in supermarkets.

In Scandinavia

In Scandinavia the mealtimes are quite different than those in the UK. Lunch is served from 11 am onwards and dinner about 5.30 pm when people come back from work.

Bread, butter and milk is served with most meals and so are potatoes. The breakfast used to consist of porridge, eggs or cheese with bread. It now tends to be fruit juice and cereal because the Scandinavians are getting very health conscious. Children still have an open sandwich for breakfast, perhaps with some fruit juice. Tea is the usual drink, served without milk, but as we drink more coffee than most people in Europe some people have coffee first thing as well.

Lunch starts early and can be a very simple snack unless you choose to make it your main meal of the day to avoid cooking at home. If you don't have a canteen for your lunch you tend to go to a cafeteria to have an open sandwich, a bun and some coffee. If you choose a 'dish of the day', it often includes a salad starter which is very welcome. The patisserie is very good and you might have a cake instead of dessert with your coffee. Most people have their main meals when they come home from work. Increasingly some of the meals are bought ready-made, but there are some excellent casseroles, baked dishes and thick soups with meat and fish which are very filling and do not require very much work. As your dinner was so early you may have a supper, a cup of tea and an open sandwich, about 9 o'clock.

General comment

I get a feeling that the French are changing more slowly in their eating habits than the British. The French family, out for Sunday lunch, still look for the traditional slow-cooked dishes. The food revolution we have had in the U.K. has not really happened in France or in Scandinavia. However, increasing foreign travel has made Mediterranean food very popular everywhere.

As regards more casual entertaining, the Scandinavians still entertain a great deal by offering coffee with home-made cakes and biscuits and perhaps a fine gateau bought from a specialist shop. If the occasion is very special such as a big birthday or a reception after a funeral, some alcohol might also be served. I suppose a tea party in the UK would be the equivalent of a coffee party in Scandinavia. In France you entertain either by a little aperitif or a proper meal such as lunch or dinner.

Trends of eating more healthily and buying more prepared dishes seem to be increasing everywhere, but in France they still think that spending time and money on eating well is worth the effort of cooking it oneself.

Blood Pancakes

I am not going to give you the recipe for this, but just to mention that I remember as a child, going to the butchers with a milk can to get the blood for this dish! The blood pancakes were delicious, black in colour and were made with blood mixed with beer or milk, flour, some syrup and chopped onion and spices. We used to eat heaps of these with a kind of cranberry jam made of Lingonberries. It can also be made in an oven dish, baked in the oven rather than fried into thin pancakes.

I suppose the English black pudding we eat with our breakfast is an English equivalent of this dish.

Ingredients that can be added to a SALAD for extra flavour or as a garnish.

HERBS – **Parsley** is the most useful, all purpose herb, but beware of its coarse texture in salads.

Savoury is a very useful herb supposed to have a peppery flavour but can be combined with most things.

Fresh dill is especially good with fish and cucumber

Fresh basil is excellent with tomato

Fresh fennel bulb will add an interesting aniseed flavour and crunch to a mixed salad

Fennel fronds (leaves) are very pretty as a garnish. Only use them, chopped, when very young on fish dishes.

Tinned asparagus – this is very good drained and used with vinaigrette dressing as part of a mixed salad.

Sweet and sour gherkins – these can be used in potato, rice, bean or pasta salads, and with cold meat, charcuterie and frankfurters.

Dried fruit or fresh fruit – such as apple or grapes go well with white cabbage salad, coleslaw, and in the case of apple, with herring salad.

Radishes – are very good sliced in most salads. They are fragrant and look jolly.

Water cress – is excellent for decorating and for mixing with a green salad. Leave it undressed for decoration as it tends to go black very quickly.

Cooked peas – are a useful addition especially to rice and pasta salads.

NUTS – In France they often sprinkle whole or chopped walnuts over a green salad dressed with walnut oil. Other nuts which are a nice addition to a salad are hazelnuts, pine nuts and unsalted peanuts.

SEEDS – such as sunflower seeds.

SPROUTING SEEDS AND BEANS – such as alfalfa, and beansprouts. You may get them in health food shops.

Suggestions on making canapés

You can use different bread for canapés, but not bread which is too floppy so that you cannot hold the canapés properly once they have the topping on. You need a firm bread or a bread with crust. I suggest the following:

Bridge rolls, cut into slices.
Thin baguettes, cut into slices.
Brown or black German bread which is solid in texture.
Italian country bread in a round shape that you can slice thickly.

Spread these with softened butter before you add the toppings.
Canapés are usually 1" x 1½", but on black bread make them smaller, say ½" x 1".

Toppings:

German liver sausage or any other paté with a slice of gherkin on the top.
Hard-boiled, chopped eggs mixed with mayonnaise topped with anchovies or capers.
Blue cheese and egg mixture (see recipe).
Smoked mackerel and scrambled eggs, on black bread.
Brie or soft blue cheese such as Cambozola garnished with black or green, halved grapes.
A roll of smoked ham with a quartered, cooked prune on top (buy tinned prunes, ready cooked – drain well).
Parma-type ham, garnished with a slice of melon, or wrapped around by the ham.
Mock caviar, black or red, bought in little jars, piled on small crackers.
Smoked oysters or mussels, served on black bread. (You find them in all supermarkets near the tinned fish.)
Tinned, white crab meat, drained and mixed with a little mayonnaise, served on sliced baguettes.
Smoked salmon roulades stuffed with smoked trout mousse, mixed with a little cream cheese, on black bread.
Roasted mixed peppers with olive oil, garlic and herbs.

DRINKS PARTIES can be great fun and easy to do. Generally they do not work out very expensive. It cheers people up if you have prepared some trays with little eats which are easy to pick up with your fingers. Some of the toppings can be prepared the day before, but in general, canapés should be made at most, a couple of hours before they are eaten. Cover them with clingfilm as soon as they are ready. Decorate the serving trays with paper doilies, and fronds of fennel, parsley or water cress, slices of lemon, or halved cherry tomatoes.

If you make any of these mini-sandwiches full size with perhaps lettuce and other garnishes such as tomato and cucumber, you can serve them as a simple supper; but remember these open sandwiches have to be eaten with a knife and fork. The Danes have these <u>Smørrebrod</u> for lunch almost every day. Two or three of these sandwiches are enough, but it is nice if they are followed by a little sweet, such as a yoghurt.

Instant snacks for the drinks party

Nuts including home-salted almonds.
Olives, not stuffed, whole, such as Spanish queen olives.
Olives in oil, stuffed with herbs, often Greek, or anchovy's from Spain.
Thin slices of salami, such as cervelat, rolled and pinned with cocktail sticks or in small, thick slices.
Cheesey biscuits, such as cheese straws – the Dutch makes are good.
Cubes of tasty hard cheese.
Crisps – Kettle crisps are excellent and substantial enough with dips. They do not break easily.

Sauces and gravy

A sauce should compliment the flavour of the dish with which it is served, not overshadow it. Allow 2½ tbs. of sauce per person. This is not very much, but if the sauce has a really good flavour, you will not need any more.

If you roast a joint of meat and you don't get much juice from it, for instance in the case of roasting potatoes around the meat, you may have to make a sauce from scratch. If you do have juice from the joint:

1. Lift the joint off its oven dish onto a cutting board to rest before carving, lightly covered with foil.
2. Pour off the juices from the joint into a bowl.
3. Pour some boiling water into the oven dish and scrape off all the little bits that have stuck to the pan but which are not burnt.
4. Add to the juices.
5. Boil the juices together for a few minutes.
6. Put aside to let the fat rise. You can then skim it off.
7. Strain the rest of the juice into a small pan and season it and thicken it with 1 tsp. of cornflour mixed in ½ cup of water.
8. If you think your gravy has not much flavour, add a small part of a stock cube.

The juice that comes out of roasted or microwaved fish should also be amalgamated with the sauce that you serve with the fish.

To thicken gravy: Add 1 teaspoon cornflour to ⅓ cup of cold water, stir and add to gravy.

STARTERS

SMOKED HADDOCK IN CREAM & SPRING ONION SAUCE

Serves 4 as a main course, 6 as a starter. (If used as a stuffing for pancakes or omelettes this recipe will be sufficient to serve 8.)

Ingredients:

2 lbs. of smoked haddock fillet
4 spring onions
¼ pint double cream or creme fraiche
½ pint milk
2 teaspoons lemon juice
bay leaf
1 tbs. flour
salt & white pepper
1 tbs. chopped parsley
½ oz butter

Method:

1. Simmer milk, bay leaf and seasoning for 5 minutes.
2. Add haddock and cook gently until easy to flake.
3. Drain but keep the milk
4. Clean pan and sauté chopped spring onions in butter for 3 minutes.
5. Add flour and when absorbed add ¼ pint of the milk from the fish to make a sauce.
6. Whisk well.
7. Add double cream, parsley, seasoning and some more milk if it seems too thick.
8. Simmer for 2 minutes.
9. Add the boned and skinned haddock into the sauce and simmer for 5 minutes.
10. Check seasoning.
11. Serve with steamed vegetables or boiled rice.

Note:

This dish was a favourite of the author Arnold Bennett. This is easy comfort food when you feel a little fragile! You do not have to use cream, you can use all milk instead.

Variations:

Make **large pancakes** in advance. Fill them with the fish mixture and some of the sauce. Place in an oven dish. Sprinkle the pancakes with parmesan cheese. Heat for 20 minutes in a medium hot oven 200° C.
Make one 2-egg **omelette** per person and fill each with a couple of spoonfuls of the fish mixture.

FINNISH FISH SOUP

Serves 6

Note:

Soups often take the place of the main course in Finland. They are filling and eaten in large quantities with bread and butter. I always associate the fish soup with Summer, and our stay on the islands where one catches the fish in the near-by lake. All kinds of fish is used in Finland for the soup: but because of the bones, I suggest you use filleted fish.

Ingredients:

1 large fillet of fresh cod – about 2 lbs.
Fish trimmings from the fishmonger (bones, heads, etc.) – optional
2 carrots, peeled and sliced
3 medium onions
4 medium potatoes
1 oz butter
2 pints of milk
3 tbs. of cream, (optional)
4 tbs. of parsley and the stalks
2 bay leaves
salt, pepper, 1 tsp. dried dill

Method:

1. Peel and cut potatoes and onions into medium sized pieces.
2. Skin the cod fillets and cut into strips, about a finger thick.
3. Combine the milk, onions, potatoes and carrots (and possible fish trimmings) and cook for 20 minutes.
4. Now remove the fish trimmings and add the pieces of fish and the herbs. (If you add the fish at an earlier stage it will be overcooked.)
5. Cook 10 minutes over a low heat, until fish is done.
6. Add the cream and butter.
7. Adjust seasoning and decorate with more chopped herbs.

Note:

The soup has a very gentle flavour, so do not overdo the seasoning.

Variations:

Add peas, sweetcorn or the carrots from the fish stock for a dash of colour. You can also do this soup with tinned crabmeat. Crab meat is already cooked so only needs to be added a couple of minutes before the end.

CUCUMBER MOUSSE

Serves 6 to 8

Note:

A lovely fresh tasting summer lunch dish.

Ingredients:

1 large cucumber
6 oz full-fat Philadelphia cream cheese, softened with a wooden spoon
2 tsp. finely chopped onion
½ oz gelatine
¼ pint boiling water
2 tbs. white wine vinegar
1 tbs. caster sugar
pinch of mace
¼ pint of whipped cream

Method:

1. Magimix the un-peeled cucumber until fine dice. **Do not** process for too long!
2. Sprinkle with salt and leave weighted down by a plate for 15 minutes.
3. Drain off juices.
4. Add onion to cucumber.
5. Dissolve gelatine in some of the hot water and add to softened cream cheese.
6. Add vinegar and sugar.
7. Add mace and seasoning to cucumber and mix thoroughly.
8. Chill in refrigerator.
9. When mixture is beginning to set, add whipped cream by folding it in gently.
10. Check seasoning. The mixture should be tangy, but not too salty.
11. Pour into an oiled mould and leave to set overnight. Leave in the mould, if attractive or turn out onto a whetted plate. (The wetness allows you to move the mousse into the centre of the plate.)
12. Decorate with cucumber slices and a little watercress.
13. Serve with Melba toast or toast triangles.

SWEDISH GRAVAD LAX WITH DILL & MUSTARD SAUCE

Takes 3 days. Serves 12 as a starter

'Gravad' means 'buried' salmon. It is not smoked but 'cured' with sugar, salt and dill in the refrigerator.

<u>Ingredients</u>:

1 x 6 lb. salmon (ask fishmonger to fillet it and take the small bones out, but to leave the skin on)

<u>For the marinade:</u>

4 tbs. salt
4 tbs. sugar
2 tbs. milled fine black pepper
4 heaped tbs. dried dill weed or 1 cup of freshly chopped dill

Swedish Mustard Sauce

14 tbs. vegetable oil (not olive oil)
4 tbs. wine vinegar (white)
4 tsp. Dijon mustard or 3 of English
2 egg yolks
1 tsp. salt and ½ tsp. fine, white pepper
3 tsp. dried dill or 2 tbs. of fresh, chopped dill
2 dsp. caster sugar

<u>Method to cure the salmon</u> – <u>Takes 3 days</u>:

1. Mix salt, sugar, pepper.
2. Place one side of salmon, skin down, in a china dish with a rim.
3. Rub salt mixture into exposed flesh and sprinkle with dill.
4. Place the other fillet on top, skin side up.
5. Cover dish with greaseproof paper or foil.
6. Put weight on top, such as heavy tins.
7. Leave in fridge for 3 days, basting the fish twice a day and turning over once so top fillet lies in the brine.
8. When the fish is cured, remove from brine.
9. Wipe with kitchen towel.
10. Slice **fairly** thinly, (but not as thinly as smoked salmon) with your knife held diagonally against the skin so that each slice has a green ribbon of dill along its edge. The skin is left behind.
11. Serve with thinly sliced brown bread and mustard sauce.

<u>Method for creating the sauce:</u>

1. Add the oil slowly to the egg yolks, while whisking to produce an emulsion, as in mayonnaise.
2. Add sugar, salt, pepper, dill and lastly the wine vinegar while mixing all the time.
Keep in screw-top jar in the fridge for up to 2 weeks.
Shake well before using.
The sauce should have a strong piquant flavour, with sweetness combined with the mustard.
It is also excellent with smoked salmon.

Note:

You can use other fish too, but it is not then 'lax'. We do this even with sprats in Scandinavia. There is a difference between dill weed (the fine thread-like leaves), and the flower of the plant with its seeds. For most things one uses the leaves only, but say, for pickling cucumber or boiling Cray fish, you use the flower as well.

Do not mix dill with fennel which looks very similar, but tastes of aniseed.

FINNISH YOGHURT
(Viili)

In the summer, eating Viili (the Finnish name for yoghurt) takes the place of porridge as a breakfast or lunch dish. It is a special type of yoghurt, which you cannot buy in the U.K. I hope one day the Scandinavians may introduce it to the UK.

Housewives make the yoghurt by keeping a little of the last batch they had, a teaspoon or so, which they place in a bowl and pour a quarter of a pint of milk over. You then leave the bowl at room temperature until it sets and you then transfer it into the fridge. Viili can only be made in the summer when the temperature is right.

What you get is a rather elastic, thick yoghurt, which is sweet rather than sour, and covered by a thin skin of cream which has risen to the surface. You eat the yoghurt chilled, sprinkled with sugar and a little cinnamon.

In Sweden the yoghurt is similar but often homogenised and consumed as a drink rather than eaten with a spoon. You can buy it in a very rich form, which is made of cream and resembles our sour cream here. This kind of yoghurt is generally used for adding to cold fish dishes as a sauce.

EGG MOUSSE

Serves 8 as a starter

Note:

This mousse was a revelation to me. I first had it as a starter at a dinner prepared by one of my real foodie friends. It was served in ramekins and was a most delicious way of presenting eggs. A large bowl of this mousse is good for a party table, and it is excellent with smoked salmon.

<u>**Ingredients:**</u>

6 hard-boiled eggs
half pint of mayonnaise
½ oz gelatin
½ pint chicken stock or vegetable stock
½ tsp. salt
½ tsp. curry powder
a good pinch of pepper
¼ tsp. or a good pinch of mace
¼ pint lightly whipped cream

<u>**Garnish:**</u>

Slices of cucumber and chopped parsley.

<u>**Method:**</u>

1. Separate egg yolks from the whites by cutting eggs in half lengthways.
2. Mash the cold egg yolks into the mayonnaise and beat well.
3. Soften the gelatine in hot stock.
4. Cool to blood heat.
5. Stir the gelatine into the mayonnaise. Leave the mixture in the fridge for about 1-2 hours to set a little.
6. Chop the egg whites fairly finely (you can do this in a Magimix) and add them to the mixture with the seasonings and spices.
7. Add the softly whipped cream and check for seasoning.
8. Put into a glass bowl or individual ramekin dishes and leave to set.

<u>**Garnish:**</u>

Before serving, garnish with halved thin slices of cucumber (with the rind on) around the edge of the dish and sprinkle some parsley in the middle.
Other serving suggestions: Serve scoops of mousse on plate surrounded by slivers of smoked salmon or decorate with 'caviar' or watercress.
If you are using lump fish roe, which is the 'caviar', add it immediately before serving as it tends to discolour the dish.

SWEDISH INNKEEPER'S PÂTÉ
Serves 6

A baked terrine, light in texture, a very useful starter.

Ingredients:
1 lb. Pork Liver, sliced
1 lb. sweetcure streaky bacon, sliced
½ lb. thinly sliced streaky bacon, stretched
6 anchovies fillets, chopped
½ medium onion, finely chopped, sautéed and cooled
5 eggs
1 tbs. plain flour
1 cup double cream
1 cup single cream
salt (be careful as bacon is salty) 1 tsp. may be sufficient
pepper
¼ tsp. Quartre Épices (if not available, ½ tsp. curry powder)
eggcup of brandy – optional

Method:
1. Grind liver in a food processor.
2. Chop up 1 lb. bacon roughly and grind in the food processor.
3. Add bacon to liver.
4. Add rest of ingredients and mix thoroughly.
5. Fry 1 tbs. of the mixture and taste to see if the seasoning is correct.
6. Line loaf tin with foil and ½ lb. of thinly sliced bacon.
7. Fill the tin with liver mixture and fold the bacon over it.
8. Bake in a bain marie covered with foil at approximately 200° C until risen (about 1 ¼ hours).
9. Leave to cool in tin.
10. Chill in fridge overnight with a weight on top (such as a full jam jar).
11. Turn out of the tin onto a serving dish.

Note:
If you use an earthenware dish, there is no need to use foil or bacon to line container as one can serve the paté straight from dish.
Makes a very pleasant soft everyday paté, not too rich, but with a delicate flavour. (Tends to crumble a bit when sliced.)

Quatre Épices is a very useful mixture of spices for paté and meat dishes. You may have to buy it in France, as it is not very common in England.

To **'stretch' bacon**, place rasher on a board and press a knife at an angle along its surface to make the rasher longer. This stops the bacon from contracting too much in the oven; particularly useful when you wrap little cocktail sausages in bacon.

AVOCADO MOUSSE
Serves 6

An unusual mousse, recommended by avocado growers. It is an elegant starter.

Ingredients:

1 level tbs. gelatine
¼ pint water
3 avocados
lemon juice
1 level tsp. finely chopped onion
2 tsp. Worcester sauce
¼ pint chicken stock
salt and pepper
¼ pint mayonnaise
¼ pint double cream, whipped
2 egg whites (optional)

For garnish:
1 small green pepper, chopped
4-6 spring onions, chopped
2 oz black olives, whole
¼ pint French dressing

Method:

1. Dissolve gelatine in the hot water and cool.
2. Peel, stone and purée the avocadoes.
3. Add lemon juice, onion, Worcester sauce and, when smooth, the stock and gelatin.
4. Leave in the fridge to begin to set.
5. Fold in mayonnaise and then the cream, softly whipped. (If it is whipped too hard, it is difficult to mix with the mousse.)
6. Put in a rinsed ring mould if available (any basin will do) and cover with cling film.
7. Leave to set in the fridge.

For Garnish:
8. Chop pepper.
9. Mix with chopped spring onion and dressing.
10. When the mousse has set, turn it out and surround it with the peppers, etc.
11. Decorate with black olives and put some sprays of parsley in the centre, if you like.

Note:
The mousse discolours if kept exposed to the open air for a long time, so only tip it out ½ an hour before the event. While it is setting in the fridge it is wise to cover it

with cling film.

To help getting the mousse out easily, rinse mould with cold water or oil it lightly before filling it. If for some reason the top does not come out looking smooth, use your garnish to sprinkle over the top to cover any blemishes.

To dissolve Gelatine:

Heat gently in a little water, in a small saucepan. Do not allow to boil. Do not stir, but shake the pan until the liquid is clear.

CRAB MOUSSE
Serves 4

Ingredients:

1 packet of powdered aspic
a few slices of cucumber or some chopped parsley
½ lb. cooked white crab meat
4 tbs. mayonnaise
2 tsp. gelatin
¼ pint whipping cream
salt and pepper, Tabasco, lemon juice

Garnish:

Mustard and cress for decoration

Method:

1. Dissolve the aspic in half a pint of hot water.
2. Pour half of it in a wetted mould.
3. Float slices of cucumber or chopped parsley on top and chill in fridge until set.
4. Flake crab and mix with the remaining aspic and mayonnaise.
5. Dissolve gelatine in a little hot water and add to shellfish.
6. When cool and beginning to set, add whipped cream.
7. Season very well with lemon juice, a few drops of Tabasco, salt and pepper.
8. Pour onto set aspic in mould and leave to set for at least 1½ hours or overnight in the fridge.
9. To turn out, dip bowl in hot water for half a minute and loosen sides of mousse.
10. When mousse starts to move when bowl is tilted, turn it upside down onto a serving dish.
11. Surround with mustard and cress.

Serve with Melba toast or ordinary toast triangles.

Note:

If you are not sure how the mousse is going to land on your serving plate, wet the serving plate first so that you can move the mousse around into the correct position.

AVOCADO PURÉE (Guacamole)

Serves 6

Useful as a cocktail dip as well as a starter, perhaps served in scooped out tomatoes, cut in half.

Ingredients:

3 large ripe avocadoes
small tin of tomatoes, drained, or 1 large fresh beef tomato, peeled
2 cloves garlic, squeezed
2 tbs. lemon juice
salt, pepper Tabasco (a few drops)

Method:

1. Halve avocadoes, remove stone and scoop out the flesh into a liquidizer.
2. Remove liquid from tomatoes, chop roughly and add to avocado. (If you use a fresh tomato, peel, de-seed, drain and chop.)
3. Add garlic, salt, pepper and lemon juice while liquidizing mixture.

Note:

It is very important to put enough salt and lemon juice to get a really tasty mix.

Eat with Mexican corn chips or pitta bread.

How to peel tomatoes:

Score tomato around the middle. Place in bowl with boiling water. Leave for 2 minutes. Remove with a fork and peel skin off with a knife. The same method can be used for peeling peaches, but they must be ripe.

LEEKS PROVENÇAL
Serves 4 to 6

<u>**Ingredients:**</u>

2 lbs. fine straight leeks with a long white part
4 large beef tomatoes or 1 x 14 oz can of tinned tomatoes
3 cloves garlic
3 tbs. chopped parsley
1 dsp. dried basil – if fresh available, 2 tbs.
¾ cup olive oil
salt and freshly milled black pepper
1 bay leaf

<u>**Garnish:**</u>

some more fresh parsley
Black olives

<u>**Method:**</u>

1. Trim off the outer layer of the leek and the top and bottom, cutting off the tough green top.
2. Check that the leeks are clean, otherwise rinse well under the tap.
3. Cut the rest of the leeks into 1½" lengths.
4. Fry leeks in olive oil for 10 minutes.
5. Remove from pan.
6. Add peeled, chopped garlic, some more oil and roughly chopped tomatoes, herbs and seasoning.
7. If you have any wine leftover, this is a good thing to add, it can be white or red.
8. Cook the mixture for about 10 minutes and add the leeks.
9. Stew gently for about 15 minutes.
10. The leeks should still be a little bit crunchy when you have finished cooking.

<u>**To serve:**</u>

A simple starter eaten with white bread on its own or as an accompaniment to cold meat. Serve hot or cold, decorated with more parsley and a few black olives. An excellent part of a buffet.

HERRING EYE
Serves 6

Ingredients:

10 oz Danish spiced herrings (these have a reddish marinade on them)
6 eggs, hard-boiled
2 medium onions, finely chopped
2 tbs. Capers, drained
2 cups fresh parsley, chopped

Method:

1. Chop your onion finely.
2. Hard boil the eggs and halve them. Keep whites and yolks separate.
3. Chop the whites roughly and mash yolks with a fork.
4. Arrange the ingredients in the following way, on a round platter:
   In the middle, put the pile of drained herrings. Round the herrings, sprinkle the capers. Round the capers sprinkle the onion, round the onion sprinkle the yolk of egg, round the yolks sprinkle the whites of eggs and finally, round the whites sprinkle the parsley.

To serve:

Offer black bread and butter and invite guests to help themselves from the platter by drawing the serving spoon from the centre of the dish towards the outside so that they get some of everything on their plate.

Ice cold schnapps or beer is very good with this dish.

If you can boil an egg you can prepare this dish! It is an interesting and easy starter for the nervous cook.

AUBERGINE PÂTÉ

Serves 5 to 6

This is a Middle Eastern starter.

Ingredients:

3 aubergines
½ cup vegetable oil
½ small onion, finely chopped
2 tbs. lemon juice
2 cloves of garlic
a few drops of Tabasco or some chilli powder

Garnish:

2 tbs. chopped spring onion
chopped cucumber
chopped green pepper
chopped tomato
3 tbs. chopped parsley
lettuce

Method:

1. Wash and prick aubergines.
2. Cook approximately 40 minutes in medium oven until really soft. Cool them.
3. With a spoon scoop out the flesh from each halved aubergine.
4. Liquidize to a smooth purée.
5. Add lemon juice, squeezed garlic, Tabasco, salt and pepper.
6. While the machine is going, pour in the oil slowly as for mayonnaise.
7. Taste for flavour, check seasoning.
8. Add chopped onion.
9. Pour into shallow serving dish lined with lettuce.
10. Decorate edges with the above garnish and sprinkle with parsley.

Serve with hot pitta bread.

JANSSON'S TEMPTATION

Serves 6 to 8

A Swedish starter, excellent for a dinner party in the Winter, accompanied by nicely chilled Schnapps. Skål!

Ingredients:

6 large potatoes
1 tins anchovy fillets, chopped
1 pt. double cream
2 large Spanish onions
2 oz butter

Method:

1. Cut potatoes into fine (julienne) strips.
2. Drain anchovies and keep oil.
3. Chop onion and sauté in butter for 15 minutes with a lid on.
4. Arrange a layer of potato sprinkled with pepper and a little salt in the bottom of a greased shallow oven-proof dish.
5. Sprinkle on onion and anchovies.
6. Put on another layer of potatoes, sprinkle with pepper and a little salt.
7. Pour on some anchovy oil and half the cream.
8. Dot with butter and bake in a hot oven for 1 hour.
9. Pour on the rest of the cream and continue baking for another 20 minutes (or more), until the potatoes are really soft and the top is brown, turning up the heat if necessary.

Note:

You should really use the Swedish type of anchovies for this dish. They are very different, but hard to come by. The usual Spanish anchovy fillets will do.

Julienne strips means you cut the potato into slightly thick 'matches'. Some blenders have a disk for doing this job. I cut mine by hand.

Many stories are told about the origin of the name of this dish. One version goes like this:

A priest visited a lonely farmhouse in winter and had to stay the night because of the bad weather. He was given a good dinner which included this dish, and loved it. In the middle of the night, he kept thinking about the potato dish and could not resist coming downstairs to have some more from the larder. He was caught by his host and felt very embarrassed, but the temptation had been too great for him!

FRENCH FISH SOUP

(á la Bouillabaisse) with garlic croutons and rouille
Serves 8 as a starter, 6 as a main course

This is a classic Mediterranean fish soup which we can only try to emulate with our Northern fish.

<u>Ingredients:</u>

FISH: 2 lb. cod or whiting, 2 lbs. squid rings, ½ lb. shelled prawns, ½ lb. any firm fish, such as Icelandic halibut or monk fish.
1 oz butter
1 large onion, chopped
3 cloves of garlic, squeezed
2 x 14 oz tin chopped tomatoes or 2 lb. fresh tomatoes, skinned and chopped
1½ pt. water or fish stock
1 cup olive oil
2 glasses dry white wine
6 stalks parsley
2 bay leaves
1 dsp. mixed herbs
1 tsp. oregano
fresh basil or the *herb* fennel, if available
salt and freshly milled black pepper
pinch of saffron threads, steeped in ½ cup hot water for 15 minutes, strained and added to stew

<u>Garlic Croutons:</u>

1 stale French bread stick, cut into ¼ inch slices
1 cup olive oil
4 cloves garlic, squeezed

<u>Rouille:</u>

¼ pt. mayonnaise
2 tsp. paprika
2 cloves garlic, squeezed
generous pinch of chilli
3 tbs. fresh, white bread crumbs

Mix all ingredients together in blender and check seasoning.

<u>Method:</u>

1. Buy squid rings, ready prepared.
2. Cut fish in largeish chunks.

3. Sauté onion.
4. Add tomato, oil, wine, stock or water and cook for 15 minutes.
5. Add all the fish (except prawns) and cook for 15 minutes.
6. Remove fish and discard any bones and skin.
7. Add dry white wine, herbs and seasoning and cook soup for ½ hour.
8. Remove bay leaf and parsley stalks.
9. Return the fish to the soup with strained saffron stock and add the prawns.
10. Taste soup for seasoning.

Note:
You may add a little tomato pureé to intensify the flavour.

Crôutons:

1. Arrange bread slices on greased oven dish.
2. Mix crushed garlic with oil and brush this mixture onto bread slices.
3. Turn over and brush also onto the other side.
4. Roast until crisp in med. oven 200° C, for 15 minutes or until golden.

Note:

Serve soup with garlic crôutons and rouille separately. Every person adds a dollop of rouille on some croutons and floats them in his soup.

Grated cheese (Gruyère) can also be served with it.

If you haven't got time to cook the soup from scratch, there are some perfectly acceptable jars of Provencale fish soup in Fish Mongers or Delicatessens. You can also buy Rouille in jars nowadays in good supermarkets.

TARAMASALATA

(smoked cod pâté)
Serves 6 to 8

Note:
The roe can be obtained in tins but beware of buying paté instead, it tends to be bland. If you get freshly smoked roe still in its skin from the fishmonger, it will look dark reddish brown.

Ingredients:

4 oz smoked cods' roe
½ pt. vegetable oil
2 cloves garlic
Freshly milled black pepper
3-4 tbs. lemon juice

Garnish:

black olives
chopped parsley

For a milder version: add ½ cup mayonnaise or sour cream.

Method:

1. If using freshly smoked roe soak it first hot water for 10 minutes. Cut the skin and pull off to expose contents.
2. Put in the mixer and add oil slowly, as if for mayonnaise.
3. Halfway through, add 3 tbs. lemon juice.
4. When all oil is absorbed add garlic, and if the roe is too thick, add 2 to 3 tbs. of boiling water.
5. If the flavour is too salty dilute with mayonnaise or cream.
6. Serve chilled in a bowl garnished with parsley and olives, accompanied by warm pitta bread.

Note:

Keeps well in the fridge.

There is a Finnish delicacy of the same type, where we use fresh raw turbot roe, mixed with a little finely chopped onion and fresh or sour cream. This is much prized and eaten with white toast as a starter. In fact, we can use many different types of fish roe for this dish. In Finland we call the dish caviar, but of course real caviar is exclusively sturgeons' roe and is not mixed with cream.
Smoked cods' roe can be used on its own, well blended, with lemon garnish, as a topping for cocktail canapés. It has a very strong, salty flavour, so use sparingly.

RILLETTES
(Potted pork)
Serves 12

A dish from the Loire in France.

Ingredients:

3 lb. belly or shoulder of fresh pork
¼ pint dry white wine
water to cover meat
3 cloves of garlic, chopped
10 peppercorns
2 bay leaves
salt
parsley, thyme or rosemary

Method:

1. Remove skin from pork and cut into ½" slices.
2. Put in a pot to cook on the stove or in the oven, with the rest of the ingredients.
3. Pour on water, almost to cover meat and a glass of dry white wine. Cover with a lid.
4. Cook for about 3 hours at medium heat (simmering) or in the oven at 180° C.
5. Remove from pot, strain the meat but keep the liquid.
6. Remove peppercorns, bay leaves and bouquet garni.
7. Crush meat with a fork (in France they tear it apart with 2 forks).
8. Skim off fat from juices and keep aside.
9. Add 3 tbs. of the melted fat to the meat.
10. Taste for flavour.
11. Pack into a bowl and cool.
12. Before the fat, left in a separate bowl, has congealed, pour a thin layer of it on top of the meat to protect it.
13. Refrigerate.

Note:

Keeps for 2-3 weeks.

Very tasty and rich paté. Serve with crusty French bread and sharp little cocktail gherkins (cornichons).

The origin of this dish is that since the French never waste a single bit of an animal they kill for food, there are many little bits left when a pig has been killed, and the larger pieces of meat have been cut off. These little bits and trimmings are stewed by slow cooking until very tender. They are then sorted by hand and bones etc. extracted. The good meat is packed into jars, as above. In country areas in France, you often see pigs ears and tails and the gizzards of poultry, cooked and packed in their own fat, for turning into tasty dishes such as fried pigs' ears. One of the specialities of the Lot region is salad with 'gesiers' which are sliced, cooked gizzards arranged over a dressed green salad and decorated with walnuts. Very good it is too! The gizzards are then quite tender.

COLD APPLE & PARSNIP SOUP

Serves 6

An interesting soup. Make your guests guess what it is made of!

Ingredients:

1 small onion, chopped
3 parsnips, peeled and cubed
4 Golden Delicious apples, peeled, cored and cubed
¼ pt. whipping cream
1½ pt. vegetable stock
1 tsp. curry powder
seasoning and lemon juice to taste
1 oz butter

Method:

1. Chop onion and sautée in the butter.
2. Add curry powder.
3. Peel and cube parsnips and add to onion.
4. Add stock and continue cooking gently until parsnips are soft. (About 10 minutes.)
5. Cook apples in butter in a saucepan with a lid on, for 10 minutes.
6. Add a little stock if they begin to stick.
7. Combine with parsnip and onion mixture.
8. Pour on the rest of the stock and simmer for 20 minutes.
9. Liquidise soup.
10. Add cream, lemon juice, salt and white pepper to taste.
11. Serve hot or chilled.

CHICKEN & AVOCADO SOUP

Serves 4 to 6

An interesting light soup, suitable for the start of a rich lunch.

Ingredients:

1 medium onion, finely chopped
2 cloves garlic, squeezed
1 14 oz (420g.) tin chopped tomatoes
1 ripe avocado
3 oz cream cheese
1½ pints chicken stock (made from roast a chicken carcass with some fresh vegetables) or 1 stock cube
1 chicken breast or a couple of chicken thighs
2 tbs. chopped parsley
2 tbs. tomato purée
bay leaf
1 tsp. each of dried basil or tarragon
2 tbs. olive oil
seasoning, including a few drops of Tabasco sauce

Method:

1. Fry chopped onion gently, in olive oil.
2. Add tomatoes, herbs, bay leaf, garlic, chicken breast and some of the stock.
3. Cook for about 20 minutes.
4. Take out chicken, remove skin and cut into small slices.
5. Add cream cheese to soup and whisk so it is well distributed.
6. Put back the chicken breast into the soup with the tomato purée and the rest of the stock.
7. Check the seasoning.
8. Finally peel and cube the flesh of the avocado and add to the soup with the parsley and Tabasco.
9. Remove the bay leaf.
10. If the soup is too thick, add a little more stock.

Note:

This is a colourful and fragrant soup, surprisingly tasty and refreshing. It looks good in a white tureen.
Serve with crusty, white rolls.

Variation:

Vegetarians could substitute the chicken with fish or shell fish, and use fish or vegetable stock.

How to peel and cube an avocado pear

1. This works well if the avocado is *really* ripe.
2. Cut the avocado in half, lengthwise. There is a big stone in the middle.
3. Hold both halves in your hands and twist them in opposite directions.
4. Pull the two halves apart.
5. Remove the stone.
6. Score the skin of the halves and peel it off.
7. Cut the flesh into cubes.

SOUP OF JERUSALEM ARTICHOKES

Serves 6

Ingredients:

1½ lbs. of Jerusalem artichokes, (they grow in the ground like potatoes)
1 medium onion, chopped
1½ pts. milk
3 tbs. cream
½ oz butter
½ cup chopped parsley
Salt and white pepper

Method:

1. Peeling raw artichokes is a chore, they are so knobbly. Boil them in water until tender.
2. Leave them to cool. The skin can then be rubbed off and the flesh extracted with your hands or with a teaspoon.
3. Combine with other ingredients.
4. Liquidize and check seasoning.

Note:

This soup is a rare treat, and a lovely start to a Sunday lunch. It has a very distinct flavour. If the flavour is a little too strong, dilute the soup with a little more milk.

BUCKWHEAT PANCAKES WITH SMOKED SALMON

Serves 2 per person

This is a Russian recipe and one of my favorites.

Ingredients:

For the pancakes:
2 oz plain flour
2 oz Buckwheat flour
¼ tsp. salt
2 eggs
½ pint milk
1½ oz butter
4 oz smoked salmon

Method:

1. Mix the flours and salt.
2. Add the eggs one by one.
3. Lastly add the milk.
4. Whisk the batter well. Leave to stand for 30 minutes.
5. Heat a frying pan.
6. Cook 3 small pancakes at a time They are meant to be quite thick.
7. When one side of the pancake looks well set, turn over to brown the other side.
8. Continue until the batter is used up.
9. Arrange a slice of smoked salmon on top of each pancake and place a spoonful of sour cream in the middle.
10. If you really want to gild the lily, place a teaspoonful of 'Caviar' (Lump fish roe will do) on top of the cream.

Note:

If you cannot be bothered to make the pancakes, you may be able to buy ready made small ones, warm them and top them as above.

FENNEL BAKED WITH CHEESE
Serves 4

Ingredients:

4 fennel bulbs
2 oz butter
3 tbs. parmesan

Method:

1. Remove outside tough leaves and some of the stalk.
2. Halve fennels.
3. Simmer in salted water until tender and drain.
4. Place cut side down in buttered ramekin dishes, 2 halves of fennel for each dish.
5. Sprinkle on the parmesan.
6. Dot with butter.
7. Bake at 200° C until golden brown, about 10 minutes.

Note:

You eat these with a small spoon and fork.

SIMPLE DANISH PÂTÉ

Serves 4 to 6

A quick and easy chicken liver pâté.

Ingredients:

1 lb. frozen chicken livers
3 oz butter + 2 oz for covering
4 tbs. sour or whipping cream
2 tbs. brandy or sherry (optional)
1 tsp. mixed dried herbs
½ tsp. quatre épices or mixed spice
1-2 tsp. salt
freshly ground black pepper
bay leaf
2 cloves garlic, crushed
½ small onion, finely chopped

Method:

1. Allow livers to defrost on a plate.
2. Cut off any sinews and discoloured bits.
3. Heat 3 oz butter in a frying pan, add onion and garlic.
4. Cook for 2 minutes.
5. Add livers (minus their juices), seasoning, bay leaf and spices.
6. Cook gently, stirring now and then for about 5 minutes.
7. Add cream and brandy or sherry.
8. Cook for a further 5 minutes.
9. Remove bay leaf.
10. Liquidise and taste for seasoning.
11. Pack into a small bowl or individual ramekins. Leave in the fridge for 3 hours.
12. When cool, heat the remaining 2 oz butter and pour over the paté to protect it.
13. Cover with clingfilm.

Notes:

Keeps for a week in the fridge.
Serve the paté with sweet gherkins and toast.
This is a quick and easy paté. A safe starter for a dinner party, especially over a busy weekend.
It is best made a day in advance.

EGG MAYONNAISE

Serves 8 as a starter

Can be made in advance and assembled 1 hour before. A most useful dish and universally popular.

Ingredients:

12 eggs
1 pint of vegetable or olive oil
3 tbs. white wine vinegar
1 tsp. salt
½ tsp. white ground pepper
1 clove garlic, crushed (optional)

Garnish:

Watercress, or shredded lettuce

Alternatives:

Decorate with little rolls of anchovy fillets.
Decorate with little rolls of smoked salmon.
Add some curry powder to the mayonnaise.
Sprinkle with chopped parsley and capers.

Method:

1. Hardboil 8 eggs for 8 minutes.
2. Plunge into cold water.
3. Crack each egg and peel.
4. Leave in cold water while preparing mayonnaise.

To make the Mayonnaise:

1. Take the four remaining eggs and separate the whites from the yolks. **Only the yolk is used in this recipe**. Keep the white (if not flecked by yolk) in a screw-top jar in the fridge for meringues.
2. Put yolks into a blender.
3. Add the oil in a very thin stream until the mixture 'takes', i.e. begins to get thick. (If you add the oil too fast, the mixture never thickens.)
4. When half the oil has been absorbed add the vinegar, salt, pepper and garlic (if liked).
5. Add the rest of the oil in a steady stream, while processing.
6. You can add 1 tsp. of English mustard for an extra 'kick'.
7. If the mayonnaise gets very thick you can add a small amount of hot water to thin it out.

To assemble the dish:

8. Smear a porcelain dish with the mayonnaise.
9. Halve the hard-boiled eggs and place yolk side down in the bottom of the dish.
10. Smear rest of the mayonnaise on top. (You may have some mayonnaise left over.)
11. Decorate sides with watercress or lettuce and any topping you have chosen, such as anchovy fillets.
12. Cover with clingfilm until used.

Note:

This is a very pleasant starter served with good brown bread or brown toast.
You can dilute the mayonnaise with some Greek yoghurt if you prefer it less rich.

It is very useful to keep home-made Mayonnaise in the fridge. It can form the basis of sauces by adding fresh herbs, spring onions or chives.

To rescue mayonnaise that has gone wrong (curdled or become runny)

1. Take mixture out of the blender.
2. Wash and start again with two fresh egg yolks.
3. Add curdled mixture *very slowly*.

Alternatively

1. Put two fresh egg yolks in a bowl.
2. Add some oil *very slowly* until the mayonnaise 'takes'.
3. Then add curdled mixture little by little.

Good luck!

BRUSSELS SOUP

Serves 4

You can use this recipe for making soups out of spinach, parsley or watercress as well.

Ingredients:

2 oz butter or margarine
l lb. Brussels sprouts (see variations or alternatives)
l medium onion, chopped
l oz flour
¾ pint vegetable or chicken stock
½ pint milk
Seasoning
1 small bunch of parsley, chopped
Cream, optional

Method:

1. Trim and halve Brussels sprouts.
2. Boil in ¾ pt. of stock or stock cube mixture until soft (chicken stock for non-vegetarians).
3. Melt butter in a pan and sauté the onions for a few minutes.
4. Sprinkle on the flour and cook for a few minutes.
5. Add some of the stock from the sprouts into the mixture, whilst stirring.
6. Simmer for l5 minutes.
7. Add the sprouts.
8. Season with salt, pepper and a pinch of nutmeg.
9. Pour into a liquidizer and process until smooth.
10. Stir in the milk and re-heat in a pan.
11. Just before serving add the cream, (if liked).
12. Sprinkle with chopped parsley.

Alternatives additions:

Use sweetcorn and a tin of drained tuna fish.
Chopped watercress.
Cauliflower.

CRAB GUMBO

Serves 6 to 8

A thick and colourful soup from Central America.

Ingredients:

1 large onion chopped
1 med. pepper, de-seeded, chopped
2 cloves garlic
1 lb. crabmeat (half white and half brown)- frozen is fine
2 lbs. of white fish cut into fingers
2 x 14 oz tin chopped tomatoes
¾ lb. okra (green pods – remove hot seeds, wear rubber gloves to do this)
1 bay leaf
2 tsp. mixed herbs
1 tsp. oregano
¼ pt. double cream
1 to 2 tbs. tomato purée
olive oil
salt and pepper
a few drops of Tabasco
1½ pints of water

Method:

1. Top and tail the okra, remove seeds.
2. Fry onion and chopped pepper in olive oil until soft.
3. Add tomatoes, crushed garlic, herbs and the trimmed okra.
4. Add water.
5. Cook with seasoning for 20 minutes.
6. Add crabmeat, fish, tomato purée and more water to cover.
7. Simmer 10 minutes.
8. Stir in cream (optional).
9. Check seasoning.

RED PEPPER MOUSSE

Serves 6 as a starter

A very pretty mousse. Looks good served on lettuce leaves.

Ingredients:

½ finely chopped onion
3 red pepper, de-seeded and chopped
2 tbs. oil
½ tsp. cayenne pepper
2-3 tsp. gelatin
½ cup water
2 tbs. wine vinegar
½ pint whipping cream
salt and white pepper

Method:

1. Sweat onion and peppers in oil.
2. Add cayenne.
3. Cook until very soft under a lid.
4. Liquidise in a Magimix with vinegar until you have a fine purée.
5. Gently dissolve gelatin in water by warming and shaking pan until the mixture is clear.
6. Add dissolved gelatin to the purée with salt and pepper.
7. Leave in the refrigerator until the mixture begins to thicken.
8. Whip cream into soft peaks.
9. Stir into the pepper mixture.
10. Now taste mixture and adjust seasoning. (You may have to add a little more vinegar.)
11. Stir in the cream gently but thoroughly so you have an even pink colour.
12. Pour into a wetted mould and allow to set in the fridge.

To serve:

1. Dip tablespoon in hot water and scoop out mixture onto serving plates lined with lettuce.
2. Decorate with a little lettuce, watercress or parsley.
3. Serve with Melba toast and butter.

MELBA TOAST

Ingredients:

1 medium sliced white loaf

Method:

1. Toast each slice lightly, in a toaster, until golden but not brown.
2. Place the slices of toast flat on a board.
3. With a sharp, serrated knife halve each slice horizontally by pressing down on the slice while moving the knife through the toast with the other.
4. You now have two, very thin slices half toasted.
5. Place the un-toasted side under a grill until slightly coloured. Be careful not to let it burn!

Leave the slices to cool without touching one another or they might go soft.
Keeps well in an airtight tin.

ONION QUICHE
Serves 6

Only the people in Alsace can do this one really well. It is one of their famous dishes. You will be amazed at how delicate it can be.

Ingredients:

Pastry ingredients:

4 oz plain flour
1 oz butter & 1 oz lard
pinch of salt
water

Filling ingredients:

3 large Spanish onions, sliced thinly
2 oz butter
3 eggs
¾ pint milk
2 oz grated cheese
1 tbs. fresh, chopped parsley
seasoning

Method:

1. Magimix pastry adding fats to flour and salt.
2. When crumbly, add a little water (about 2 tbs.),until the pastry becomes a ball.
3. Roll out and line a 9" flan tin.
4. Prick pastry and bake for 15 minutes. (It should look cooked but not coloured.)
5. Melt butter and sweat onion under a lid until soft, but not coloured.
6. When cooked (after 10 minutes) arrange on the cooked pastry.
7. Whip the eggs.
8. Add the milk and seasoning.
9. Pour on top of the onion.
10. Sprinkle with cheese.
11. Bake in the oven for about 20-30 minutes, until quiche has risen and is golden brown.

RISOTTO WITH SPRUE ASPARAGUS

Serves 4 to 6

A dish inspired by Elizabeth David's story about her tasting 'wild asparagus' in Italy.

Ingredients:

1 small bundle of thin green asparagus
2 tbs. olive oil
1½ oz butter – (reserve some for finishing the dish)
1 onion chopped and gently sautéed
6 oz Arborio rice (special Italian risotto rice)
1 pt. chicken stock (or vegetable stock)
2 oz Parmesan cheese
salt and black pepper
2 tbs. chopped parsley
1 glass of dry, white wine

Method:

1. Sweat onion in butter and oil.
2. Cut asparagus into ½" pieces and reserve until the rice is cooked.
3. Add rice and toss with onion.
4. Add hot chicken stock, wine and seasoning.
5. Simmer and stir now and then for about 15-20 minutes.
6. Top up with stock, if necessary, until the rice is cooked and looks creamy but not dry. Add blanched asparagus, i.e. boiled in water until just tender.
7. Check seasoning.
8. Add a lump of butter.
9. Serve immediately, generously sprinkled with Parmesan.

Venetian story:

One of my heroes in cookery is Elizabeth David, who wrote her first book about French food at a hotel in Ross on Wye, just after the war. In her book 'An Omelette and a Glass of Wine', there is a story about a trip she made to Venice in the spring and 'discovered' the wild asparagus. A neighbour in a restaurant, where she had lunch, was eating this green risotto, and she decided to try it. The dish was 'magical'. Apparently the season for this asparagus is very short – just 2 or 3 weeks: and she was lucky to be able to taste it.

As I and my husband were in Venice at the same time of the year, I kept looking for the wild asparagus in the shops. I found it in a little back street grocer-cum-green-grocer, and brought several bunches home with me to England. The asparagus is very thin but has the same shape as our asparagus. I experimented with it to make a risotto. The recipe is above. The recipe works quite well with ordinary English Sprue asparagus. (The thin, all-green asparagus that grows in this country.)

SMOKED TROUT PÂTÉ

For 20 canapés

(See also recipe for Smoked salmon roulades with a cheese and herb stuffing.)

This can be used as a topping for croutons with cocktails, or to fill smoked salmon roulades for a drinks party.

Ingredients:

4 fillets of smoked trout, any bones removed
3 oz softened cream cheese
1 teaspoon of finely chopped onion
1 tbs. finely chopped parsley
1 tbs. lemon juice
sour cream or yoghurt for mixing (less than a small carton)
salt and pepper to taste
4-5 drops of Tabasco

Method:

1. Mix trout, cream cheese, onion and lemon juice in a blender. (Do not blend for more than a few seconds as it might curdle.)
2. Stir in a little sour cream or yoghurt until you get a thick paste that holds its shape.
3. Add parsley and seasoning and Tabasco.

For smoked salmon canapés:

1. Wrap a teaspoon of the paste in a small square of smoked salmon and place, (seam down), on a buttered piece of rye bread 1" x ½".
2. For decoration, cut oval shapes out of black Greek olives (you get about 4 from each olive).
3. With a little of the trout mousse stick the olive on top of the salmon roulade.

Note:

The black olives look very pretty on the pink salmon and the canapés taste delicious.

CRÈME VICHYSSOISE
(Leek & Potato soup)
Serves 6

My daughter's favourite soup.

Ingredients:

1 oz butter
3 leeks
2 large potatoes
1½ pts. milk
3 tbs. chopped parsley
1 bay leaf

Garnish:

1 or 2 tbs. cream

Method:

1. Wash and slice leeks.
2. Peel potatoes and chop them.
3. Sweat leeks in the butter for 5 minutes, without browning.
4. Add potatoes.
5. After a few minutes, add milk, parsley and bay leaf.
6. Simmer soup until potatoes are tender: (use a heat diffuser to stop the milk 'catching').
7. Remove bay leaf. Liquidize soup in a blender.
8. Add a little cream, if liked, salt and pepper.
9. Serve hot or chilled.

Note:

Heat diffusers: You can buy these to stop food 'catching' while cooking. Separate diffusers are used for gas and electricity. You can also buy a flat, glass disk to place in a pan of milk to stop it boiling over.

FINNISH SUMMER SOUP

Serves 6

My mother's favourite soup. Much appreciated due to the tender, new, fresh vegetables.

Ingredients:

1 pt. water
4 young carrots
1 cup of shelled peas
1 small cauliflower
2 or 3 potatoes
1 handful of fresh spinach
2 tbs. fresh parsley, chopped
2 tbs. fresh dill, chopped
2 pts. milk
1 tsp. salt
1 tbs. flour
2 tbs. butter
white pepper

Method:

1. Clean and chop all the vegetables.
2. Boil all, except the spinach, in the water with seasoning.
3. Mix some of the milk with the flour until no lumps remain.
4. Pour this, with the rest of the milk into the soup.
5. Add parsley, dill and butter.
6. Check seasoning.

Note:

This soup should be very gently flavoured so be careful with the seasoning.

MARINADED KIPPERS

Serves 8

This is a surprising dish. Some people prefer it to smoked salmon as a starter.

Ingredients:

2 lbs. boneless kipper fillets – frozen or vacuum packed
½ pt. good French dressing with a little less salt than usual
½ Spanish onion, thinly sliced
2 tbs. black peppercorns
4 Bayleaves
2 tbs. parsley, chopped

Method:

1. Defrost kippers, if frozen.
2. Remove the skin: it comes of quite easily by pulling, if you start at the tail end.
3. Cut into two fillets.
4. Cut each fillet into 1" pieces.
5. Make dressing.
6. Mix fish with dressing, onion, spices and herbs.
7. Marinade in fridge for three days, stirring it occasionally.
8. Serve with buttered black or brown bread.

MELITZANES
TOMATO & AUBERGINE BAKE
Serves 6

Ingredients:

6 slices toast – enough to cover the base of a shallow dish
2 medium aubergines
1½ lbs. tomatoes
1¼ lb. grated cheddar
oil for frying

Method:

1. Place toast in the bottom of a 3" deep dish.
2. Slice aubergines into ¼" thick slices and fry in oil until golden brown.
3. Cool the aubergines and spread half the slices on the toast.
4. Sprinkle with some of the cheese.
5. Slice tomatoes and place on top.
6. Sprinkle with salt and cover with some cheese.
7. Add remaining aubergine slices.
8. Add the rest of the cheese.
9. With a sharp knife, cut the dish up into serving pieces – 6 squares.
10. Cook in the oven for 30 to 40 minutes at 200° C.

Note:

Serve with a plain green salad as a starter or supper dish

This recipe was given to me by my Greek Cypriot business partner.

SPINACH TART
Serves 6 to 8

Ingredients:

½ lb. frozen leaf spinach (or 1½ lb. of fresh spinach, lightly boiled, drained and coarsly chopped)
2 oz cottage cheese
3 oz cream cheese
2 oz parmesan
2 eggs
4 oz double cream
salt and pepper

Shortcrust pastry made with 6 oz flour and 3 oz fat

Method:

1. Prepare pastry and fit it into a 9" flan tin and bake until cooked.
2. De-frost spinach and drain thoroughly.
3. Mix the cheeses, cream and eggs.
4. Add the spinach and seasoning.
5. Pour this mixture into the pastry case.
6. Bake for 30 to 40 minutes at 200° C, until barely set.

Note:

It can be served hot or cold

TUNA & SWEETCORN SOUP

Serves 4

Ingredients:

1 medium tin of sweetcorn
1 small tin Tuna in oil, drained
1 onion, fincly chopped
1½ pints, chicken or vegetable stock
½ pint milk
2 oz butter
1 heaped tbs. plain flour
2 tbs. chopped parsley
seasoning
3 tbs. cream – optional

Method:

1. Chop onion and sweat in butter.
2. Sprinkle on the flour.
3. Add the stock and milk, gradually.
4. Simmer for 15 minutes.
5. Add drained sweetcorn and flaked tuna.
6. Finish with cream and parsley.
7. Check seasoning.

Note:

This soup has a very mild flavour which seems to be appreciated by most people.

MUSSELS GRATINÉE – FAÇON MARIANNE

Serves 6 to 8

This is a very tasty starter from Sweden. It is useful in that it can be prepared in advance and just put in the oven when the guests arrive.

Ingredients:

3 x 15oz tins of mussels in brine, drained
4 oz butter
4 tbs. finely chopped parsley
4 cloves garlic, squeezed
1 cup crème fraiche
1 tin anchovy fillets
black pepper, (but NO salt)

Topping:

4 oz fresh breadcrumbs
1 oz grated parmesan cheese

Method:

1. Drain and chop anchovies, but keep the oil.
2. Squeeze garlic.
3. Melt the butter.
4. Mix these with the parsley and the creme fraiche and the pepper.
5. Butter a shallow oven dish and fill with drained mussels.
6. Distribute the anchovy sauce over the mussels.
7. Mix breadcrumbs and parmesan and sprinkle on top.
8. Dribble the anchovy oil over the whole dish.
9. Bake in a hot oven, about 200° C for 30 minutes.
10. Serve with plenty of crusty bread.

Note:

A little, ice cold Swedish Schnapps would go well with this dish!

SMOKED SALMON PÂTÉ

Serves 6 to 8

This is excellent on black bread served as canapés or as a starter served with Melba toast.

Ingredients:

12 oz smoked salmon trimmings
3 oz melted butter
3 dsp. lemon juice
3 tbs. soured cream or Greek yoghurt
6 to 8 drops of Tabasco
1 tsp. salt (or to taste)
Plenty of freshly ground black pepper

Method:

1. Cut up salmon roughly and chop up in the Magimix.
2. Stop Magimix before it becomes a fine purée.
3. Pour on melted butter while the blender is turning.
4. Stop the machine and add the rest of the ingredients.
5. Pack in a pottery dish and leave in the fridge for 3 hours.

Note:

One of the quickest and easiest starters to make.

GAZPACHO

Serves 6 to 8

A delicious iced soup, no cooking involved.

Ingredients:

1 carton tomato juice
1/3 pint cold water or chicken or vegetable stock
2 tbs. vinegar
3 cloves garlic, squeezed
3 tbs. olive oil
1 medium Spanish onion, finely chopped
1 small cucumber, finely chopped, with rind on.
4 tbs. finely chopped parsley
seasoning

Accompaniments:

4 slices of bread, cubed and fried in a mixture of oil and butter and garlic until golden
3 large tomatoes, skinned, de-seeded and chopped
1 whole cucumber, chopped
1 onion finely chopped
2 peppers, de-seeded and finely chopped

Method:

1. Prepare vegetables for soup and for accompaniments.
2. Mix soup ingredients.
3. Taste for seasoning.
4. Chill in the refrigerator.
5. Serve soup in a large tureen.
6. Serve the garnish separately in little bowls for people to help themselves.

Note:

This is a very colourful soup and refreshing on a hot day. It MUST be really cold.

ASPARAGUS & EGG MOUSSE

(a Belgian recipe)
Serves 6

Ingredients:

1 lb. (500 g) tin of Asparagus
8 hard boiled eggs
1 pint of mayonnaise
3 tsp. Gelatine
salt
cayenne pepper
salad to garnish

Method:

1. Melt the gelatine in a little hot water, or stock from the asparagus tin.
2. Chop the eggs roughly and mix with the mayonnaise.
3. Add the salt and cayenne pepper.
4. Purée them all in a food processor for a few seconds and add the gelatine mixture.
5. Chop the asparagus by hand and combine with the egg pureé. Stir into the mixture.
6. Check seasoning.
7. Turn into an oiled or wetted ring mould.
8. Leave to set overnight.
9. To serve, turn out and fill the centre of the mould with salad greens.

Comments:

I sometimes do the mousse in a bowl and scoop out each serving onto a plate. Garnish it with asparagus spears and water cress.

Serve it with toast or brown bread rolls.

Note:

This recipe is quite rich. One could replace ¼ pint of the mayonnaise with vegetable stock from the asparagus tin.

ONION, TOMATO & BASIL FLAN

Serves 6

Ingredients:

6 oz shortcrust pastry (this means that you make pastry with 6 oz flour and 3 oz
fat, best done in a blender)
2 Spanish onions, thinly sliced
3 medium tomatoes
2 tbs. fresh basil (or 2 tsp. dried basil)
salt and pepper
3 eggs
¼ pt. double cream
2 oz strong cheddar, grated
oil for frying

Method:

1. Fry onions gently, until soft.
2. Slice tomatoes.
3. Chop basil.
4. Mix eggs, cream and seasoning.
5. Roll out pastry and line a 9" flan tin with it.
6. Prick and bake 'blind' for 15 minutes at 200°C.
7. Arrange onions at the bottom, then tomatoes, then herbs, followed by the egg mixture.
8. Top with the cheese.
9. Place in the oven at 200°C.
10. Cook for about 35 minutes until risen and brown.
11. Leave to cool before you cut it as it needs to set a little.

SMOKED MACKEREL PÂTÉ

Serves 4 to 6

Ingredients:

2 packs of smoked mackerel (NOT peppered)
3 oz melted butter
1 tub of sour cream or a small tub of crême fraiche
6 – 8 drops Tabasco sauce
1 tbs. chopped parsley
a little salt and some freshly ground black pepper
2 tbs. lemon juice

Method:

1. Skin the mackerel fillets.
2. Blend the mackerel in a food processor.
3. Add hot melted butter and the rest of the ingredients.
4. Taste for seasoning.
5. Pack into a small earthenware bowl.

Note:

If kept for a few days, cover with clingfilm. Keep in the fridge. Serve with brown toast and lemon wedges.

SMOKED HADDOCK MOUSSE

Serves 4 to 6

Ingredients:

¾ lb. smoked haddock
milk mixed with water to poach it
½ pint aspic – made as per packet
1 tsp. gelatine
2 tbs. lemon juice
¼ pint mayonnaise
¼ pint double cream
salt and white, fine pepper
a few drops of Tabasco

Method:

1. Poach haddock in milk and water for 10 minutes.
2. Remove fish onto a plate.
3. Skin, bone and flake it.
4. Prepare aspic, as per packet.
5. Dissolve the gelatine in it.
6. Rinse glass serving dish with cold water.
7. Pour some of the aspic into the bottom of the dish.
8. Place in fridge to set. (You may wish to put a few slices of cucumber in the bottom of the dish too, to set in the aspic for decoration.)
9. Whip cream until soft peaks.
10. Mix the rest of the aspic with the fish in the blender.
11. Remove from blender.
12. Fold in mayonnaise and cream.
13. Add lemon juice and seasoning.
14. When the aspic in the serving dish has set, pour the mixture on top and leave that to set.
15. Serve from the dish or turn out by dipping bowl in hot water and turn it upside down onto a plate.

Note:

Aspic is like powdered stock which has gelatine in it so that it both flavours and sets the liquid that it is in. It is generally multi-purpose so that you can 'set' any savoury dish with it. Vegetarians may not approve so it may be necessary to use an alternative setting agent.

MUSHROOMS À LA GRÈCQUE
Serves 4

A delicious, light starter for preceding a heavy meal.

Ingredients:

1 carrot
1 small onion
4 tbs. olive oil
4 tbs. corn oil
1 cup dry white wine
2 cloves garlic, crushed
Bouquet garni
1 lb. whole button mushrooms, washed
½ lb. tomatoes skinned and chopped
salt and pepper
a little white wine vinegar if necessary
3 tbs. chopped parsley for garnishing.

Method:

1. Chop carrot and onion finely and sauté in half the oil for 5 minutes.
2. Add wine, herbs and garlic.
3. When the onions are soft, add button mushrooms and chopped tomatoes.
4. Cook gently for 10 to 15 minutes while turning them over from time to time.
5. Cool, and remove the bouquet garni.
6. Add the rest of the oil and chopped parsley.
7. Add seasoning and possibly a little white wine vinegar or lemon juice if the dish seems too oily.
8. Serve at room temperature with pitta bread.

ASPARAGUS WITH SAUCE RAVIGOTE

Serves 6

A light but delicious spring starter.

Ingredients:

2 lbs. (about 4 bunches) fresh asparagus

Sauce:

1 cup French dressing
2 tbs. finely chopped onion
1 tbs. capers
2 tbs. chopped parsley
2 tbs. any other fresh herb such as tarragon or chervil
1 gherkin, finely chopped
2 hard-boiled eggs finely chopped

Method:

1. Trim the bases of the asparagus and peel away some of the skin from the bottom ends.
2. Poach or steam, gently, until barely tender. (The tips cook very quickly but you have to cook a bit longer for the stalks to cook.)
3. Drain and leave on a plate to cool.
4. Mix up the sauce ingredients but keep parsley and egg apart.
5. Arrange asparagus on six plates.
6. Pour on the dressing.
7. Sprinkle with egg and parsley.
8. Serve with fresh, white bread rolls and butter.

CEVICHE
Serves 6

This is raw, marinated fish that 'cooks' in the lime or lemon juice and turns white. It should be eaten cold and perhaps accompanied by some ice-cold vodka and some bread. The dish comes from South America. It is *important* that the fish is **very fresh**.

Ingredients:

2 lbs. fish, e.g. filleted salmon and any firm white fish such as cod, haddock or monkfish
4 lemons or limes
2 medium onions
1 green pepper
1 fresh chilli
2 tbs. chopped parsley
1 tbs. capers
salt and black pepper
4 tbs. olive oil
2 more lemons for garnish

Method:

1. Remove skin and bones from the fish.
2. Slice salmon fairly thinly.
3. Cube the white fish.
4. Chop onions and peppers small.
5. Squeeze juice from the lemons or limes.
6. Open chilli (use rubber gloves as the seeds can burn you) and remove the seeds.
7. Chop chilli finely.
8. Arrange fish and vegetables on a dish.
9. Cover with lime/lemon juice and leave for 4 hours turning the fish occasionally.
10. Arrange salmon around the edge of a serving dish with the cubed white fish and the vegetables in the middle.
11. Pour the olive oil over the dish.
12. Scatter on the parsley and arrange the lemon wedges or slices around the plate as a garnish.
13. Serve with white bread.

SPARE RIBS OF PORK
CHINESE STYLE
Serves 6

Not a dish for formal dinner parties!

These ribs are cooked twice. They are first boiled and then baked as they need a really long cooking time to become tender.

<u>Ingredients</u>:

2½ lbs. spare ribs of pork (get the *actual ribs* not the joint of pork called 'spare ribs')
1 to 2 chicken stock cubes
<u>For the sauce:</u>

4 tbs. tomato sauce
2 tbs. Worcester sauce
2 tbs. soya sauce
2 tbs. vinegar
4 tbs. oil
1 tsp. mustard
3 tbs. runny honey
3 cloves of garlic, crushed
½ tsp. Tabasco sauce
seasoning

<u>Method</u>:

1. Make up chicken stock and cover spare ribs with it.
2. Boil for about 1 hour.
3. Meanwhile, make the sauce combining all the ingredients with salt and pepper.
4. Oil a large oven dish and spread the drained spare ribs over it.
5. Brush them well with the sauce.
6. Roast in an oven at 200° C for about 1 hour, adding more sauce when necessary.
7. In the end the spare ribs should look brown and appetising and there should be a little sauce left over.
8. Turn several times while baking to make sure that all sides get covered with the sauce. Add a little water if sauce dries up.
9. When ribs are ready, separate them and serve 2 to3 ribs per person.

Note:
Provide your guests with 2 large paper napkins each, 1 to go under the chin and 1 to wipe the fingers.
Provide fingerbowls if you have them.
Good for a barbecue party outdoors.

GARLIC MUSHROOMS
Serves 6

These grilled mushrooms can be prepared in advance and cooked while the guests are having their aperitif.

Ingredients:

1½ lbs. fresh, button mushrooms
oil and butter for frying
1 cup fresh breadcrumbs
2 tbs. parsley, chopped

Garlic butter
6 oz softened butter
1 medium onion, finely chopped
4 cloves garlic, squeezed
2 tbs. lemon juice
salt and pepper

Method:

1. Wash mushrooms.
2. Remove any dirty stalks.
3. Dry carefully.
4. Sauté gently for about 7 minutes in a mixture of oil and butter.
5. Place in an oven-proof dish that will fit under the grill.
6. Mix the softened butter with the onion, garlic, lemon juice, salt and pepper.
7. Wrap in foil and roll into a sausage shape.
8. Cool in the fridge or freezer for ½ an hour.
9. Remove the foil and slice into ½ cm. thick slices which you dot over the mushrooms.
10. Scatter with breadcrumbs and chopped parsley.
11. Place under a hot grill for about 10 to 15 minutes. Take care not to burn top.
12. Serve hot on heated plates, with crusty bread.

Note:

The dish smells beautifully of garlic and butter and there are lots of buttery juices to mop up.

MAIN COURSE DISHES

STUFFED PARTRIDGES
Serves 2 to 4

<u>Ingredients:</u>

2 partridges/2 poussins/4 quails
4 rashers of stretched, streaky bacon
2 oz butter
1 tbs. lemon juice
1 glass dry vermouth
4 oz double cream
1 onion
1 stick celery, chopped
6 shallots chopped
2 tsp. cornflour & water
watercress for decoration

<u>Method:</u>

1. Put half of the butter and some shallots in the birds. (Not in the quails if they are stuffed.)
2. Rub birds with butter, season and cover with bacon.
3. Cook for 25 minutes altogether, starting at 220° C but lower heat to 190° C after first 15 minutes.
4. Transfer birds to an oven dish and keep them warm.
5. Add onion, any remaining shallots, chopped, and the rest of the butter to the pan juices and cook 3 minutes.
6. Add vermouth, 1 cup of water and lemon juice and seasoning.
7. Mix cornflour with a little water and stir into sauce.
8. Finally add cream.
9. Cook on a low heat for 5 minutes to amalgamate flavours and cook onion.
10. Add seasoning.
11. Spoon 3 tbs. of the sauce on each plate and place a partridge on top (or half a poussin or a whole quail).
12. Decorate with watercress.

<u>Stuffing:</u>

½ lb. of fresh sausage meat
1 small onion, chopped and fried
1 cup of fresh bread crumbs
1 egg
2 tbs. parsley
1 tsp. dried thyme
salt, freshly ground pepper

<u>Method:</u>

1. Mix all well together and check seasoning.
2. Cook any surplus stuffing separately for about 15 minutes and serve some with the birds.

Serving suggestion:

Roast potato slices and spiced red cabbage and red currant jelly go well with this dish.

PRAWN & FETTA RAGOUT
Serves 6 to 8

Ingredients:

1 lb. peeled prawns
butter and oil to sauté, about 2 tbs. of each
1 14 oz tin chopped tomatoes
1 tbs. tomato purée
6 oz button mushrooms
3 cloves garlic
2 med. onions chopped
1 tbs. tarragon or oregano (1 tsp. if dried)
1 tsp. mixed dried herbs (including dill)
4-5 drops Tabasco
¼ pt. sour cream
salt and pepper
8 oz full fat fetta cheese, cubed

Method:

1. Chop onion and garlic, slice mushrooms.
2. Fry onion and garlic in oil and butter until soft.
3. Add mushrooms and the tin of chopped tomatoes.
4. Combine tomato purée and herbs with wine and cook gently for 10 minutes.
5. Add prawns, salt and pepper and finally sour cream.
6. Add the fetta cheese and let mixture bubble very gently for about 10 minutes to allow sauce to mature and reduce slightly.
7. Stir gently now and then, do not put a lid on.
8. This is best cooked in a large sauté pan.
9. Put the rice on to cook when you add the prawns and both will be ready at the same time.

This meal can be cooked in under half an hour. Check flavouring, the sauce should be tangy. A Greek salad, with fetta cheese cubes, is rather nice with it.

Served with Basmati rice and a green salad.

Greek Salad

Ingredients:

1 crisp iceberg lettuce
chunks of un-peeled cucumber
tomatoes
slivers of raw onion
Garnish:

whole black olives
serve with vinaigrette dressing made with olive oil

How to cook Basmati rice

Allow 1 cup of rice to 2½ cups of water. Add salt. Cook with a lid on for 10 minutes. Taste rice. The rice appears to have holes in it when all the water has been absorbed, but if it is not cooked add a little more water and continue cooking for a few minutes.

Brown rice takes from between 15 to 35 minutes to cook, depending on which rice you use.

SALMON COULIBIAC

Serves 10 to 12

An excellent party dish that can be made in advance. See Book Cover.

This is a Russian fish pasty filled with cooked fish, rice and eggs. It is served with melted butter or sour cream. Suitable accompaniments would be new potatoes, a sweet and sour cucumber salad or a green salad. No cooked vegetables except potatoes are appropriate. Serve hot or tepid.

Small cocktail-sized versions of the pies, half-moon shaped, are nice with drinks if they are warmed up slightly and contain an extra juicy filling (some extra cream and mushrooms).

Ingredients:

Pastry: 2 lbs. ready-made puff pastry (you can get it ready rolled out)

Filling:

3 lbs. salmon or salmon-trout (whole fish or a piece)
1 cup white long-grained rice, cooked
6 oz button mushrooms
6 eggs, hard boiled
2 tbs. dried dill or ½ cup of fresh dill
3 tbs. fresh herbs – fennel, parsley, savoury
2 medium onions
4 oz butter
2 tbs. lemon juice

Glaze:

1 egg and a little milk

Method:

1. Poach salmon in a court bouillon (this is water in which you have boiled 2 bay leaves, 10 black peppercorns, salt, 3 tbs. wine vinegar and 2 sliced carrots for 10 minutes).
2. The fish should be cooked very gently for 25 minutes and then allowed to get cold in its liquid, preferably overnight.
3. The stock should cover the fish completely. (If skin is exposed it will be difficult to get it off the next day.)
4. Boil rice.
5. Peel and chop eggs fairly small by hand or in the food processor.
6. Chop onion and sweat in half the butter.
7. Add sliced mushrooms and the rest of the butter until melted (no need to cook).
8. Prepare stuffing mixture by adding onions, mushrooms, eggs and herbs to rice

with all the juice from the pan, salt and pepper.
9. Add 2 tbs. lemon juice.
10. Skin and fillet fish.
11. Roll out 1 lb. of pastry into an oblong piece, fairly thinly.
12. On one half of the oblong, place ½ of the stuffing, then half the fish on top. Then cover with the rest of the pastry square.
13. Roll out second piece of pastry into a similar oblong. (You should have 2 pastry 'loaves' altogether.
14. Place remaining ½ of the stuffing and fish on top.
15. Fold pastry over, wet edges and pinch together.
16. Brush pastry with beaten egg all over both 'loaves'.
17. Make some decorative 'leaves' of pastry trimmings, and brush these with beaten egg as well.
18. Place the 'leaves' on the parcels as decoration. Fixing them with egg wash.
19. Cook for about 50 minutes in medium oven, 180° C.
20. Turn heat down if the pastry gets too brown, or cover with foil.

Accompaniment:

8 oz melted butter or 10 fl oz sour cream served separately
Danish cucumber salad
boiled new potatoes.

Recipe for Danish cucumber salad:

Ingredients:

1 cucumber
1 cup of water
1½ dsp. of white vinegar
2 tbs. fresh dill (or 1 tbs. of dried dill)
a little salt and white pepper
1-1½ dsp. sugar

Method:

Best made in advance.
1. Wash and slice cucumbers very thinly.
2. Salt and leave for 10 minutes with a weight on top.
3. Dissolve sugar in water.
4. Add vinegar, salt, pepper and herbs.
5. Check for seasoning, the dressing should have quite a strong sweet and sour taste.
6. Rinse and dry the cucumber.
7. Add to the dressing.
Leave 2 to 3 hours, if possible, before serving.

BEEF STEW WITH RED WINE

Serves 6

This is a stew that used to be made on the Rhône barges in Provence.

Ingredients:

3 lbs. of chuck steak, cut into large chunks 1½" x 1½"
¼ lb. streaky bacon cut into strips and fried until the fat runs
1 tbs. flour
salt to taste
½ tsp. allspice
3 cloves garlic, crushed
½ bottle red wine
2 tbs. olive oil
¾ pint beef stock
bouquet garni (bay leaf, 2-3 sprigs parsley, sprig of thyme and rosemary)
6 fillets of anchovies

Method:

1. Brown meat in olive oil.
2. Dust with flour.
3. Add the rest of the ingredients.
4. Bake in the oven at 180 ° C for 2-3 hours until really tender.
5. Add water if the stew dries up.
6. Adjust seasoning before serving.

Serve with garlic croutons (2 pieces of French bread sliced and rubbed with garlic fried in olive oil.
A green salad would also be welcome.
No other vegetables.

STEAK & KIDNEY PUDDING
Serves 4

This is such a hearty dish for the winter, I bet many of us have forgotten how to make it so here is a recipe:

Miss Lydia Cook, whom I interviewed on her 80th birthday, gave us many recipes for the cookery book. She does not remember any big parties from the past, and even Christmas was celebrated with a cockerel or two that one had fattened up oneself for the occasion. But judging by her recipes Miss Cook and her family ate very well and people could really cook in those days.

Ingredients:

For the pastry:

8 oz plain flour
1 tsp. baking powder
3½ oz shredded suet
salt, water to mix.

For the filling:

1 lb. of chuck steak
1/4 lb. of kidney
l tbs. seasoned flour
l onion
½ pint stock or water
salt and pepper

Method:

Pastry
1. Sieve the flour, baking powder and salt in a bowl.
2. Add the suet and enough water to make a soft dough.
3. Turn onto a floured board and knead lightly.
4. Cut off a piece of pastry to save for the lid. (about ⅓)
5. Roll out the larger piece of pastry to fit a 2 pint pudding basin.
6. Grease the basin and line with the pastry.

Filling
1. Trim and cut the meat and kidney into neat pieces.
2. Roll in seasoned flour.
3. Put into the lined basin with the sliced onions, and stock.

To assemble the pudding

1. Damp the edges of the pastry. Fill with the meat mixture.
2. Roll out the smaller piece of pastry and fit over the pudding to form a lid. Seal the edges well.
3. Cover the pudding with a cloth and tie it around with string.
4. Lower basin into a pan of boiling water, but do not allow the water to reach more than halfway up the basin, and do not allow the water to touch the cloth.
5. Put the lid of the pan on, and boil steadily for 2-3 hours, **replenishing the boiling water as necessary**.

Serve the pudding in the basin in which it was cooked with lightly boiled cabbage and creamy mashed potatoes.

Note:

It is wise to make a little extra gravy for this dish by using any meat and kidney trimmings, a bit of onion and seasoning. Add some water and half a beef stock cube. Boil together for 10 minutes. Strain and thicken with 1 to 2 teaspoons of cornflour in cold water.

FISH PIE

Serves 4

Fish pie was a popular dish during the war as it allowed a family to have a good meal from a small amount of cod.

Ingredients:

1 lb. of cod or any other white fish
¾ pt. of milk
2 oz butter
2 tbs. plain flour
2 tbs. parsley, and 1 tsp. anchovy essence, or 2 oz grated cheese
3-4 potatoes boiled and mashed with a little milk and butter and seasoning

Method:

1. Cook fish in milk.
2. Remove the fish and take out any bones.
3. Melt butter in a small saucepan.
4. Add flour and stir until well blended.
5. Add the milk from the fish, cook for 2 minutes.
6. Season and add chosen flavouring of parsley, and anchovy essence or cheese.
7. Place fish in a greased oven-proof dish.
8. Pour over the sauce and pile on the mashed potato.
9. Dot with butter.
10. Bake in a hot oven 200° C for 20 to 30 minutes.

Serve with peas and carrots.

CHICKEN BREAST STUFFED
WITH HERB CHEESE
Serves 4

Ingredients:

4 chicken breasts, boned, with skin on
4 oz full fat cream cheese
2 tbs. chopped spring onions (or replace with 2 cloves of garlic, squeezed)
2 tbs. chopped parsley
½ cup of flour, seasoned with salt and pepper
l oz butter and l tbs. cooking oil
some lemon juice
2 tbs. grated Parmesan cheese

Method:

1. Open up the chicken breasts horizontally so that you have a pocket.
2. Work the spring onion or garlic, parsley and some salt and pepper into the cream cheese.
3. Stuff the chicken breasts with this.
4. Close firmly so the breasts look whole again, and so no cheese is showing.
5. Turn in seasoned flour.
6. Heat butter and oil and sauté chicken on both sides until golden brown.
7. Place chicken in an oven-proof dish.
8. Sprinkle with lemon juice and Parmesan cheese.
9. Bake for 30 minutes at Gas Mark 6 (200° C), loosely covered with foil.
10. Remove foil towards the end of the cooking period to brown the chicken.

Serve with some of the pan juices and with plain boiled rice and fried courgettes.

How to cook courgettes:

Ingredients:

4 courgettes, washed and sliced fairly thickly
1 tbs. butter
1 tbs. oil
1 tsp. dried tarragon
salt and pepper

Method:

1. Sauté courgettes gently in a frying pan for 8 minutes.
2. Sprinkle with tarragon and seasoning.
Best cooked just before eating. If they stand for a long time they go limp and lose

their charm.

This dish is good for a dinner party as you can prepare it in advance until the oven stage. You can also cook the rice beforehand and put it in the oven dotted with butter, to keep hot provided it is well covered with foil. The best way to heat rice is in the microwave oven for 2 minutes.

The chicken is also a delicious cold dish, served with mango chutney.

FISH IN DILL SAUCE

Serves 4

Ingredients:

Fish stock: about 2 cups, made from fish trimmings, some onions, a bay leaf, peppercorns and a tablespoon of vinegar

1½ lbs. of firm white fish, such as monkfish or halibut, turbot etc. Fresh salmon would be good, too
1 small onion
2 oz butter
¼ pint of double cream
1 glass dry white wine
salt and pepper
2 tbs. finely chopped fresh dill or 2 tsp. dried dill. Parsley can be substituted

For garnish:

Some peeled prawns.

(If you have used salmon or salmon trout, this is not necessary as the colour is there already.)

Method:

1. Cut fish into large pieces, (if monk fish, cut into large cubes).
2. Melt butter, add onion and sweat for two minutes.
3. Add the fish and sauté gently, turning pieces over after 5 minutes.
4. Now add the fish stock and some dry white wine, (half a wine glass will do).
5. Let the fish stew for 10 minutes until done.
6. Add cream and check for seasoning.
7. Add prawns if you wish.

Note:

Cream makes everything taste bland, so seasoning is important. If the stock was well seasoned you may not have to add much.
A couple of spoonfuls of buttery white rice or a few delicate vegetables of a bright colour, such as mange tout are nice with this dish.
This is a dish which would **not** go well with salad, you need cooked vegetables, but just a little.

Variation:
Egg sauce: This is the same sauce as above but without the dill. In its place, include 2 hard boiled eggs, chopped.

ROAST HAKE

Serves 4 to 6

Sunday lunch with a whole roast pike was one of my childhood treats. Hake is a good substitute, which is normally used for roasting. It is a delicious firm fleshed fish, also excellent cold, poached, with mayonnaise for a buffet.

Ingredients:

1 large Hake
3 oz butter
1 cup of fresh white bread crumbs
2 tbs. chopped parsley

Method:

1. Rinse cleaned hake.
2. Place on a buttered oven dish.
3. Season the inside of the hake with salt and pepper, a knob of butter and some parsley.
4. Cover the top with breadcrumbs, mixed with some parsley.
5. Dribble top with melted butter.
6. Roast in the oven at about 180° C, covered with foil for about 45 minutes.
7. After ¼ hour, remove foil to brown the surface slightly.
8. Baste with more melted butter.
9. Check that fish is done by sliding a pointed knife in the thickest part.

Serve with egg sauce, boiled potatoes and seasonal green vegetables.

To make egg sauce:

Make an ordinary white sauce and add to it 2 chopped hard boiled eggs.

HAM IN JELLY – JAMBON PERSILLÉ

Serves 10

Ingredients:

4 lb. piece of gammon – middle cut preferably
2 pig's trotters – split and soaked for 24 hours
2 pints stock
½ bottle dry white wine
1 onion roughly chopped
1 oz gelatine per pint
4 cloves garlic
3 carrots peeled and cut into chunks
bouquet garni
2 large cups chopped parsley
1 tbs. salt and 20 peppercorns

Method:

1. Soak ham and trotters overnight in cold water.
2. Place the above in a large pan in cold water and bring to the boil.
3. Take off the scum, when it rises.
4. Add onion, carrots, garlic and bouquet garni, salt and peppercorns.
5. Boil ham 30 minutes to the pound and 30 minutes over, about 2½ hours, simmering with the trotters.
6. Leave to cool in the liquid.
7. Remove ham from liquid. Discard trotters.
8. Skin it and slice it, cutting slices further into approx. 2" x 2" pieces.
9. Boil up the liquid and strain it.
10. Taste it for flavour.
11. Measure and calculate the amount of gelatine required to set it. (see gelatin packet) and measure your stock. The trotters help to set the stock and give flavour.
12. Heat gelatine in a little water and add to the stock.
13. Layer meat and parsley in a serving dish and pour stock over it.
14. When cool, leave in fridge overnight.

The ham can be decorated with some additional sprigs of parsley and slices of gherkins.
Nice dish for a summer buffet.

MEAT GALANTINE
Serves 10 to 12

A suitable dish for the buffet table or as a splendid starter for a summer lunch.

Ingredients:

2 lbs. shin of beef
2 lbs. shoulder of pork
2 carrots
1 small onion
water
3 tbs. white wine vinegar
½ cup chopped parsley
1 bay leaf
salt
10 peppercorns
½ oz gelatine per pint of stock used
2 egg whites to clear the stock

Method:

1. Place meat in a large saucepan with carrots, spices and herbs.
2. Pour over cold water.
3. Bring to the boil and cook until meat is tender.
4. Take out meat and cut into neat little cubes, the size of dice.
5. Strain stock and clarify it with two egg whites whisked and placed in the hot stock.
6. Strain again and leave to cool.
7. Measure the amount of stock and calculate the amount of gelatine required to set it.
8. Taste for seasoning and adjust if necessary.
9. Pour meat, some of the carrots boiled with the meat and fresh parsley into a round pudding basin rinsed with cold water.
10. Dissolve gelatine and add to the stock. Pour enough stock to cover the meat.
11. Leave to get cool and when cold, leave to set in the refrigerator.

To serve:

Dip dish in hot water and turn out contents onto a plate. Serve decorated with sprigs of parsley. Slice as a cake.

Note:
You can use the same recipe but exchange meat for fish and use the fish stock to mix with the gelatine. In this case, decorate the base of the pudding basin with some slices of hardboiled eggs and herbs such as fennel, before adding the fish and its liquid containing the gelatine.

JELLIED BEEF

Serves 12

This is a lovely buffet dish for a summer luncheon.

Ingredients:

6 lbs. lean beef in a piece
2 pigs trotters, split and soaked for 24 hours – if available
1 large onion
3 carrots
2 sticks celery
bunch of parsley
¼ bottle white wine or 3 tbs. wine vinegar
6 Juniper berries
3 bay leaves
20 peppercorns
1 tbs. salt
gelatine or aspic

Method:

1. Place beef in a large saucepan, covered with cold water and bring to the boil. When scum rises, skim it.
2. Now add the rest of the ingredients (except the gelatine) and boil the beef for 2½ hours. Check that it is tender, boil for 30 minutes longer if not.
3. Remove beef from liquid and strain the liquid.
4. Taste it for flavour and measure the amount of liquid to calculate the amount of gelatine or aspic powder needed. (Aspic powder can be bought in sachets in grocers' or supermarkets.)
5. You may need about 2 pints of liquid to cover the beef once it is sliced, so make up the jelly or aspic accordingly.
6. Slice beef into manageable slices, not too thinly. Arrange on an oval serving dish with a rim.
7. Dot with some of the carrot and cover with the jelly stock.
8. Leave to set in a cool place.
9. Refrigerate when cold.

BEEF STROGANOFF

Serves 4 to 6

This is the Finnish version of a Russian dish, which is very popular.

Ingredients:

1½ lbs. of braising beef
4 oz butter
½ tbs. salt
¼ tsp. white pepper
½ onion
2 tbs. flour
water or stock
½ cup cream
1 – 2 tbs. tomato purée
2 tsp. mustard
2 gherkins, chopped

Garnish:

1 small tub of sour cream, a little poured on each serving

Method:

1. Cut the beef into fingers about ½" wide and 1½" long.
2. Brown them quickly in butter.
3. In the same butter, brown some onion and add to the meat.
4. Sprinkle meat with salt, pepper and the flour.
5. Add the stock or water.
6. Simmer until meat is tender, about 45 minutes to 1 hour.
7. Add the cream, the tomato purée, mustard and the gherkins cut into medium-sized cubes.

Serve with boiled rice and a green salad.

MOUSSAKA
Serves 4

This is the Greek form of Shepherds' Pie.

Ingredients:

2 medium aubergines
4 tbs. olive oil
1 large onion chopped
3 cloves garlic
1 lb. minced lamb or beef
1 tsp. cinnamon
1 tsp. oregano
sprig of thyme and parsley
seasoning
2 x 14 oz tins of tomatoes

For sauce:

1 oz butter
1 tbs. flour
½ pint milk
seasoning
1 bay leaf

Topping:

breadcrumbs
a little grated cheese

Method:

1. Fry onion until golden.
2. Fry lamb until slightly brown.
3. Slice Aubergines (½" thick) and salt them. Leave them to sweat for 15 minutes, then rinse and pat dry.
4. Fry Aubergines 2 minutes on each side in hot oil.
5. Chop cloves of garlic.
6. Layer the ingredients as follows: start with the tomato, garlic, cinnamon and herbs, then add the aubergines, the meat, and continue until the dish is full.
7. Make the white sauce by melting butter, adding the flour, and add the milk slowly whilst whisking. Add the seasoning and simmer for 10 minutes.
8. Cover the top of the Moussaka with the white sauce.
9. Sprinkle with breadcrumbs and cheese.
10. Bake at 180° C for 1 hour, until golden.
Serve with a Greek salad and Pitta bread.

Note:

If you replace the meat with sliced mushrooms, lightly fried, you will have a vegetarian version of this dish. This is a good party dish as it can be made in advance.

PORK WITH PRUNES

Serves 8

A dish from Tours on the Loire.

Ingredients:

8 pork steaks
1 lb. large prunes
½ bottle red wine, preferably from the Loire
2 tbs. redcurrant jelly
¼ pint double cream
butter and oil for frying
seasoning

Method:

1. Soak prunes in red wine over night.
2. Boil them in this liquid until soft. Add some water if necessary.
3. Strain the prunes and keep the juice.
4. Remove the stones keeping the prunes whole.
5. Fry pork steaks in butter – for two minutes on each side.
6. Add the wine juice in which the prunes cooked, and a little more water if necessary.
7. Simmer steaks for 20 minutes.
8. Remove steaks and keep hot.
9. Add redcurrant jelly to the sauce and when it has melted, add the cream and seasoning.

Serve steaks covered with some of the sauce and decorated with the prunes.
Serve the rest of the sauce separately.

Note:

This dish is very rich and tasty and should have very plain vegetables to accompany it – such as a little potato purée and mange tout peas.

BAKED PLAICE OR SOLE

Serves 4

Ingredients:

4 fillets of sole or plaice
1 tbs. parsley chopped
2 tbs. lemon juice
2 tbs. dried white breadcrumbs
2 oz grated strong cheese
1 cup of single cream
salt and pepper

Method:

1. Grease oven-proof dish.
2. Season fillets of fish and lay skin side down on dish.
3. Sprinkle with lemon juice and parsley.
4. Add cream.
5. Add breadcrumbs and lastly grated cheese.
6. Bake in oven at 200° C for about 20 minutes, then grill for a few minutes to brown the top.
7. Serve with plain vegetables.

A slimming alternative:

Steamed fish

Butter a dinner plate. Place fish upon it. Sprinkle with salt, pepper, lemon juice and fresh herbs. Cover with foil or greaseproof paper. Place over a saucepan of boiling water and cook until done. (About 10 minutes.).

Serve with steamed vegetables.

TURBOT AIOLI
Serves 6

This is a really simple dish to make as long as you have a good mayonnaise. It is quite expensive, so share it with friends for a special occasion.

Ingredients:

How to make fish stock:
fish bones
½ cup vinegar
12 pepper corns
2 carrots
2 onions
2 bay leaves
salt
1½ pts. water
1 large piece of turbot (allow ½ lb. per person)

Garnish:

2 lemons
fresh parsley
3 hard boiled eggs, cut into wedges
lettuce, tomatoes and sliced cucumber

Method:

This dish is very easy to cook for a large number of people. If you cook a whole turbot, poach it in an oven dish covered in foil, in the oven.

1. Make fish stock by simmering the stock ingredients with water for 20 minutes.
2. Poach turbot in stock. (Test if it done by using a skewer or knife.)
3. Leave to cool in the liquid.
4. Remove from liquid and drain and skin the fish.

Mayonnaise: (Aioli)

Ingredients:

½ pt. vegetable oil
½ pt. olive oil
4 egg yolks
salt and pepper
wine vinegar to taste (2-3 tbs.)
3 cloves of garlic, squeezed

Method for Mayonnaise:

1. Put yolks in a blender and add half the oil slowly in a thin stream.
2. When blended add vinegar.
3. Continue adding the rest of the oil.
4. Season with salt, white pepper – taste.
5. Add the garlic and more vinegar if necessary. Leave mayonnaise fairly thick.

Serve with following vegetables:

2 lb. potatoes
1½ lb. french beans
3 carrots

Method:

1. Cut beans in half.
2. Peel and cut potatoes into chunks.
3. Peel carrots and cut into large pieces.
4. Steam the vegetables starting with potatoes and carrots for 10 minutes.
5. Add beans for another 6 or 7 minutes, until tender.

How to present the dish:

Place poached Turbot, skinned, in the middle of a large serving dish. Surround with garnish neatly arranged vegetables, and decorate with hard boiled eggs, parsley and lemon wedges. Serve Aioli separately.

Note:

This is a good dish for a summer luncheon. As a caterer, I once served Turbot for a special dinner for 160 people! For the cold buffet, we also served jellied beef and coronation chicken from 3 different serving points. Everybody queued for the Turbot and kept coming back for seconds and thirds. We soon ran out, as you can imagine!

SPICY YOUNG CHICKEN
(Á LA BANGKOK)
Serves 6

Ingredients:

3 young chickens, (poussins). Serve half to each person. Alternatively use 6 chicken breasts.
Spicy butter:
½ lb. softened butter
1 tsp. coriander
½ tsp. cloves
1 tsp. ginger
¼ tsp. cayenne
1 tsp. cinnamon
2 tsp. turmeric
1 tsp. salt
½ tsp. white pepper
2 cloves garlic, squeezed
Glaze: ½ cup green label mango chutney

Method:

1. Prepare the chickens so they lie flat in 'butterfly style'; i.e. place a chicken, breast down, hold firmly with one hand while you cut through along the back bone from front to back. Open up chicken and press down on board, breast down. Cut off any surplus skin and fat. Remove the wing tips and tips of the legs. Place chicken with breast up on an oven tray.
2. Mix butter with seasoning and spices and smear over the chickens.
3. Roast for 20 min. on 200° C near the top of the oven.
4. Baste from time to time.
5. Take dish out and smear chicken with mango chutney.
6. Cook for a further 10 minutes.
7. Carve each chicken into two halves along breast bone. Remove the breast bone.
8. Serve each half on a hot plate with buttery juices from the oven tray.

Serve plain rice and a simple salad with this dish.

Note:
One can also cook a **leg of lamb** in this way. Slivers of garlic are inserted into slits in the boned meat. (Ask the butcher to bone the leg for you.) Rub oil, herbs and garlic into the meat in the usual way. This is an Italian recipe.

This dish lends itself well to a barbecue as it cooks fast and is easily carved.

POACHED CHICKEN WITH
PEPPER MAYONNAISE
Serves 10

A cold buffet dish, easy to prepare and can be made well in advance.

Ingredients:

2 x 3½lbs. chickens
1 onion
2 sticks celery
1 leek (leaves left on)
handful of parsley
2 bay leaves
salt and teaspoon of peppercorns
water to cover

Mayonnaise:

¾ pint of vegetable oil
2 tbs. white wine vinegar
3 egg yolks
2 cloves of garlic crushed
salt and pepper
1 tsp. English mustard

Flavouring:

2 red peppers, roasted and pureéd

Garnish:

1 iceberg lettuce shredded
1 cup of halved green seedless grapes
1 red pepper, sliced thinly

Method:

1. Poach the chickens for about 1¾ hours in water with onions, celery, leek, parsley, bay leaves, salt and peppercorns.
2. When the chickens are tender leave in water to cool, preferably overnight.
3. Skin, bone and cut flesh into bite-sized pieces, draining off any stock.

Mayonnaise:

1. In a food processor place egg yolks and while blending, add oil very slowly at

first, then faster as it thickens.
2. Add vinegar and seasoning, garlic and mustard.
3. Add puréed peppers, prepared as described below.

Prepare peppers:

1. Wash and halve them and remove core, seeds and stalk.
2. Place halves skin side up in a hot oven and roast for 10 min.
3. Turn them over and roast another 10-15 min. until tender.
4. While hot put in a plastic bag and leave until cool.
5. Then with a sharp knife and your fingers skin peppers and purée in food processor.
6. Add to mayonnaise. (This sauce can be thinned with a little hot water.)
7. Check seasoning.

Continue as follows:

1. Mix dressing with cold chicken pieces.
2. Arrange on a platter surrounded by chopped iceberg lettuce.
3. Just before serving, spoon a little spare dressing over the top and decorate with strips of raw pepper and halves of green seedless grapes.

TOMATO & SPINACH LASAGNA

Serves 6

Ingredients:

6 sheets of plain lasagna

Tomato sauce:

1 x 15oz tin of chopped herb tomatoes
1 medium onion, chopped
1 stick of celery chopped
1 large carrot finely chopped
2 cloves of garlic squeezed
¼ pint of red wine
2 teaspoons sugar
salt and freshly milled black pepper
½ cup of olive oil
fresh parsley and basil

Method:

1. Fry chopped vegetables in oil until transparent (about 10 minutes).
2. Add tomatoes, herbs and wine and seasoning.
3. Cook for 15 minutes.
4. Check for flavour. Add seasoning.
5. Add some water, if necessary, as the sauce should be fairly runny.

Béchamel sauce with spinach:

2 oz butter
2 tbs. of plain flour
1 pint full cream milk
1 bay leaf, salt

For this sauce we add:

1 tsp. English mustard
6 oz grated, strong Cheddar cheese (some of which is used for the topping)
1 lb. of fresh spinach

Method:

1. Melt butter, add flour, and cook until well mixed.
2. Add milk slowly, whisking the mixture all the time.
3. Add bay leaf and seasoning and cook for 10 minutes.
4. Add English mustard, grated cheese, spinach.

5. Add seasoning.
6. Cook gently for a few minutes or until ingredients are well blended. Remove bay leaf.
7. Check seasoning.

To assemble main dish:

1. Butter large, square earthenware dish.
2. Place half the tomato sauce at the bottom then spoon over 1/3 of the spinach sauce.
3. Then place 3 uncooked sheets of lasagna on top.
4. Repeat, and put the last 3 leaves of lasagna on top.
5. Cover with last 1/3 of the spinach sauce.
6. Sprinkle with breadcrumbs and the grated cheese kept back.
7. Cover with foil for the first half of the cooking period.
8. Bake in an oven at 200° C for about 30 minutes.
9. Then remove foil and cook for a further 20 minutes, or until you feel the lasagna is soft and cooked and nicely brown.

Note:

Sheets of lasagna can be used without pre-cooking.
A Béchamel sauce is the usual, all-purpose, white sauce. By adding certain ingredients you get the following variations of it.

Mustard sauce = Add 1 tsp. of English mustard.
Cheese sauce = Add 6 oz grated strong cheddar for use with macaroni cheese or cauliflower cheese.
Parsley sauce = Add 2 tbs. chopped parsley, used with fish dishes.
Egg sauce = Add 2 chopped hard boiled eggs.

Note:
The lasagna can be prepared in advance and just put in the oven 50 minutes before you eat.

QUICK SEAFOOD PILAU
Serves 4 to 6

An easy supper dish, and very healthy, too. Experiment with different kinds of sea food or use the ready made mixture you can buy in the supermarkets.

Ingredients:

1½ lbs. mixed cooked seafood or use cooked prawns, and tinned mussels (tinned in brine, not vinegar) and fillet of cod, skinned and cut into fingers
1 ¾ cup of brown Basmati rice
¾ tin of chopped tomatoes
1 medium onion, chopped
1 glass of dry, white wine, (optional)
5 tbs. olive oil
2 cups water
3 cloves of garlic, squeezed
2 bay leaves
2 tbs. chopped parsley
1 dsp. dried dill
2 tbs. lemon juice
6-8 drops of Tabasco sauce (or a good pinch of chilli powder)
salt and pepper

Method:

1. Heat some oil in a large deep frying pan.
2. Gently sauté the onion and garlic for 3-4 minutes.
3. Add the rice and sauté for 5 minutes more.
4. Add tomatoes, herbs, seasoning and Tabasco or chilli, and some water to cook the rice in.
5. Cook gently stirring from time to time, covered by a lid or foil. About 30-40 minutes.
6. Add water, as rice absorbs the juices, and dribble on some olive oil towards the end.
7. When rice is nearly cooked, add the seafood mixture and some more water if the pilau becomes dry.
8. Cook for 5 minutes tossing gently, and to heat through.
9. Taste for flavouring.
10. Add more salt and lemon juice and Tabasco if necessary.
11. The pilau should be moist with some sauce still left in the pan.
12. A knob of butter stirred in before serving helps the flavour.

Serve with a crisp salad.

ROAST LAMB WITH CRUST
Serves 6 to 8

Ingredients:

1 leg of lamb, at least 4 lbs.
1½ cup of fresh white or brown breadcrumbs
3 cloves of garlic
2 tbs. fresh parsley
1 tbs. dried thyme and rosemary
2 tsp. salt
2 tsp. black pepper
4 tbs. French mustard (fine or coarse)
Oil to dribble on crust

Method:

1. It is important to trim the leg of lamb of some of its skin and surplus fat.
2. Then smear with mustard all over.
3. Mix breadcrumbs with crushed garlic, herbs and seasoning and pat into mustard.
4. Dribble some oil over the crust.
5. Roast leg about 1¾ hours at 200° C degrees. Cover loosely with foil, if crust gets too dark.
6. Spoon the fat that comes out of the joint over the crust from time to time.
7. Take out of oven and leave to rest for 15 minutes before carving.

To carve:

Cut into thick slices. This keeps the crust more intact.

Note:

As this way of roasting lamb does not produce much juice for gravy (just a little moisture under the joint), I either take some trouble to make a separate gravy with stock, or serve redcurrant jelly with the meal.
Roast potatoes go well and can be roasted in the same oven, but not on the same dish as the lamb as they may become covered by crumbs from the lamb. The second vegetable could be a moist one such as leeks or courgettes.

To make gravy for lamb:

Any juice left in the roasting pan – fat removed
1 stock cube – lamb if possible
1½ cups of water
1½ tsp. corn flour, mixed with a little water for thickening
1 bay leaf
A pinch of herbs

a little red wine
2 tbs. redcurrant jelly
seasoning if required

<u>Method:</u>

1. Dissolve cube in ½ pint of water in a small saucepan.
2. Add redcurrant jelly and the juices from the joint.
3. Thicken with cornflour mixture.
4. Taste and add seasoning as required.

FILLET STEAK
WITH BÉARNAISE SAUCE

Serves 4

Ingredients:

4 fillet steaks, 1" thick – about 1 lb. total weight
Butter and oil for frying
Seasoning – salt and freshly milled black pepper
4 tbs. Bearnaise sauce (or mayonnaise mixed with 1 tsp. finely chopped cocktail
gherkins, 1 tsp. capers and a little onion would also be suitable)

Method:

1. Cook 2 or 3 minutes on each side, and season.

For a special treat serve with Béarnaise sauce see recipe below.

Bearnaise Sauce:

Ingredients:

4 tbsp. White wine vinegar
6 peppercorns, ½ bay leaf, fresh herbs chopped, preferably tarragon
1 small onion, chopped
2 egg yolks
3 oz Butter

Method:

1. Cook vinegar with onion herbs for 5 minutes, then strain. Place liquid in clean
   pan.
2. Add yolks, one by one, while stirring. Then add butter, cut into small cubes
   allowing each cube to be absorbed before adding more.
3. If you have meat juices, add at this stage, but do not overheat as sauce can easily
   curdle. (If it does, put it in a blender and it may come together again.)

FINNISH STEAK WITH ONION
Serves 4

This steak is served well done because it has stewed with the onions in a little stock. This is a good idea if the meat is not very tender.

Ingredients:

4 large pieces of frying steak – 1½ lbs. total weight, slightly flattened with a rolling pin
2 onions – sliced
butter for frying
seasoning and 1 bay leaf

Method:

1. Brown steak in a frying pan for 2 minutes in butter on a fairly high heat.
2. Remove meat from pan and, brown sliced onions in the same pan for 5 minutes.
3. Return steaks to the pan with the onions.
4. Add a cup of water.
5. Add seasoning and bay leaf.
6. Cook until onions are soft, about 5 minutes.

Serve with mashed potato.

Note:

These steaks can be kept warm without spoiling.

RUMP STEAK WITH STILTON

Serves 4

Ingredients:

4 Rump steaks about ½" thick, total weight about 2 lbs.
oil for brushing steaks
seasoning
½ lb. stilton cheese

Method:

1. Pre-heat the grill and trim the steaks.
2. Season with salt and freshly milled black pepper.
3. Grill for about 3 minutes on each side.
4. Slice Stilton thinly and place on the steaks.
5. Melt the cheese under the grill.

An alternative to rump steak with stilton: Serve steak with garlic or herb butter. Mix softened butter with squeezed garlic and chopped herbs.

MINUTE STEAK

Serves 4

Ingredients:

**4 large rump steaks cut ¼" thick and slightly beaten. – total weight about 2 lbs.
oil and butter for frying**

Method:

1. Heat the oil and butter in a large frying pan.
2. Season the steaks on both sides.
3. Fry 2 steaks at a time for 30 seconds on each side.

Serve with the juices from the pan.

Garlic or herb butter would go well with these steaks. See Recipe for Rump Steak.

GRILLED FRESH MACKEREL
WITH MUSTARD
Serves 2

A quick, simple supper dish.

Ingredients:

2 fresh mackerel which have bright eyes and feel very stiff, not limp
4 tbs. French mustard
salt, pepper and lemon juice

Garnish:

Wedges of lemon for serving

Method:

1. Slit each Mackerel at 1" intervals on each side.
2. Fill slits with French mustard.
3. Season with salt, pepper and lemon juice.
4. Place on foil under a hot grill.
5. Grill for approximately 3 minutes on each side.

Serve with wedges of lemon, new potatoes and some greens.

STEAMED FISH WITH
BEURRE BLANC SAUCE
Serves 4

This is one of my favourite dishes in France. The Beurre Blanc is very rich but wonderful with a fish of solid texture.

Ingredients:

4 portions white fish steaks, eg. Halibut, Turbot, Cod or Haddock
1 tbs. lemon juice
1 oz butter
1 tbs. chopped parsley
seasoning

Method:

1. Place the fish on a plate that fits on a pan above boiling water.
2. Sprinkle with lemon juice.
3. Dot with butter.
4. Add seasoning and parsley.
5. Cover plate with foil.
6. The fish takes about 15 minutes to cook.

BEURRE BLANC SAUCE

Ingredients:

½ small onion, finely chopped
4 oz butter
2 tbs. white wine vinegar
3 tbs. dry white wine
a little parsley, tarragon and bay leaf
4 or 5 peppercorns, and a little salt

Method:

1. Boil the onion, peppercorns and herbs with the wine and vinegar for about 5 minutes.
2. Using a fine sieve, strain the remaining juices into a clean pan.
3. Cut butter into small cubes.
4. Add 2 or 3 at a time while stirring, until they have been absorbed and the sauce begins to thicken.
5. Continue adding a few pieces of butter at a time, until all has been absorbed.
6. Taste and add a little salt and perhaps a little extra vinegar, if the sauce is not piquant enough.

CURRIED MEAT BALLS

Serves 6

This is a homely curry, and improves with re-heating.

Ingredients:

1½ lb. minced lean beef or lamb – you can mix meat such as pork or lamb with turkey
1 large onion, chopped
3 cloves of garlic, squeezed
1 tin of tomatoes
1 tbs. tomato purée
2 eggs
salt
1 pt. beef stock – use a cube
2 tsp. butter
2 tsp. oil
1 small carton plain yoghurt

Spices:

½ tsp. chilli powder
2 tsp. coriander and turmeric
1 tsp. cumin seeds
1 tsp. ginger (if using fresh ginger chopped and peeled, add 1 tbsp)

Method:

1. Fry onion in butter.
2. Add oil and spices, fry for 2 minutes.
3. Add tomato purée, garlic and 1 cup stock.
4. Cook for 5 minutes.
5. Take some 3 tbs. of the onion mixture and mix well with the meat.
6. Add seasoning to the meat, taste for flavour.
7. With wet hands roll into balls about 1" in diameter.
8. Place these on a wetted tray.
9. Fry the meatballs in oil and butter.
10. Add stock to the rest of the onion mixture and drop fried meatballs into the stock.
11. Add yoghurt.
12. Simmer for at least 30 minutes.
13. Thicken sauce, if liked, with cornflour (1 tsp) and water (½ cup cold water).
14. Taste for seasoning.

If you do not find that this curry is spicy enough for you add 1 tbs. Garam Masala or curry paste.

Serve with some of these:

Boiled Basmati rice.

Poppadums fried in oil until expanded and crisp, then well drained (or bought already fried).

Nan bread – warmed in the oven.

Indian chutneys – one hot and one sweet.

A simple salad of lettuce, tomato, cucumber and slivers of onion garnished with hard boiled eggs, quartered.

HOT MADRAS CURRY
Serves 4

Ingredients:

2 lbs. stewing steak or shin of beef cut into strips
2 oz butter + 2 tbs. oil
2 med. onions, chopped
2 cloves of garlic, squeezed
2 tbs. lemon juice
¾ pt. of stock made with a beef cube
Spices:- 1 tsp. ground coriander
   ¼ tsp. chilli powder
   1 tsp. cumin seeds
   ½ tsp. cinnamon and cloves
   1 tsp. ground ginger
   2 tsp. turmeric
1 carton yoghurt (optional)

Method:

1. Melt some butter, cut up onion and beef.
2. Fry onion, until lightly brown.
3. Remove from pan.
4. Add oil and fry spices for 2 minutes.
5. Add some stock and simmer.
6. In a clean frying pan, add some butter and oil, fry meat until coloured.
7. Add the onion and spice mixture and stock to cover.
8. Simmer for 1½ to 2 hours, until meat is tender.
9. Check seasoning
10. If curry is not spicy enough for you, add 1 dsp. Garam Masala or curry paste.

Serve with boiled Basmati rice, Indian chutneys (I use a hot and one sweet), shredded coconut and some salad, sliced bananas, and chopped spring onions.

Also yoghurt salad: **(Raita)**

Ingredients:

½ pt. yoghurt
½ cucumber chopped finely, with peel on
1 tsp. fresh mint
2 cloves garlic crushed
salt and pepper

Method:

1. Mix all ingredients together and chill before serving.

This Yoghurt dip is cooling if you find the curry too hot.

Variations:

EGG CURRY

Make curry as above, omitting meat, thicken sauce with cornflour and water, add 6 hard boiled eggs, peeled and halved a few minutes before serving.

PRAWN CURRY

Omit the meat. Add 8 oz of de-frosted and drained prawns to the curry and thicken the sauce with a little cornflour and water.

VEGETABLE CURRY

Omit meat and add to sauce, par-boiled potato chunks, cauliflower florets, chunks of aubergine and frozen peas. Stew until soft, about 30 minutes. Vegetarians will need to use vegetable stock to make the sauce.

BUTTERFLY CHICKEN

Serves 4

Ingredients:

1 x 3½ lb. oven ready chicken
olive oil
2 cloves garlic in slivers
thyme, marjoram, tarragon (about 2 tbs. in all) Fresh rosemary, chopped, is
also good
salt and pepper
1 tbs. lemon juice

Method:

1. Un-truss the chicken.
2. Place breast side down on a carving board and with a sharp, heavy knife, cut along one side of back bone.
3. Open up the chicken and spread out by pressing on the two halves.
4. Trim off any visible fat and extra skin.
5. Turn chicken round and press down with the skin side now up.
6. Treat both the skin side and the inside of the chicken in the following way:
7. Insert slivers of garlic under the skin, here and there.
8. Brush with olive oil.
9. Sprinkle with salt, pepper and lemon juice.
10. Sprinkle with herbs.
11. Place on an oven-proof dish and cook for 1 hour at 200° C.
12. To carve, take off the wing tips and the ends of the legs.
13. Cut into 4 joints and each side of the breast into 2 pieces.

Serve with a little rice and salad. You could also serve them with a few quartered, unpeeled potatoes wedges baked with the chicken and dribbled with olive oil.

TARRAGON & BUTTER CHICKEN

Serves 4

This is a lovely simple dish, especially in spring when the tarragon is out.

Ingredients:

1 x 3 ½ lb. oven-ready chicken
2 oz butter
1 glass dry, white wine
1 tsp. lemon juice
2-3 tbs. tarragon leaves
salt and pepper
1 tbs. flour to thicken sauce slightly

Method:

1. Remove string from chicken.
2. Rinse inside of chicken and dry all over.
3. Rub chicken with butter and season.
4. Put breast side down in an oval Pyrex dish and sprinkle with the tarragon.
5. Add wine and a little water and cook for 1 hour at 180° C, basting a few times.
6. Turn chicken round to brown breast side up.
7. Cook for another ¼ hour.
8. Test that it is well done by piercing between thigh and body. If liquid is quite clear it is done.
9. Allow to rest in a warm place for a few minutes.
10. Strain juices from pan into a bowl.
11. Strain off the fat that rises, but keep it to one side.
12. In a clean saucepan put 2 tsp. of the fat and 1 tbs. flour and mix.
13. Now add the juices you have saved.
14. Simmer the sauce for 5 minutes and adjust seasoning if required.

Carve chicken, pour over some sauce and serve rest separately.
Serve with boiled rice or new potatoes and a green salad, lightly dressed.

Note:

When my Husband and I were newly married and learning about wine, we ordered about 2 doz. half bottles, all different, from Berry Brothers, the famous old wine merchants. They must have been intrigued with the order. Every Saturday night we dined on this Tarragon chicken and tried a different bottle of wine. We discussed the wine and made very serious notes about it. I think it taught us to pay proper attention to the wine, if nothing else. A few years later on, we visited the various wine regions, mostly in France, and saw how the wine we had tasted is grown. It certainly helps to memorise the taste of the wine if you have drunk it in the area where it is made.

CABBAGE PARCELS
in Greek, Dolmas – in Swedish Kåldolmar
Serves 8

Dolmas appear in various forms all over Europe. In Greece they wrap rice in vine leaves. Cabbage replaces vine leaves in Northern Europe.

Ingredients:

2 large green cabbages, boiled in salted water until tender
1 cup long grained rice, boiled
2 lb. minced beef (or 1 lb. mushrooms)
1 large onion, chopped
salt and pepper
3 tbs. of parsley and 2 heaped tsp. mixed herbs
stock and tomato juice – 1 pint of each or more, as necessary
butter for frying
2 tbs. sugar

Method:

1. Fry onion in butter.
2. Fry meat until lightly coloured – vegetarians can use mushrooms instead of meat.
3. Mix with onion and herbs and rice.
4. Season well.
5. Separate the leaves of the cabbages, carefully, keeping them a whole as possible.
6. Trim off the thick part of the stems.
7. Make a parcel of each leaf, filled with 1 tbs. of stuffing.
8. Place in an oven dish, 'seam' side down.
9. Pack the parcels tightly together, to stop them opening.
10. Pour on ½ pt. of stock and tomato juice.
11. Dot with butter.
12. Sprinkle with sugar.
13. Cook under foil for 1½ hours.
14. Remove foil and cook for a further ½ hour to brown.
15. Add more stock and tomato juice as necessary.
16. If you have any pan juices left, thicken them with a little cornflour and water and pour over the Dolmas before serving.

Serve with boiled or mashed potatoes. In Finland we often have Lingonberry jam with this dish. You might like to try Cranberry sauce instead.

Note:

An excellent buffet dish. It re-heats well, and is very cheap to make.

PORK STEAKS WITH PAPRIKA SAUCE

Serves 6

I had this dish by Lake Constance and we had the most wonderful 'Knockerln' (fresh noodles) with it.

Ingredients:

6 Pork escalopes, (slightly beaten to make them thin)
oil and butter for frying, flour with salt and pepper

Sauce:

1 small onion, chopped very fine
2 tbs. white wine vinegar
1 tbs. paprika
½ pint sour cream
2 tsp. capers
salt and pepper
juice from the pan
seasoned flour
butter for frying

Method:

1. Turn escalopes in seasoned flour.
2. Fry in oil and butter until slightly browned, about 2-3 minutes on each side.
3. Put in a serving dish in a warm oven.
4. Rinse out the pan juices with a little water and boil up – keep this liquid.
5. Clean pan and fry a finely chopped onion.
6. Add paprika and stir until absorbed.
7. Add vinegar and juices from the meat.
8. Cook for 3 minutes.
9. Slowly add the sour cream.
10. Finally add the capers and seasoning.
11. The sauce should be quite sharp.
12. Serve the escalopes partly covered by sauce and serve the rest of the sauce separately.

To serve:

Noodles or new potatoes are very nice with this dish, accompanied by a crisp salad.

SIMPLE CORONATION CHICKEN
Serves 6

This dish was devised for the 25th anniversary of the coronation of Queen Elizabeth II, and has remained popular ever since.

Ingredients:

1 x 3½ lb. chicken
1 stick of celery
1 carrot
1 onion
bouquet garni
parsley
seasoning
¾ pint mayonnaise, thinned out slightly with 3 tbs. boiling water

For the curry sauce:

2 tbs. vegetable oil
1 heaped tbs. curry powder or paste
2 tsp. tomato purée
2tbs redcurrant jelly

Serve with boiled Basmati rice.

Method:

1. Boil chicken for 1½ hours in water with the vegetables, herbs and seasoning. (Can be done the previous day).
2. Skin chicken, remove bones and cut chicken into bite-sized pieces.
3. To make the sauce:
4. Heat oil in a small saucepan.
5. Add curry powder and cook gently for 2 minutes.
6. Add jelly and tomato purée and cook for 5 minutes whilst stirring.
7. Add 1 tbs. water if mixture gets too dry.
8. Cool slightly.
9. Add this curry mixture to the mayonnaise.
10. Taste for seasoning – it should have a sweetish curry flavour.
11. Toss chicken in mayonnaise, mixing well.
12. Pile onto a dish surrounded by cold, boiled basmati rice.
13. Decorate chicken with a little chopped parsley and little blobs of redcurrant jelly along the top.

Note:
An alternative flavouring for the mayonnaise could be red peppers which you roast until soft and purée, adding the purée to the mayonnaise.

CHRISTMAS HAM

Ingredients:

a whole Danish smoked leg of gammon, (or 10-15 lb. piece of Danish middle cut of gammon).
10 peppercorns
3 bay leaves
bouquet garni
½ pt. dry cider (optional)
DO NOT ADD SALT

Method:
To cook the ham:
1. Soak overnight in cold water.
2. Throw away the water and put in a large pan and cover with fresh cold water.
3. Bring to boil and remove scum as it forms.
4. Add the herbs, spices and cider.
5. Note time of boiling. A 15 lb. ham takes 4 hours to cook, check after 4 hours by piercing with a skewer. If meat feels tough, cook a little longer. If you use middle cut of Gammon, test after 3 hours.
6. Turn ham over halfway during the cooking time.
7. When ready, take off the heat and leave to cool in the water.
8. When cold, remove from water and place on a large tray.
9. With a sharp knife, tear the skin off the ham. It comes off quite easily.

Ingredients for crust:

1 cup fresh brown breadcrumbs (make these in a blender)
1 cup demerara sugar
40 whole cloves
6 tbs. mustard powder mixed with water to make a thick paste

Method continued:

1. Smear mustard all over the fat of the ham.
2. Mix breadcrumbs with sugar and sprinkle and pat onto the mustard.
3. Push in cloves at intervals into the fat to form a nice pattern.
4. Place on oven dish. Bake in oven 200° C for about ½ hour or until sugar coating has started to melt and the crumbs to colour. TAKE CARE not to burn it.
5. Serve cold with boiled potatoes, swede purée and carrot purée.

Note:
Ham is normally cooked for 30 minutes per 1 lb. and 30 minutes over but in the case of a very large joint, the cooking time is considerably REDUCED.

CASSEROLED PHEASANT OR PIGEON

Serves 6 (**pheasant**), 4 (**pigeon**)

Ingredients:

2 pheasants or 4 pigeons
4 rashers streaky bacon cut into ½" pieces
½ pt. red wine
2 oz whole walnuts
3 sticks celery
6 juniper berries, crushed (optional)
¼ pt. whipping cream
seasoning
bouquet garni
butter and oil for frying

Method:

1. Wipe birds and remove any leftover feathers.
2. Brown birds in hot butter and oil on each side and put in heavy saucepan.
3. In the remaining fat, brown streaky bacon.
4. Add to the birds.
5. Now fry celery, cleaned and chopped into ½" chunks.
6. Add to the birds.
7. Finally brown walnuts slightly and combine with the rest of the ingredients.
8. Pour on wine, ½ pt. of water, (enough to cover the birds).
9. Add seasoning, juniper berries and bouquet garni.
10. Stew birds gently on top of the stove with the lid on 1½-2½ hours, depending on how tough the birds are.
11. Test them with a skewer.
12. Remove birds from pan and carve the pheasant into serving pieces. (The pigeons are served whole.)

Place in a shallow serving dish and keep them warm while you make the sauce.

To make the sauce:

1. Remove bouquet garni from stock and some of the bacon, walnuts and celery for garnish.
2. Strain sauce.
3. Thicken sauce with a little cornflour and water.
4. Add cream.
5. Test for seasoning.
6. Finally spoon some sauce over the birds and decorate with celery, bacon and walnuts.
7. Serve rest of the sauce separately.

Suitable accompaniments:

Potato and celeriac purée, red cabbage with apple, redcurrant jelly.

Note:

A good pheasant can serve 4 people if accompanied by a rich sauce. A pigeon only serves one person because the legs are often not edible.

KEDGEREE
Serves 6

A wonderful dish at any time, for breakfast, lunch or supper! Excellent for a Sunday 'brunch' party as it can be made in advance.

Ingredients:

2 lb. smoked haddock
1 lb. basmati rice
3 hard boiled eggs
lemon juice
3 oz butter
salt and white pepper
3 tbs. chopped parsley
½ pt. milk
¼ pt. whipping cream
6 drops tabasco

Method:

1. Poach haddock in half milk, half water.
2. Remove fish from pan and skin and flake into large pieces. Keep some of the stock.
3. Take out any bones.
4. Meanwhile hard boil the eggs and boil the rice for 10 minutes and strain if done.
5. Rinse rice once with boiled water, to separate the grains.
6. Fork the rice gently and keep warm.
7. Peel and cut up eggs with a fork, or in a blender.
8. Combine rice, fish and eggs.
9. Add butter in little cubes.
10. Add parsley, a sprinkling of lemon juice and a few drops of Tabasco.
11. Season.
12. Add cream just before serving.
13. Test again for seasoning.
14. Place in a heated oven-proof dish with lid or covered with foil to keep warm in the oven before serving.

Note:

Can be left in the oven for about half an hour on a low heat. The cream will help to keep it moist. If it is likely to dry up, add a little of the milk in which the fish was cooked.

Serve on its own. Poached broccoli goes well with it.

ROAST GOOSE DINNER

Serves 8 to 10

Ingredients:

1 dressed goose – about 18 lbs. plus giblets
1 large onion
1 sprig of rosemary
6-7 leaves of sage
2 bay leaves
1 chicken stock cube
salt and pepper
2 tsp. cornflour mixed with a little cold water
2 tbs. redcurrant jelly – optional
1 glass Port – optional

Method:

1. Pre-heat the oven to 220°C.
2. Rinse out the goose.
3. Pour scalding water over the breast.
4. Prick the bird all over with a fork.
5. Place on an oven rack in a roasting tin.
6. Add ½ inch of water to the tin.
7. Place the herbs in the water with the neck of the goose.
8. Roast the goose for 30 minutes, then lower the heat to 180°C.
9. Protect the wings and legs with foil to prevent them burning.
10. Baste occasionally and cover lightly with foil if the breast gets too dark.
11. Cook for a total of 3 hours, until the leg meat feels tender when you insert a skewer.
12. Take out of the oven and leave to rest on a cutting board before carving.

Comment:

There is not much meat on the breast, but there is plenty around the thighs and wings. Serve each helping with some crispy skin, stuffing and apple sauce.

For the gravy:

1. Drain the contents of the oven dish into a bowl and pour off the fat which will be plentiful. Keep the latter for cooking other dishes. (It is especially good to fry potatoes in.)
2. Place the rest of the juices into a small saucepan.
3. Add some water, a stock cube and some wine to make a sufficient quantity, about 1¼ pints.
4. Simmer for 10 minutes, while you carve the goose.
5. Add seasoning.

6. Thicken slightly with 2 tsp. of cornflour mixed with a little cold water, and pour this into the gravy whilst stirring. Cook for 2 minutes.
7. Check seasoning. Add the port and redcurrant jelly at this stage.

LAMB ROGAN GOSH
Serves 5 to 6

This is quite a mild lamb curry.

Ingredients:

3 lbs. of cubed lean lamb
¾ pt. yoghurt
2 onions chopped
2 tbs. paprika
2 tbs. tomato puree
2" fresh ginger, peeled, scraped into strands or chopped
salt and pepper
3 cloves garlic, squeezed
oil for frying
basmati rice, to serve with it.

Method:

1. Brown onions lightly, for about 10 minutes.
2. Add garlic and paprika.
3. Continue frying for 2 minutes.
4. Add meat, ginger and tomato purée.
5. Put meat in a saucepan with the yoghurt and ½ pt. of water.
6. Simmer for 2 hours. (The yoghurt transforms the sauce into a rich gravy.)
7. Add a pinch of cayenne if you wish to make it hotter.
8. For a stronger curry flavour, add 1 heaped tbs. Garam Masala or curry paste and cook for a further 10 minutes.
9. Serve with rice and a tray with Indian chutneys, Naan bread and banana slices.

BEEF NASI GORENG

Serves 4 to 5

I first had this dish in Holland and have enjoyed various versions of it since, as it lends itself to experimentation.

Ingredients:

2 lb. beef slices cut fairly thinly
8 oz basmati rice
4 oz mushrooms, sliced
1 large onion, finely chopped
2 cloves of garlic, squeezed
1 pepper, chopped (with inside membranes and seeds removed)
3 tomatoes, peeled and chopped, you can use chopped, tinned tomatoes
1 tbs. nasi goreng ready-made sauce. This thai sauce may not be available, but you could replace it with 3 tbs. soya sauce
1 tsp. pepper sauce (Tabasco)
2 eggs
3 spring onions
oil and butter for frying
salt and black pepper

Method:

1. Cut beef into fingers, about ½" thick.
2. Prepare vegetables.
3. Cook rice for 10 minutes, or until it is done.
4. Strain and run boiling water through it in a wire sieve. Keep hot.
5. Fry onion in oil and butter until soft, about 5 minutes.
6. Add chopped pepper, sliced mushrooms and chopped tomatoes.
7. Cook for about 10 minutes on gentle heat.
8. Remove vegetables and keep hot.
9. In a clean frying pan, fry beef in butter and oil until it is no longer red (2-3 min.).
10. Add garlic, nasi goreng sauce and pepper sauce.
11. Add the vegetables and mix with seasoning. Keep hot.
12. Whisk the eggs with seasoning and make an omelette.
13. Fry it on both sides.
14. When omelette is ready put it on a plate and cut into strips.
15. Clean and peel off outer layer of spring onions, cut into 1" lengths.
16. Take a large oven-proof dish.
17. Arrange rice along the edges.
18. Place beef and vegetable mixture in the middle.
19. Decorate rice with strips of omelette and spring onion.
20. Reheat for a few minutes if necessary.
21. Serve with a green salad with a sour cream dressing.

Sour cream dressing:

1 tub sour cream
4-5 drops of tabasco
salt and white pepper
1 dsp. wine vinegar

<u>Method</u>:

1. Stir well and toss the green salad lightly with the dressing immediately before serving.

ROAST DUCK WITH
APPLE & CELERY STUFFING
Serves 4

Duck is so delicious, but there is not much meat on it, so make a good stuffing and make sure the skin is really crisp and nice to eat.

Ingredients:

1 duck, oven-ready 4-5 lbs. (frozen is fine)

Stuffing:

2 Granny Smith apples, peeled, cored and chopped
4 sticks celery, sliced and coarsely chopped
2 tbs. parsley, chopped
2 oz walnuts, coarsely chopped
2 thick slices of bread, turned into breadcrumbs with the Magimix
1 onion
½ lb. pork sausage meat
2 oz butter
salt and pepper
1 egg

Gravy:

3 tbs. orange juice
1 glass dry white wine
2 tsp cornflour with a little water to thicken it
Degreased juices from roasting tin (Pour off the fat)

Method:

To roast duck:

2. Rinse the duck inside and out removing the giblets.
3. Dry the duck and season with salt and pepper.
4. Pierce it all over with a fork (at least 20 times).
5. Place on a rack over an oven dish, so that all the fat drips into the dish and the duck keeps dry.
6. Place a little water and a bouquet garni in the oven dish.
7. Cook at 200° C for about 2 hours. DO NOT baste, as the skin should be really crisp and brown.

To make the stuffing:

1. Fry the duck's liver and heart from the giblets, (if available) in some butter.
2. When done, chop finely and use for stuffing.
3. Chop onion and celery and fry gently in butter.
4. Combine all the rest of the stuffing ingredients i.e. sausage meat, apples, walnuts, breadcrumbs, egg, herbs and seasoning. Mix well.
5. Taste for seasoning.
6. Cook stuffing separately in an oven-proof dish for about 1 hour.

To make the gravy:

1. When duck is cooked, place on an oven dish in a warm oven.
2. Strain the juices off from the dish in which the duck cooked.
3. Place in a bowl and skim off the fat as it rises.
4. Put the juices in a clean saucepan, add white wine, orange juice and thickening. (1 tsp. cornflour mixed with a little water.)
5. Add seasoning and simmer for 5 minutes.

To serve:

Carve duck, allowing a joint and some breast meat and crispy skin for each person.
Serve stuffing and sauce separately.

Accompaniments:

Rice and a salad of chicory and orange. (Chicory leaves mixed with thinly sliced orange and lightly dressed with olive oil.)
Mange tout also go well with this.

CHICKEN WITH A WINE
& MUSTARD SAUCE
(Dijonnaise)
Serves 8

Ingredients:

1 x 4½ lb. Chicken (You can also use frozen turkey)

Stock:

2 stalks celery
1 onion
2 carrots
bouquet garni
8 peppercorns
salt

Sauce:

3 oz butter
2 tbs. flour
½ pt. whipping cream
½ pt. white wine
½ pt. chicken stock
2 tsp. dried tarragon or 2 tbs. fresh tarragon
1 tbs. strong dijon mustard
2 oz parmesan, grated
2 oz gruyere, grated

breadcrumbs and some parmesan for topping

Method:

1. Rinse out chicken.
2. Cover with water.
3. Simmer chicken with the vegetables, herbs and seasoning until tender (about 2 hours).
4. Leave to cool in liquid, if possible.
5. Drain chicken.
6. Discard skin and bones and cut meat into medium sized pieces (size of a tablespoon).

To make the sauce:

1. Melt butter, add flour and cook for 5 minutes, without browning.
2. Add wine, stock and tarragon and simmer for ½ hour.

3. Add mustard, cheese, cream and simmer for 10 minutes very gently.
4. The sauce should be well flavoured and pungent. Add more mustard if it is too bland.
5. Cover an oven dish with some sauce.
6. Add a layer of chicken and alternate with sauce, finishing with sauce on top.
7. Sprinkle with breadcrumbs and cheese.
8. Bake in the oven at 200° C for about 45 minutes or for an hour if the chicken was cold to start with.

Serve with plain rice. A green salad is nice with it.

LEMON CHICKEN
Serves 6

Ingredients:

6 chicken breasts, skin removed
2 lemons
1 medium onion, finely chopped
4 oz butter
seasoned flour: 4 tbs. flour mixed with salt and white pepper to taste
½ cup white wine
½ cup water
bouquet garni
½ pt. double cream
cornflour for thickening

Method:

1. Trim chicken breasts and turn in seasoned flour.
2. Grate the rind of one lemon and squeeze the juice.
3. Squeeze the juice from second lemon.
4. Fry chicken breasts lightly in butter.
5. Remove these from the pan and fry the onion lightly.
6. Cover the fried chicken and onions with foil and cook in the oven for about 30 minutes at about 200° C.
7. When done, strain the juices into a saucepan with a cup of white wine and ½ cup of water, seasoning and the bouquet garni.
8. Simmer for about 5 minutes.
9. Add lemon peel and juice.
10. Strain sauce and thicken slightly with about 2 tsp. cornflour and water.
11. Add the cream to the sauce. Cook gently for 2-3 minutes.
12. Adjust seasoning.
13. Transfer chicken to a warm serving dish.
14. Spoon some sauce over the chicken and serve the rest of the sauce separately.

Serve with a little plain Basmati rice and a few mange tout.

Note:

For a party, garnish with slices of lemon.

BEEF OLIVES
Serves 8

A very useful Sunday lunch dish which can be made in advance.

Ingredients:

4 lb. beef, sliced thinly (topside or similar cut)
1 lb. streaky bacon
1 jar of sweet and sour gherkins
2 oz butter
2 oz flour
1 tbs. tomato purée
bouquet garni
2 bay leaves
beef stock or water (use ½ beef stock cube)
parsley
wooden cocktail sticks

Method:

1. Ask the butcher to slice the beef thinly and to beat it out slightly.
2. Cut beef into slices about 3" x 3".
3. De-rind bacon and cut into 2" lengths.
4. Cut gherkins into 4, lengthways.
5. Roll up a piece of beef round 1 slice of bacon and quarter of a gherkin and fix with cocktail stick.
6. Brown rolls in butter and oil mixture.
7. Transfer to a large saucepan.
8. Add a little cold water to the frying pan and let it bubble up, scraping off all bits from the sides.
9. Keep juices and transfer them into the large saucepan.
10. Clean out frying pan.
11. Add 2 oz butter and when melted, 2 oz flour.
12. Brown gently until nut coloured.
13. Add ½ pt. stock, tomato purée, bay leaves, and bouquet garni.
14. Stir until sauce is smooth, and then pour sauce over the beef.
15. Add pepper, parsley and enough water to cover the beef.
16. Cook for 40 minutes.
17. Remove rolls of beef onto a dish.
18. Take out sticks.
19. Check sauce for seasoning (the bacon may give out enough salt).
20. Put beef back in sauce.

Serve with mashed potatoes and glazed carrots.

VEGETARIAN RISOTTO WITH MUSHROOMS

Serves 2 to 3

Ingredients:

150g risotto rice (looks a bit like pudding rice)
1/2 medium onion, finely chopped
3 cloves of garlic, finely chopped
1 stick of celery, chopped
6 oz mushrooms, sliced, any kind
1 pt. (500ml) good stock (you can use stock cube)
1 wine glass of dry white wine
1 ½oz (50g) grated parmesan cheese
1 teacup of chopped, fresh herbs (e.g. parsley, basil, a little rosemary or thyme)
2 bay leaves
4 tbs. olive oil
salt and black pepper

Variations:

If not vegetarian, 2oz of some coarse, dried Italian sausage, sliced thinly, can be added 10 minutes into cooking. Or substitute the sausage with some sun-dried tomatoes for extra flavour.

Method:

1. Put two tablespoons of olive oil in a large sauté pan, with a lid.
2. When hot, add chopped onion, garlic and celery.
3. Cook slowly, without colouring, for 5 minutes with the lid on.
4. Add the rest of the oil and rice.
5. Cook for 5 minutes on medium heat.
6. Add one cup of stock and bay leaves.
7. Cook for 5-10 minutes.
8. Add mushrooms and sausage (if used) and the wine and half the herbs.
9. Cook while stirring gently so the rice does not stick.
10. Add more stock as it is absorbed.
11. Keep lid on when not stirring.
12. Towards the end of the cooking time (about 25 minutes) add the rest of the herbs and Parmesan cheese.
13. Leave in a warm place.

Note:

When ready, the Risotto should be creamy with some liquid around the edges. Add a little more water or stock if necessary.

Serve with a very simple green salad, dressed with olive oil and a few drops of balsamic vinegar. This dish has a very gentle flavour but it 'grows' on you and is wonderful 'comfort food'. Good for you, too!

When asparagus is in season, you can add that in pieces to the risotto, but allow 15 minutes for it to cook. Alternatively, you could poach the asparagus separately and add when cooked.

MOROCCAN LAMB
Serves 6

A good party dish as it can be prepared in advance and carved before the guests arrive.

Ingredients:

1 leg of lamb (New Zealand frozen lamb is fine)
1 aubergine – washed and cut into 1" cubes
3 courgettes – washed and sliced into ½" thick slices
2 large onions, – chop each into 8 pieces
4 cloves of garlic – peeled and roughly chopped
1 x 14 oz tin of chopped tomatoes
1 pint stock – use a beef stock cube if you have no stock
herbs: thyme, rosemary and 2 bay leaves
spices: 1 heaped tsp. Turmeric and cinnamon
2 heaped tsp. coriander
¼ tsp. chilli powder
olive oil and butter
6 ready to eat apricots – chopped
6 ready to eat prunes – stoned and chopped

Note:

Find a casserole large enough so a leg of lamb can lie flat in it. If the dish does not have a lid, use foil to cover.
The dish can be cooked in the oven, but it is easier to braise on top of the stove as you can stir it, and prevent the meat and vegetables burning.
Cooking time alone is 3 hours on low heat. The meat should be so soft that it almost falls off the bone.

Method:

1. Trim excess fat off lamb.
2. Stick little wedges of garlic into cuts in the meat.
3. Brown the meat in oil and butter on all sides.
4. Prepare the vegetables and fruit – the aubergines are washed, cut up (1" x 1"), sprinkled with salt, left for 10 minutes to 'sweat', rinsed, dried with kitchen paper.
5. Prepare the stock. (I often include any left over wine I have to the pot, but not if the pot is an untreated, an old cast iron one, as the metal may interact with the acids in the wine.)
6. Once the meat is browned, add onion, garlic and brown in the fat next to the meat.
7. Add water, up to 1½", and cook meat with herbs for about 1½ hours, turning from time to time, adding stock (and wine if used) if liquids dry up.

8. Add aubergines, courgettes, spices and fruit.
9. The vegetables braise gently by the side of the meat. There should be plenty of liquid to mix vegetables in and turn the meat, but never more than 2" as the vegetables ooze of their own juice.
10. Add salt and plenty of pepper.

To serve:

1. Take out lamb.
2. Cut into thick slices.
3. Place in a hot serving dish.
4. Test the flavour of the juices in the pan, correct seasoning.
5. Arrange vegetables round the meat with some of the juice.
6. Serve the rest of the juice separately.
7. I serve new potatoes with this dish but more appropriate is couscous or boiled rice.

Couscous:

1. Buy fine couscous and boil for 3 minutes in salted water until tender.
2. Line a colander with muslin or a napkin and pour in couscous.
3. Keep colander covered over steaming water to keep it hot until needed.
4. Stir in a knob of butter before serving.

Note:

I recently did this dish with 3 legs of lamb and used a fish kettle and an old ham kettle to cook the dish. It was a much appreciated dish and seemed to go a long way. The gravy has a wonderful flavour from the lamb and vegetables.

FINNISH MEAT BALLS
WITH PIQUANT SAUCE
Serves 6 to 8

The most popular, traditional dish in Finland, especially among children.

Ingredients:

1½ lbs. minced beef, (or 1 lb. minced beef and ½ lb. of minced pork)
½ cup breadcrumbs
½ cup water mixed with ½ cup cream
1 onion chopped
2 eggs
seasoning
1 tsp. mixed herbs
1 tsp. chopped parsley
salt and pepper

For the sauce:

2 tbs. flour
2 tbs. butter
½ cup cream
seasoning

Method:

1. Soak breadcrumbs in water and cream.
2. Brown chopped onion.
3. Add breadcrumbs and onion to meat with seasoning and some parsley.
4. Roll with your hands into little balls about 1" in diameter.
5. Place these on a wet board or plate.
6. Fry the balls in oil and butter until brown.
7. Set aside.
8. Add butter to pan to make sauce.
9. Add the flour and brown slightly.
10. Add some water and cream and mixed herbs and seasoning.
11. Boil for 15 minutes.
12. Place meat balls in a spacious saucepan.
13. Pour sauce over them.
14. Cook for about 25 minutes. Adjust seasoning.

To Serve:

Serve with boiled potatoes, glazed carrots and side dishes of sweet and sour gherkins or cranberry sauce. (Lingonberry jam is the usual accompaniment.)

191

Note:

The fried meat balls can be used on their own, heated as a cocktail snack. I serve them with a rather spicey, hot tomato sauce. Serve yourself by picking up a meatball with a cocktail stick and dipping it in the sauce. They are very popular at drinks parties.

Piquant sauce with tomato:

2 cups chopped tinned tomatoes
1 small onion finely chopped and fried
2 cloves of garlic, squeezed
2 tbs. tomato purée
1 bay leaf
¼ tsp. chilli powder
salt and pepper

Method:

1. Combine all ingredients and cook for about 5 minutes.

PASTA WITH BLUE CHEESE SAUCE
Serves 2

This is a quick and easy dish to make and real 'comfort food'.

Ingredients:

1 pack fresh tagliatelli – about 1 lb.
2 oz Danish blue or stilton cheese
2 oz garlic roulade or garlic cream cheese
1 tub sour cream
¼ pint milk
2 tsp. cornflour
½ lb. courgettes
1 tbs. oil
1 tbs. tarragon
sprinkling of lemon juice
1 cup grated cheddar

Method:

Sauce:

2. Heat milk in saucepan.
3. When hot add cornflour mixed with water.
4. Add the 2 cheeses a little at a time and whisk.
5. Add seasoning and sour cream and simmer for a few minutes.
6. Taste for flavour – it should be fairly strong.

Courgettes:

1. Wash, top and tail and cut into fairly thick slices.
2. Fry these in oil until slightly brown, turning once, (about 5 minutes).
3. Sprinkle with Tarragon, seasoning and lemon juice.

To boil pasta:

1. Place in a pan of boiling water with salt and a tablespoon of oil.
2. Boil pasta until almost done – about 4 to 5 minutes, if fresh pasta is used.
3. Drain and mix with hot sauce and courgettes.
4. Sprinkle with some cheddar and serve the rest separately.

Note:

If you have no courgettes you can substitute them with poached broccoli or fried mushrooms.

CHICKEN LIVER PILAU
Serves 6

Ingredients:

6 oz long grain rice
chicken stock (or vegetarian)
butter for cooking rice
1 medium onion, chopped
4 oz butter
½ lb. chicken livers, de-frosted, drained and trimmed
1 pepper, de-seeded and chopped
8 oz button mushrooms, washed and sliced
1 tbs. chopped parsley
1 tsp. fresh thyme
seasoning

Method:

1. Boil rice in some chicken stock in the usual way (1 cup rice to 2-2½ cups stock).
2. Prepare chicken livers – cut each liver in half. (Remove stringy bits.)
3. Fry onion and peppers in butter until soft.
4. Add chicken livers and fry for a further 5 minutes until almost cooked.
5. Remove from pan and keep warm.
6. Fry mushrooms in more butter.
7. Mix boiled rice with the other ingredients and the herbs.
8. Check seasoning.
9. Add a little hot stock to moisten mixture if it seems too dry.

Note:

For a vegetarian option, use vegetable stock and 8 oz cubed aubergine instead of chicken livers.
This dish re-heats well in the microwave.
Serve with a green salad.
If you like, add a few sultanas or nuts to the pilau, say, fried cashews.

MINI SMÖRGÅSBORD

Serves 4 to 6

This is a nice lunch or supper collection for a busy hostess and a pleasant surprise for the guests.

Ingredients:

1 tin sardines in tomato sauce
1 jar spiced herring or mustard herring (available from Waitrose)
1 tin red salmon
4 oz mayonnaise
4 hard boiled eggs
¼ lb. sliced salami
6 oz fine liver paté
rice salad bought or home-made containing cooked rice mixed with chopped ham, tomato, peas and parsley, moistened with french dressing.
new potatoes, boiled, served hot
rye and white bread

small salad tray:
lettuce, tomato, cucumber and gherkins

Method:

1. Prepare rice salad the day before.
2. Prepare salad tray.
3. Arrange red salmon, (drained if tinned) with mayonnaise on top.
4. Quarter the hard boiled eggs and place on top.
5. Remove herrings or sardines from their tins or jars and arrange on cereal bowls or small plates.
6. Similarly, the sliced salami and the pâté.
7. Boil the new potatoes just before serving the meal.
8. Put out the bread and the butter.

Your meal is ready!

Note:

For pudding, fresh or stewed fruit, topped with cream is quite nice. Swedish ice cream will be welcome (available from Waitrose).

PORK GOULASH
Serves 6 to 8

This is a hearty Hungarian dish for a winter evening.

Ingredients:

3 lbs. pork steaks
2 large onions
2 tbs. paprika
¼ tsp. cayenne pepper
1 small tin tomato purée
1 x 14 oz tin chopped tomatoes
1 bay leaf
1 heaped tsp. thyme
8 oz button mushrooms
oil and butter for frying
¼ pt. double cream
¼ pt. soured cream for decoration
1 wineglass dry sherry
1 tbs. plain flour

Method:

1. Cut pork into fingers.
2. Chop onion finely.
3. Fry meat first then remove it to a separate saucepan adding the tin of tomatoes and the tomato purée.
4. Fry onion until beginning to colour adding some more butter if necessary.
5. Sprinkle on the flour, paprika and the cayenne pepper.
6. Fry gently for 2 minutes.
7. Add sherry, seasoning, herbs and cold water to make the sauce, stirring all the time.
8. Pour sauce over the meat making sure all the meat is covered. Add more water if necessary.
9. Simmer for 1½ hours. **Meanwhile...**
10. Wash and fry the mushrooms, halved
11. Ten minutes before the goulash is ready add the mushrooms and the cream
12. Check the seasoning, the flavour should be strong and a bit sharp.
13. At the last minute add the soured cream, in swirls, on top.
Serve with noodles and a green salad.
Drink 'Bulls' Blood' – red Hungarian wine, with it!

Note:

Some people add small chunks of potato half and hour before the dish is ready.

HAMBURGERS A LA LINDSTRÖM

Serves 4

Ingredients:

1 lb. minced steak
2 egg yolks
½ cup cream
1 heaped tbs. chopped or grated onion
3 tbs. finely chopped pickled beetroot
1 tbs. capers
2 cold cooked potatoes, mashed
salt & pepper

Method:

1. Season the ground mince.
2. Add the cream, a little at a time, followed by the yolks.
3. Add the finely chopped vegetables and the potatoes.
4. Test for seasoning.
5. With your hands, form the mixture into small, high hamburgers.
6. Fry them in butter for about 15 minutes, turning them 3 times.

Note:

If you wish the hamburgers to be accompanied by a sauce place a little stock, some cream and 1 to 2 tsp. of mustard in the frying pan, add the hamburgers which will flavour the gravy. Season and simmer the gravy for about 10 minutes.
Creamed carrots (turned in some white sauce or light cream) and plain boiled potatoes are nice with these.

HADDOCK & SWEETCORN BAKE

Serves 4 to 6

Ingredients:

2 medium tins of sweetcorn
1½ lbs. smoked haddock or cod
1 pint good cheese sauce made with:-
2 oz butter, 2 oz flour, 1 pint milk, bay leaf, salt and pepper and 6 oz strong, grated cheddar

Method:

1. Poach fish in a mixture of milk and water for about 10 minutes. (Just use water if you cannot spare the milk.)
2. Make cheese sauce by making a roux of butter and flour, adding milk, gradually whilst stirring, adding bay leaf, salt and pepper and 4 oz of the grated cheese (2 oz left for topping).
3. Skin, bone and flake fish.
4. Butter an oven-proof dish.
5. Drain the sweetcorn and arrange at the bottom of the dish.
6. Arrange fish on top.
7. Pour over the cheese sauce.
8. Sprinkle dish with extra, grated cheese.
9. Serve with plain, new potatoes.

Note:

We used to dine with an elderly couple who had lived in the Far East for a long time. There they had cooks, of course, so the wife never learnt to cook and hated it. I first got to know this dish at her table because she found it so easy to make. It is a very good supper dish or a hearty starter. The sweetness of the corn is a perfect foil for the salty haddock.

SWEDISH SALMON MOUSSE

Serves 8 as a main course, 12 as a starter

A pleasant summer lunch dish.

Ingredients for Fish Stock:

2 carrots
1 onion
bay leaves
parsley stalks
3 tbs. white vinegar
water to cover fish
salt and about 12 pepper corns

Method:

1. Boil all stock ingredients together for 15 minutes, before adding to the fish.
2. Add the salmon and cook for a further 30 minutes, or until done. (Stick a skewer in to see if it is done.)

Ingredients for Salmon Mousse:

4 lbs. raw salmon
3 tsp. of gelatin powder
small bunch of dill
small bunch of chives
8-10 fresh tarragon leaves (or 1 tsp. dried tarragon)
1 tsp. french mustard
½ tsp. of tabasco
½ pt. double cream
1-2 tablespoons of dry vermouth or lemon juice

Method to make Salmon Mousse:

1. Make fish stock.
2. Poach fish in it.
3. Dissolve gelatine in a little hot stock.
4. Skin salmon and remove bones.
5. Blend in a food processor.
6. Add the gelatine to the mixture.
7. Add dry vermouth, chopped herbs, French mustard and Tabasco with seasoning.
8. Transfer mixture into a mixing bowl.
9. Whip cream and fold into the mixture.
10. Check seasoning.
11. Turn mixture into a rinsed ring mould, or a round dish.
12. Chill in the refrigerator until set.

Ingredients for the piquant sauce:

2 eggs or 4 egg yolks
1 cup vinegar
1 cup water
3 tbs. mustard
1 large jar of créme fraiche or 1½ cups of whipping cream
1 tbs. of flour
1 tsp. salt
1 tbs. butter

Garnish:

Water cress

Method for making the sauce:

1. Melt butter and add flour.
2. Add water slowly, whisking all the time.
3. Add mustard and vinegar.
4. Cook for 5 minutes.
5. Season well.
6. Whisk eggs.
7. Remove sauce from heat and incorporate eggs while whisking. Cool.
8. Whisk cream until soft peaks.
9. Fold into sauce.
10. Check seasoning.

To serve:

1. Turn mousse out of mould by placing it in hot water for 1 minute and up-turning it onto a large serving dish.
2. Spoon some of the sauce over the mousse.
3. Place water cress in the centre, or around mousse.
4. Serve the rest of the sauce separately.

Note:
New potatoes and a plain green salad are suitable accompaniments.
This recipe was given to me by some Swedish friends.

It is a very useful for a party dish in the summer as it can be made in advance.

SIMON'S RED THAI CURRY
Serves 2

My son-in-law, Simon, used to woo my daughter with this dish before they married. He succeeded!

Ingredients:

7 oz raw prawns (frozen)
2 oz creamed coconut steeped in hot water to make ½ pint
1 large clove garlic
1 hot chilli – de-seeded (use half the quantity if you don't want such a hot curry)
juice of 2 limes or lemons
1 stick of lemon grass, bruised
1 red pepper, sliced, slices halved (same size as prawns)
ghee or butter
1 handful mushrooms, chopped
3 tbs. fresh coriander
seasoning

Method:

1. Lightly fry prawns, garlic, chilli, in ghee or butter.
2. Add lime juice and seasoning.
3. Only fry the prawns until they turn pink.
4. Add red pepper and mushrooms.
5. Fry for 2 minutes longer.
6. Add lemon grass, but do not eat it.
7. Fry 2 minutes longer.
8. Make up coconut milk and add it.
9. Sprinkle on coriander.
10. Simmer until curry tastes well balanced, 10-15 minutes.

Serve with basmati rice.

ROAST PORK LOIN WITH
APRICOTS OR PRUNES

Serves 8 to 10

Note:

Take your prepared apricots or prunes when you go to buy the meat. Ask the butcher to remove some of the excess fat and to give you the bones and the skin to make crackling if you wish. Ask him to place your prepared apricots or prunes into the meat and tie it up with string.

Ingredients:

6 lbs. boned and skinned pork loin
12 dried apricots or prunes, stewed with a little sugar until soft. (Remove prune stones)
2 carrots
2 onions
herbs such as fresh rosemary and sage
2 bay leaves
seasoning
½ bottle of dry white wine
¼ pt. double cream
2 tsp. cornflour to thicken the gravy

Method:

1. Fry the stuffed meat in butter and oil to brown it slightly, if you have a frying pan large enough.
2. Peel and slice the carrots and the onions and fry these in butter until slightly brown.
3. Place loin in an oven dish that will hold it comfortably without being too large.
4. Place the vegetables around it with the herbs and the white wine and seasoning.
5. Place the bones that you got from the butcher around the joint as well, to add flavour to the gravy.
6. Cover with foil and roast for about 2 hours at 180° C. If the roasting pan gets dry top up with a cupful of water from time to time.
7. Rub the scored pork skin with salt and roast on a separate shelf above the meat. (It will take about 40 minutes to roast.)
8. Test the meat with a skewer to see if it is ready. If so, the juices will come out clear.
9. Take out the meat and keep warm. Strain the juices from the oven dish.
10. Place in a saucepan and simmer to concentrate the flavour.
11. Thicken the sauce slightly with 2 tsp. cornflour mixed in a little cold water.
12. Add the cream and simmer gently.
13. Test for seasoning and add more if necessary.
14. Remove the string and carve meat into 1 cm thick slices.

15. Serve it with the sauce and crackling.

Note:

Carrots, boiled potatoes and sprouts would make a colourful mixture to accompany the meat.

RICH VENISON PIE

Serves 6 to 8

Ingredients:

2½ lbs. venison, cubed

For the marinade:

1 leek
2 carrots
3 cloves of garlic
bouquet garni
olive oil
½ bottle red wine
freshly ground black pepper

Other ingredients:

6 oz smoked bacon
olive oil
¾ pt. chicken stock
½ lb. button or field mushrooms
butter for frying
seasoning
12 oz ready-rolled puff pastry (buy frozen)
egg to glaze
3 tbs. redcurrant jelly
1 egg, chopped

Method:

1. Clean and peel the vegetables.
2. Slice fairly thinly.
3. Put marinade ingredients together.
4. Add the venison.
5. Marinade overnight in the fridge – turning occasionally.
6. Cut up the smoked bacon with scissors into small pieces.
7. Fry these gently in a little oil.
8. Clean mushrooms and halve or slice them.
9. When meat has marinaded, take out of the marinade with a slotted spoon.
10. Fry meat over high heat until slightly coloured.
11. Add marinade, bacon and the chicken stock and cook for 1½ hours in the oven at 180° C until tender.
12. Add redcurrant jelly.
13. Remove bouquet garni.
14. Check seasoning and leave to get cold.

15. When cold, place in a casserole dish.
16. Cover with pastry – Brush top with egg.
17. Cook for about 40 minutes in the oven at 200° C.
18. Cover top with foil if the pastry browns too quickly.

Serve with boiled potatoes and spiced red cabbage.

SPRING LAMB WITH HERBS

Serves 6

This recipe does justice to the good flavour of spring lamb.

Ingredients:

3 lbs. lean leg of lamb off the bone. Ask the butcher to bone the leg for you. You then trim it and cut it into chunks.
2 tbs. oil and some butter
1 large onion, sliced
1 medium turnip, peeled and sliced
3 carrots, peeled and sliced
4 or 5 runner beans, cut up
3 or 4 new potatoes
2 cloves garlic, peeled and squeezed
bouquet garni (bay leaf, sprig of rosemary, sprig of thyme, parsley)
2 tbs. chopped parsley (additional)
½ bottle dry white wine
¾ pt. stock or water
seasoning

Method:

1. Fry lamb in oil and butter until brown.
2. Prepare vegetables and cut into small chunks.
3. Cover meat with water or stock.
4. Bring to the boil and skim off any skum.
5. Add herbs, seasoning and wine and cook for about an hour until meat is almost tender.
6. Add the vegetables and cook for a further 30 minutes.
7. Remove the bouquet garni.
8. Check seasoning.
9. Serve in the casserole, sprinkled with parsley.

Note:

This is a complete dish in itself and doesn't really require any vegetables, but some mashed potato might be nice, or some fresh bread.
Optional: ½ cup of cream to enrich the sauce.

SEAFOOD LASAGNA

Serves 6

Ingredients:

1 lb. salmon fillet
8 oz frozen prawns
8 oz mixed sea food or cooked mussels
rind and juice of a lemon
1 tbs. dried dill
2 tbs. fresh chopped parlsey
2 oz flour
2 oz butter
1½ pints milk
½ pt. double cream
1 tsp. anchovy essence or a few chopped anchovies
8 sheets of lasagna
2 oz parmesan cheese
seasoning
breadcrumbs and butter for topping

Method:

1. Cube salmon and cook slowly in butter until just done.
2. Make a roux of the flour and butter and add the milk gradually, while whisking.
3. Then add the cream and check the seasoning so that the sauce is well flavoured.
4. Add lemon peel and juice, dill and parsley.
5. Add anchovies and Parmesan cheese.
6. Cook sauce for a few minutes.
7. Butter a shallow oven-proof dish.
8. Place some sauce in the bottom.
9. Some lasagna sheets on top.
10. Then some more sauce and half the seafood.
11. Add a few lasagna sheets again, on top.
12. Then some sauce and the rest of the seafood.
13. Top with last lasagna sheets and the rest of the sauce.
14. Sprinkle with breadcrumbs.
15. Dot with butter.
16. Bake for 1 hour at 200° C.

Note:

Spinach is also a suitable addition to this dish. Some pasta need not be cooked if it is baked in a sauce, but if you want to make sure, poach your sheets of lasagna for 5 minutes in boiling water before you use them in this dish.

Cocktail Meatballs with piquant sauce

Christmas Ham with whole prunes and mustard

Coeur à la crème – French cream cheese dessert
Ideally made in a special heart shaped china dish with drainage holes

Salmagundi (Swedish sillsallad)
A salad of meat, fish and cooked vegetables garnished with a sour cream
sauce coloured pink with beetroot juice

Herring Eye
Herring with egg (white and yolk separated)
Parsley and onion and capers

Cream Cheese dip with crudités (fresh raw vegetables)

Summer luncheon
Top Row: Westcoast prawn salad, Beeches wine, Scandinavian crispbread and rolls, meatballs, cheeseboard, chocolate mousses, strawberries, grilled sausages, eggs in mayonnaise, oak-smoked fresh salmon.
In Front: Salmon coulibiac, Jansson's Temptation, seafood filled pancakes.

Food for a drinks party
Hot meatballs with spicy sauce, bacon wrapped prunes, tray of
canapes, pepper salami with gouda cheese, Parma ham round melon,
stuffed eggs with mock caviar garnish, Pâté canapes with gherkin,
spicy herring on black bread, tray of Pâté canapes, cream cheese dip
with raw vegetables

Finnish Christmas Meal
Top Row: Salmagundi, rice and carrot bake, swede bake,
dessert of dried fruit
Centre Row: Christmas ham with a sugar crust,
served with mustard and prunes, Swedish pâté
Front Row: Rollmops in sour cream sauce (in jar), smoked salmon,
rollmops with tomatoes, herring eye with egg garnish and capers,
Finnish prune dessert
God Jul means Happy Christmas in Swedish

Side of oak-smoked salmon (cooked, not raw)

Rollmops with garnish of tomatoes, lettuce and gherkins

A tray of cold cocktail food: pepper salami with gouda cheese filling, Parma ham with melon stuffing, more pepper salami, smoked salmon with cream cheese filling and olive garnish, spicy marinated herring on black rye bread

The Dessert Trolley
Top Row: Green marzipan cake and South-African brandy tart
Middle Row: Coeur à la crème with strawberries and creamed rice
with apricot pureé
Bottom Right: Pavlova with cream and fresh fruit, bilberry tart,
chocolate mousses

ACCOMPANIMENTS
& OTHER DISHES

CYPRIOT MEATBALLS
Serves 6 to 8 with drinks.

Ingredients:

½ lb. minced pork + ½ lb. minced beef
½ cup fresh breadcrumbs
½ cup parsley
½ cup finely chopped onion
1 clove garlic, squeezed
1 egg
salt and black pepper

Method:

1. Mix all ingredients and knead together.
2. Leave for ½ hour in the refrigerator.
3. With your hands, form into small balls, the size of large cherries.
4. Deep fry these in oil until light brown (or roast for a short time in the oven until brown).
5. Serve hot or cold.

A tomato sauce that goes well with these meatballs is:-

SPICY TOMATO SAUCE
Sufficient for 6 to 8 people

Ingredients:

1 tin chopped tomatoes, less a little of the juice
2 tbs. tomato puree
3 cloves garlic, squeezed
½ chopped fried onion
¼ cup olive oil
1 bay leaf
¼ tsp. chilli powder
salt

Method:

1. Simmer all ingredients together for about 20 minutes.
2. Check seasoning, and remove bay leaf.
3. Serve hot as a dip for the above meatballs.

Note:
Each guest helps himself to a wooden cocktail stick, pierces a hot meat ball, dips it into the sauce and eats it!

CARROT BAKE
Serves 6 to 8

A vegetable casserole.

Ingredients:

1½ cups Patna rice (the usual rice) – cooked with 5 cups of water and 1 tsp. salt
2 cups milk
2 eggs
10 carrots
1 tbs. honey or golden syrup
butter
breadcrumbs

Method:

1. Cook rice in water and salt (about 15-20 minutes).
2. Continue cooking adding a little milk until rice is cooked.
3. Peel and boil carrots in water until soft.
4. Mash carrots with a fork.
5. Mix carrots and rice.
6. Add eggs and milk.
7. Add honey or golden syrup, seasoning.
8. Check seasoning.
9. Pour into a buttered, shallow oven dish.
10. Dot with breadcrumbs and extra butter.
11. Bake for 1 hour at 180° C, until risen.
12. Cover with foil for half of the time.

Note:

It rises rather like a soufflé. Serve with gammon steaks, or any meat.
Traditional Finnish Christmas dish.

QUICK CHEESE SOUFFLÉ

Serves 2 to 3

This is like a fluffy omelette.

Ingredients:

4 eggs
1 cup milk
2 cups of grated cheese
2 tbs. butter

Method:

1. Separate egg yolks from whites.
2. Whisk yolks, and add milk and seasoning.
3. Add cheese.
4. Whip whites until stiff.
5. Fold into the cheese mixture.
6. Melt butter in a frying pan.
7. Pour in the mixture.
8. Fry with a lid on at low heat for 7 to 10 minutes.
9. Serve immediately with a green salad and fresh French bread.

FARMER'S OMELETTE

Serves 4 to 6

Ingredients:

1½ tbs. butter
100g smoked ham, chopped
3 to 4 peeled and cooked potatoes, chopped
2 small onions chopped
4 eggs
4 tbs. water
1 tbs. parsley or chives
seasoning

Method:

1. Fry the chopped onion in butter.
2. Add chopped ham and potatoes.
3. Fry for about 10 minutes.
4. Whip eggs, salt and water.
5. Pour on top of the ham and potatoes.
6. Cook for several minutes until the egg has set. To cook the top, cover with lid for part of the time.
7. Sprinkle parsley over the top.
8. Serve in wedges.

GREEN TOMATO, APPLE & ONION CHUTNEY

Serves 20

Ingredients:

1½ lbs. of green tomatoes
l½ lbs. cooking apples
½ lb. onions
½ oz ground allspice
¼ tsp. pepper
1 oz salt
¼ lb. sultanas
6 oz demerara sugar
½ oz cloves
½ pt. vinegar

Method:

1. Put tomatoes, onions and apples through a mincer. (Or cut up by hand, or use Magimix.)
2. Add salt and leave overnight.
3. Strain off surplus liquid.
4. Put pulp in a pan.
5. Add sultanas and spices, and the cloves tied in a muslin bag.
6. Add sugar and vinegar.
7. Simmer gently, stirring occasionally until reduced to a soft pulp (about 2 hours).
8. Put in jars and cover.

STUFFING WITH PRUNES, APRICOTS & ONIONS

To accompany roast goose, duck or turkey

Ingredients:

1 lb. pork sausage meat
6 prunes, cut in slivers
8 apricots, roughly chopped
1½ cups of fresh white bread crumbs – (prepared in the blender)
2 eggs
heart and liver of the bird
1 large onion, chopped
salt and pepper
3 tbs. chopped parsley

Method:

1. Mix pork sausage with breadcrumbs, parsley and eggs (use a fork or your hands).
2. Fry heart and liver of the bird in butter and oil until almost done, and chop.
3. Fry the onion in the same pan.
4. Add these to the rest of the ingredients.
5. Season well with salt and pepper.
6. Place in an oven proof dish.
7. Cover loosely with foil and bake for 1 hour at 180°C.

Apple Sauce

Ingredients:

3 bramley apples, peeled, cored and cut into chunks
2 oz sugar
1 cup water

Method:

1. Place apples in water and boil until apples are soft and can be mashed with a fork.
2. Add sugar and cook for a further 10 minutes
3. Taste it, and add a little sugar or lemon juice if you wish. The sauce should be fairly 'tart'. It is suitable for fowl and pork.

TOFFEE BRITTLE WITH CHOCOLATE & ALMONDS

Ingredients:

1 tbs. golden syrup
1 cup sugar
1 cup butter
4 oz plain chocolate
2 oz flaked lightly toasted almonds

buttered greaseproof paper
sugar thermometer, if available

Method:

1. Heat the first 3 ingredients in a large thick saucepan.
2. Stir until the mixture boils.
3. Turn down heat and leave to cook until you measure 250° C using a sugar thermometer. This takes about 40 minutes. Do not stir the mixture.
4. If the mixture goes too dark lower the heat.
5. Butter greaseproof paper.
6. Pour the mixture on thinly and leave to cool.
7. Melt chocolate in a double boiler (or microwave).
8. Smear over toffee and scatter the almonds over the surface.
9. Leave to cool and set.
10. When quite cold, loosen from paper and break up into bite-sized pieces.

Note:

Store in a screwtop jar. Will keep for weeks in a dry place. The butter gives this toffee a really delicious flavour. It tastes exactly like 'Dime' bars and makes an excellent contribution to a bazaar or for Christmas presents.

FRUIT COMPÔTE FOR HAM

Serves 6 to 8

For a party it is nice to serve this home made fruit compôte with hot or cold ham.

Ingredients:

1 tin crushed pineapple (or pineapple rings)
1 tin sliced peaches
6 cooked prunes (½ small tin)
1 cup sultanas
2 apples, peeled, cored and sliced
6 whole cloves
1 tsp. cinnamon
1 dsp. sugar
1 dsp. lemon juice

Method:

1. Drain pineapple, peaches and prunes (if tinned), but keep juices.
2. Chop peaches and place them with chopped prunes, crushed pineapple (if using pineapple rings, crush them with a fork), sultanas, apples and spices in a saucepan and:
3. Boil for about 15 minutes.
4. Taste for sweetness.
5. Add a spoonful of sugar and lemon juice to taste.
6. Remove cloves.
7. When cold put mixture in a screwtop jar.

Keeps about 1 month.

FINNISH GREEN TOMATO CHUTNEY

Serves 20

I remember first having this chutney when I was about 4 years old, and visiting one of my Father's colleagues for lunch. The highlight of the meal, for me, was the chutney!

Ingredients:

4 pts. green tomatoes
1 cup white wine vinegar
2 pts. water

Preservation liquid:

2 lbs. sugar
1 cup white wine vinegar
4 cups water
10 whole cloves
10 cm cinnamon stick

Method:

1. Dry the tomatoes and remove the stalk.
2. Prick the tomatoes with a silver fork and place in a crock.
3. Combine vinegar and water.
4. Heat until boiling point and pour over the tomatoes.
5. Leave for 24 hours.

6. Prepare the preservation liquid by boiling the sugar, white wine vinegar and water with the spices, placed in a muslin bag, until you get a clear liquid and the sugar has melted.
7. Take out the tomatoes from the crock and lower them gently into the preservation liquid in a saucepan.
8. Simmer until the tomatoes are soft.
9. Remove the tomatoes gently, with a spoon.
10. Place in the emptied crock.
11. Boil up the syrup until thickened and pour it over the tomatoes.
12. When the chutney has cooled, cover the crock with greaseproof paper and a lid and keep in a cool place.

Note:

An excellent accompaniment to cold meat or a roast.

PICKLED MUSHROOMS IN VINEGAR

Serves 4 to 6 for 2 meals as an accompaniment

Going as a family to pick berries or fungi in the woods, generally in September, was a tremendous outing we looked forward to. Several families often went together and brought with them a coffee pot and sandwiches. Finns drink coffee on all occasions!

My Mother, who was a farmer's daughter, knew exactly under what sorts of trees you could find certain berries or fungi, and when the weather was suitable for these to grow and be plentiful. At the end of the day, we went home with baskets full of produce. We sat that evening, cleaning the mushrooms and cutting off stalks and bad bits. Everyone had mushroom charts at home and knew exactly which poisonous ones to avoid. The next day we were busy making boiled preservation solution with sugar, salt, vinegar and pickling spices. Pickled mushrooms are very useful as an accompaniment to meat dishes in the winter, when green vegetables are scarce. We used to get rather tired of only eating potatoes with everything.

By the way, there is a new law in Finland that allows you to go picking berries and fungi even from private woods. You have a right to roam and pick these during the season, generally in the Autumn. Out of politeness, you do not pick them near farms, but in the wild woodlands.

Ingredients:

2 pints of cleaned, small mushrooms, any kind

vinegar solution:

3½ cups of white wine vinegar
1 cup sugar
½ tbs. salt
½ tbs. whole, white pepper
½ tsp. grated nutmeg
1 dsp whole cloves
1 bay leaf

Method:

1. Poach the mushrooms in salted water.
2. Drain and leave to cool on a kitchen towel.
3. Arrange the mushrooms in a crock or jar.
4. Boil the vinegar with the spices for 5 minutes.
5. Strain over the mushrooms.
6. Close the jar or crock and keep in a cool place.

SPRING SANDWICHES

Dutch Spring Feast

Some Dutch friends of mine, took me on the first official day of Spring, to visit a farm where we were offered this delicacy. It consisted of plain, brown farm bread in large slices, spread with freshly made curd cheese and spring onions. We sat under the apple trees that were in blossom and drank beer with the sandwiches. It was a very charming occasion, with many families bringing their children along.

FINNISH SPRING SANDWICH

Ingredients:

crispbread
butter
cream cheese or processed, melted cheese (e.g. Laughing Cow)
parsley and chives

Method:

1. Butter the crispbread and spread with the cheese.
2. Wash the herbs and cut finely with scissors.
3. Sprinkle the herbs, liberally on the crispbreads.

Nobody can resist these!

SPINACH PANCAKES

Serves 6 to 8 large pancakes

Ingredients:

3 cups plain flour
1 tsp. sugar
1 tsp. salt
2 pints milk
1 to 2 eggs
3 tbs. melted butter
300g. 10 oz spinach

Method:

1. Wash the spinach, drain well and chop finely.
2. Make the pancake batter with the other ingredients, and add the spinach.
3. Fry in the usual way, in butter.

Note:

On its own this makes a good, filling vegetarian dish.
You can also reserve the chopped spinach and roll the pancakes around this filling.

POTATO PORRIDGE
A BREAKFAST DISH

Serves 4 hungry people

There are many different kinds of porridge in Scandinavia, and this is one of the more interesting ones. Some porridge is made with milk, some with ½ milk and ½ water and the grains used are oats, rye, rice and forms of differently milled wheat. A porridge which we use as a dessert includes fruit – see following recipe for Lingonberry Porridge.

Ingredients:

2 pints potatoes
3 to 4 pints water
2½ to 3 cups rye or barley flour
salt

Method:

1. Peel the potatoes; cut into wedges and cook in boiling water until soft.
2. Pour off the water into a bowl.
3. Mash the potato and replace some of the water.
4. Heat in a saucepan.
5. Add the rye or barley flour while whisking, into the potato mixture.
6. Cook slowly for ½ hour, over a low heat. Add salt to taste.

Sometimes we eat this porridge with a lump of butter in the middle or with milk as an accompaniment.
The Finns make many different kinds of porridge, generally eaten for breakfast or lunch with milk. A tradition from the days when there was not much else to eat.

LINGONBERRY PORRIDGE

Serves 8

If you don't have Lingonberries, cranberries will do very well for this dish. Lingonberries grow in pine forests all over Scandinavia. They are small red berries, quite hard and tart, and this jam is often used to accompany meat dishes, for instances meat balls.

Ingredients:

1½ pints lingonberries, mashed
4 pints water
1 cup sugar
½ tsp. salt
2 cups rye flour
1 tbs. cornflour

Method:

1. Crush the berries. Cook in water and strain off juice into a separate bowl.
2. Add sugar and salt to the juice and boil it.
3. Add rye flour while whisking.
4. Cook the porridge for ½ to ¾ hour whilst stirring occasionally.
5. Thicken with cornflour and boil up again for a few minutes.
6. Pour porridge into a large dish and beat it until fluffy with and electric beater.
7. Serve with milk or cream and some additional sugar.

Note:

I once served this porridge as a dessert at the end of a wedding breakfast. It looked very pretty in small glass bowls, decorated with a dollop of cream. I wonder how many guests knew how it was made!

CARROT, SWEDE & RICE PURÉE

Serves 4 to 6

Ingredients:

1 lb. carrot
1 swede
1 cup cooked rice
2 eggs
½ cup milk
1 oz butter
seasoning

Topping:

breadcrumbs and butter

Method:

1. Peel, cube and boil carrots and swede.
2. Mash these with a fork or in a blender.
3. Mix in 2 eggs, 1 oz melted butter, salt and pepper and cooked rice.
4. Place in a buttered oven dish.
5. Sprinkle with breadcrumbs and dot with butter.
6. Bake for about 1 hour at 180° C.

Note:

This is a good vegetarian dish, but also ideal to serve with hamburgers and ham.

FRIED SPRING CABBAGE
Serves 3 to 4

This was taught me by a girl married to an Indian. She used to add chilli to the dish.

Ingredients:

2 heads of spring cabbage
1 medium onion, chopped
2 cloves of garlic, chopped (optional)
2 tbs. oil
1 tsp. lemon juice
seasoning
chilli sauce, 1 tsp. or Tabasco (6 drops)

Method:

1. Remove tough, outer leaves of cabbage.
2. Wash cabbage and chop into shreds.
3. Drain.
4. Heat oil in a large sauté pan.
5. Sweat onion and garlic, if used.
6. Add lemon juice and chilli, if liked (say 6 drops of Tabasco).
7. When onion is translucent, add cabbage.
8. Cook gently under a lid for 5-10 minutes, until limp and fairly soft.
9. Check seasoning.

You can buy Tabasco sauce in most supermarkets. My friend cooks the spring cabbage without water.

GARLIC BUTTER & HERB BUTTER

Serves 4

Ingredients:

2 oz softened butter
2 cloves garlic, crushed
1 tbs. finely chopped parsley
½ tsp. lemon juice
salt and pepper

Method:

1. Mix all the ingredients together with a wooden spoon.
2. Shape into a sausage.
3. Wrap in foil.
4. Chill in the refrigerator.
5. For serving remove foil and cut into slices. Serve a slice on steaks or fish.

HERB BUTTER

Substitute garlic for a mixture of herbs such as parsley, chives and a pinch of thyme.

Serve slices of the butter on vegetables, fish or steaks.

.

OVEN ROASTED POTATO SLICES

Serves 4

Ingredients:

4 large potatoes, peeled
olive oil
mixed herbs
seasoning
2 cloves garlic, squeezed. (optional)

Method:

1. Slice potatoes, fairly thinly.
2. Arrange on an oiled baking sheet.
3. Brush with oil, seasoning and herbs.
4. Bake at 200° C for 30 minutes, or until soft.

Note:

If they haven't browned in 30 minutes turn up the heat slightly and roast for a further 10 minutes.

ROAST POTATOES

Serves 6 to 8

Ingredients:

6 large potatoes suitable for baking (they are floury)
oil
seasoning

Method:

1. Peel and cut potatoes into halves or smaller chunks.
2. Boil potatoes in water for 2 minutes.
3. Drain and let steam evaporate.
4. Place on an oiled oven dish or around the joint.
5. Brush with oil and season.
6. Roast about 1 – 1½ hours at oven temperature about 180° C.

They taste better if basted by the juices from the meat.

Variations:

HASSELBACK POTATOES

Serves 6

A Swedish way of roasting potatoes, for chops and steaks.

Ingredients:

6 potatoes, medium size
2 tbs. dried bread crumbs
2 tbs. grated Parmesan cheese
seasoning

Method:

1. Peel and halve the potatoes, lengthways.
2. Stand a potato, cut side down on a board.
3. Hold it firmly with one hand while cutting slits into it that do not quite reach the base.
4. Repeat with the rest of the potatoes.
5. Sprinkle them with salt and breadcrumbs and lastly, Parmesan.
6. Dribble some oil over them.
7. Bake in a hot oven for 1 hour approximately.

APPLE & CELERY STUFFING

Serves 4

This is ideal with Duck or Turkey.

Ingredients:

2 Granny Smith apples, peeled, cored and chopped
4 sticks celery, sliced and coarsely chopped
2 tbs. parsley, chopped
2 oz walnuts, coarsely chopped
2 thick slices of white bread, turned into breadcrumbs with the Magimix
1 onion
½ lb. pork sausage meat
2 oz butter
salt and pepper
1 egg

Method:

1. Fry the liver and heart from the giblets, (if available) in some butter.
2. When done, chop finely and use for stuffing.
3. Chop onion and celery and fry gently in butter.
4. Combine all the rest of the stuffing ingredients i.e. sausage meat, apples, walnuts, breadcrumbs, egg, herbs and seasoning. Mix well.
5. Taste for seasoning. Try a spoonful of the stuffing to see if it tastes good. Adjust seasoning if necessary.
6. Cook stuffing separately in an oven-proof dish for about 1 hour.

TABBOULEH
Serves 10 to 15

Ingredients:

¾ lb. fine or medium couscous
2 lbs. large tomatoes, finely chopped
2 large cucumbers, finely chopped
1 bunch of spring onions, finely chopped
1 large bunch of parsley, finely chopped (I use a Magimix)
1 large fistful of garden mint, finely chopped
juice of 2 lemons
4 fl. oz olive oil
1 pepper, finely chopped
salt and freshly ground black pepper
whole black olives
½ Chinese cabbage for garnish

Method:

1. Cover the couscous with hot water and leave to soak for 10 minutes. Taste it and if it is still hard, leave it to soak a little longer, and add some more hot water.
2. Drain the couscous well by putting it in a fine sieve and squeezing it with the back of a spoon.
3. Put into a bowl and stir it around a bit to let in air.
4. Add all the herbs, chopped tomatoes, cucumber and spring onions, well drained.
5. Mix dressing with oil, lemon juice, and seasoning and add some to the couscous until you feel it is moist.
6. Before serving add the rest of the dressing and toss again.
7. Serve on a plate lined with Chinese cabbage leaves.
8. Decorate with black olives.

Note:

Excellent on its own but equally good as part of a mixed salad table. Tabbouleh is a Middle Eastern dish and a lovely summer salad.
Add some extra olive oil if the salad is too dry.

COFFEE – LARGE QUANTITIES!

For large quantities of coffee, say for a party, you have to use a large saucepan and, preferably, several large thermoses to pour the coffee in.

Allow 4 moderately heaped dessert spoons of medium ground coffee per pint, (this serves 4 people)
Allow 3 moderately heaped dessert spoons per pint of coffee for a medium sized cafétière.

Method:

1. Measure the amount of water (depends on number of guests) you require and heat it in a saucepan on the stove.
2. When it is boiling, add the amount of coffee as suggested above.
3. Let it come to the boil just once and then put the lid on and leave in a warm place for three minutes.
4. Clarify coffee by adding a tablespoon of cold water. This will make the coffee grounds go to the bottom.
5. After a couple of minutes, you are now ready to strain the coffee into thermoses.
6. Pre-heat thermoses by pouring boiling hot water into them while you are making the coffee.
7. Empty the thermos.
8. Place a funnel on top of it.
9. Place a strainer over the top – You may need to steady this with a free hand.
10. Fill thermos through the strainer and the funnel.
11. Your coffee is now ready and will keep hot for 6 to 7 hours.
12. Repeat with other thermos flasks.

For 20 people I generally make 3 medium sized saucepans of coffee.
It is a great help to have the coffee ready at the end of a party, when you want to relax.

VICTORIA COOKS'
PARSNIP & SPROUT PURÉE
Serves 6

This makes a lovely green purée suitable to serve with a roast or grilled chops or turkey. The bitterness of the sprouts is tempered with the sweetness of the parsnips.

Ingredients:

1 lb. sprouts
1 lb. parsnips
2 tbs. cream
1 oz butter
1 egg
breadcrumbs
seasoning
extra butter for top

Method:

1. Peel and chop parsnips and boil in salted water until soft.
2. Peel sprouts and boil in salted water until soft.
3. Drain and blend the two together to a fine purée.
4. Add cream, melted butter and 1 egg to the purée.
5. Remove from blender.
6. Season.
7. Place in a buttered, oven-proof dish.
8. Sprinkle with breadcrumbs and dot with butter.
9. Bake about 40 minutes at 180° C until slightly risen.

HOME-MADE BEER

Makes 4 gallons

Ingredients:

2 2/3 lbs. granulated sugar
2 lbs. plain malt – from Boots
2½ oz hops
2 oz yeast
1 tsp. salt
½ egg-cup of gravy browning

Bottles with tops suitable to withstand second fermentation without 'popping'

Method:

1. Boil 2 gallon of water.
2. Add sugar, malt, hops and salt.
3. Boil for 1 hour.
4. Put 2 gallons of cold water in a large crock.
5. Tie muslin firmly over the top.
6. Pour boiling hops and malt, etc onto this muslin.
7. Tie muslin into a bag.
8. Steep in liquid for 40 minutes.
9. Squeeze liquid through the bag and remove.
10. Add yeast and browning.
11. Top up to 4 gallons with water as some may have boiled away.
12. Skim daily until the fermentation is complete (about 4 or 5 days).
13. Bottle the beer in clean bottles.
14. Put ½ tsp. sugar in each bottle and put on the screw tops.
15. Leave 14 days.
16. Be very careful _not_ to disturb the sediment when pouring.

Note:

This makes a full-flavoured, bitter beer. We used a large bread crock to make it in. This recipe was given to us by the late Marcia Eeles from Sandwich, Kent. She was a great lady and friend.

APPLE & SULTANA CHUTNEY

Makes about 10 jars

This makes a sweet chutney, slightly flavoured with ginger. Very good with ploughman's lunch.

Ingredients:

4 lbs. cooking apples
½ lb. onions
1 lb. sultanas
1½ pints vinegar
1½ lbs. soft brown sugar
¼ oz ground ginger

Method:

1. Peel and core apples.
2. Chop fairly finely.
3. Peel and chop onions, but fine chop in a blender.
4. Put apples and onions and sultanas in a large saucepan.
5. Pour on ½ pint vinegar.
6. Bring to the boil and simmer with a lid on for 20 minutes.
7. Add sugar, ginger and the rest of the vinegar.
8. Simmer without a lid for about 40 minutes.
9. Leave to stand for 30 minutes.
10. Pot in clean jam jars when cold.

Makes about 10 jars of chutney. Very good with a mellow cheddar.

STEAMED VEGETABLES

Serves 2 to 3

Ingredients:

2 or 3 potatoes
2 parsnips
½ lb. of organic carrots
½ cauliflower

Method:

Use a steamer.

1. Clean, peel and prepare vegetables in large chunks.
2. When water in steamer boils, add potatoes and carrots and steam for 10 minutes with a lid on.
3. Add parsnips and cauliflower and steam until all vegetables are soft, perhaps another 7 minutes.

FINNISH CARROT PIE

Serves 6

Suitable for the buffet table, especially for vegetarians.

Ingredients:

1½ lbs. carrots
1 egg
¼ pint cream
1 tsp. salt
1 tsp. sugar
2 oz melted butter

Pastry made with:

6 oz flour
3 oz fat
or buy ready-made puff pastry.
1 egg for brushing the top

Method:

1. Peel and boil carrots until soft.
2. Mash with a fork.
3. Add the rest of the ingredients.
4. Put in a tart tin, lined with pastry.
5. Cover with a pastry lid.
6. Brush with egg.
7. Bake for about 45 minutes at 180° C.

You can omit the top crust and instead sprinkle with breadcrumbs and butter.

SPICED RED CABBAGE

Serves 3 to 4

Ingredients:

½ red cabbage
1 or 2 oz butter
1 clove garlic (optional)
½ chopped onion
1 cooking apple, peeled, cored and chopped
1 tbs. sugar
1 tsp. ground cloves
2 tbs. vinegar
salt and pepper

Method:

1. Melt butter and add onion and apple.
2. When soft, add finely chopped cabbage.
3. Allow to sauté gently for about 15 minutes whilst stirring occasionally.
4. Add a little water so that the cabbage does not stick.
5. Add the rest of the ingredients.
6. Leave to cook for 30 to 40 minutes, stirring occasionally.

The cabbage is ready when it feels soft but not limp.

Excellent with sausages or game dishes.

CHEESE PUDDING

Serves 2 to 3

This is an old fashioned but tasty supper dish suitable for grownups and children.

Ingredients:

3 oz fresh white breadcrumbs
¾ pint milk
2 oz grated, strong cheddar
1 oz butter, melted
1 egg
salt
¼ tsp. cayenne pepper
¼ tsp. mustard powder

Method:

1. Heat milk and pour it on breadcrumbs.
2. Whisk egg and add with the rest of the ingredients to the breadcrumb mixture.
3. Bake in a small, buttered oven dish for about 45 minutes at 180° C.

Note:

For larger numbers just double the quantities. Serve with a tomato salad and fresh bread.

SAUCES, DRESSINGS & SALADS

SWEDISH SAUCE

Serves 4

This sauce is ideal with cold ham.

Ingredients:

1 cup mayonnaise
2 or 3 tbs. apple puree
1 tbs. horseradish sauce
½ tsp. strong mustard

Method:

1. Mix all ingredients and allow to stand a little before serving.

COLD HERB SAUCE FOR SALMON

Serves 2 to 3 people

Ingredients:

1 tub sour cream
salt and white pepper
a few drops of Tabasco
1 tbs. chopped parsley
2 tbs. chopped spring onions or chives
1 tsp. dried dill or 1 tbs. of fresh dill

Method:

1. Mix all the herbs into the cream.
2. Check seasoning.

HOLLANDAISE SAUCE

Serves 2 to 3

Ingredients:

125 g butter
2 egg yolks
1 large tbs. water
1 tbs. lemon juice
salt and white pepper
a good pinch of cayenne pepper

Method:

1. Melt butter in a saucepan.
2. In another pan – mix together egg yolks, water, lemon juice and seasoning.
3. Place this saucepan inside another, larger one with simmering water, or use a double boiler if you have one.
4. Whisk until the sauce begins to thicken.
5. Add melted butter, a drop at a time, and then in a thin stream while whisking all the time.
6. Serve immediately, while warm.

Note:

It is difficult to keep this sauce hot as it tends to curdle easily, but if you have to, place it in a pan of warm (not hot) water and stir occasionally.
The sauce is especially good with fish and vegetables such as asparagus.

Different additions can be made to produce different sauces, such as remoulade sauce (following recipe).

RÉMOULADE SAUCE
Serves 2 to 3

Ingredients:

As for Hollandaise sauce but you need to:

add 1 tsp. chopped capers and gherkins
parsley and tarragon or chives
2 fillets of anchovies, chopped
a little mustard

The sauce should have quite a strong flavour and can also be served with grilled meat.

BÉARNAISE SAUCE

Serves 4

Ingredients:

2 small onions or shallots, finely chopped
2 tbs. tarragon vinegar or white wine vinegar
3 crushed pepper corns
½ stock cube dissolved in 1 tbs. water (optional)
4 oz butter
3 egg yolks
3 tbs. warm water
1 tsp. each of chopped tarragon and chervil
a good pinch of cayenne pepper

Method:

1. In a small saucepan, place the onions, the herbs, the tarragon vinegar, the pepper corns and 3 tbs. water.
2. Simmer for 5 minutes with a lid on.
3. Add water if it dries out.
4. Strain this mixture into a clean pan, pressing all the juices out of the onions.
5. Add the 3 yolks to the juices and whisk.
6. Cube the butter and add a couple of cubes at a time, whilst stirring with a wooden spoon. Do not add any more butter until the previous lot has been absorbed and amalgamated.
7. Continue until all the butter has been absorbed by the sauce.
8. Taste for seasoning.

This sauce us generally served with meat such as a thick fillet steak garnished with a little paté and sliced, fried mushrooms on top with a spoonful of the Béarnaise sauce over all.

APPLE SAUCE

Serves 4 to 6

Ingredients:

3 bramley apples, peeled, cored and cut into chunks
2 oz sugar
1 cup water

Method:

1. Place apples in water and boil until apples are soft and can be mashed with a fork.
2. Add sugar and cook for a further 10 minutes.
3. Place apple pulp in a strainer and force it through into a bowl, (the last rough bits can be added as they are, or discarded).
4. Taste it, and add a little sugar or lemon juice if you wish.

Note:

The sauce should be fairly 'tart'.
Serve hot with roasted fowl or pork.

ONION SAUCE

Serves 6 to 8

Usually served with lamb. This is a useful sauce in cases where you don't have much gravy with your meat.

Ingredients:

2 medium onions, peeled
1 pt. full cream milk
3tbs. cream (optional)
1 bay leaf
2 oz butter
2 oz flour
seasoning

Method:

1. Cook onion in ½ pt. milk and ½ pt. water with bay leaf, until tender.
2. Remove onion and chop it.
3. Keep liquid.
4. Melt butter.
5. Add flour, frying gently without colouring.
6. Gradually add the rest of the milk and some of the onion liquid until the sauce has the right consistency.
7. Add chopped onion and 3 tbs. cream (optional) and seasoning.

HOT PIQUANT SAUCE
WITH TOMATOES
Serves 4

Ingredients:

2 cups chopped tinned tomatoes
1 onion finely chopped and fried
2 cloves of garlic, squeezed
2 tbs. tomato purée
1 bay leaf
¼ tsp. chilli powder
salt and pepper

Method:

Combine all ingredients and cook for about 5 minutes.
Useful pasta sauce and goes well with seafood as well as meatballs, or on top of pizza.

COLD PIQUANT SAUCE
Serves 3 to 4

Ingredients:

2 yolks of hard-boiled eggs
¼ tsp. salt
1 tsp. mustard
¾ tsp. sugar
white pepper
2 tbs. vinegar
1½ cups cream

Method:

1. Rub all ingredients, except the cream, together.
2. Whip cream until soft peaks and fold in gradually.
3. Check seasoning.

This is a nice sauce to serve with smoked fish.

COLD SAUCE SABAYON

Serves 6

Will keep refrigerated. Serve as an accompaniment to pears or peaches poached in wine.

Use a double boiler over simmering water (or cook in a pan sitting a larger pan filled with 1" of simmering water).

Ingredients:

4 egg yolks
3 oz caster sugar
¾ cup of Marsala wine or sherry

Method:

1. Put all the ingredients in a pan, preferably a double boiler over simmering water.
2. Whisk until sauce heats up, but do not allow to boil because the eggs could curdle.
3. Continue whisking until very thick. This may take some time (15 to 20 minutes).
4. Remove from heat.
5. Set pan in cold water and continue whisking until cold.
6. Keep in the refrigerator.

TOMATO SAUCE FOR PASTA OR PIZZA

Serves 4 (or an 8" pizza)

Ingredients:

1 x 14 oz tin chopped tomatoes
1 medium onion, chopped
½ green pepper, chopped
1 glass red wine
1 tsp. sugar
1 dsp. tomato puree
2 bay leaves
1 dsp. basil
3 dsp. freshly chopped parsley
salt and black pepper
oil for frying

Please note: add an extra dessert spoon of tomato puree if the sauce is intended to top a pizza.

Method:

1. Sweat the onion and pepper in some oil for 5 minutes.
2. Add the rest of the ingredients and simmer for 30 minutes.
3. Taste for seasoning. If you wish the sauce to be more concentrated, continue simmering for another half an hour.

SALAD DRESSINGS

FRENCH DRESSING

Ingredients:

6 tbs. vegetable oil
1 to 2 tbs. white wine vinegar (or Italian balsamic vinegar)
1 clove garlic, crushed
salt and pepper

Method:

1. Combine all ingredients.
2. Put in a jam jar.
3. No need to keep it in the fridge.
4. Shake jar well before use.

BLUE CHEESE DRESSING

Ingredients:

6 tbs. single cream
2 tbs. oil
3 tbs. mashed Roquefort or Danish blue cheese softened with some of the cream until liquid
1 tbs. lemon juice
2 tbs. hot water
salt and pepper

Method:

1. Shake all ingredients well in a jam jar.
2. Keep refrigerated.

PARISIAN DRESSING

Ingredients:

6 tbs. oil
2 boiled egg yolks
1 tsp. salt
½ tsp. pepper
1 tsp. mustard powder
2 tsp. lemon juice
2 tsp. sugar
1 clove garlic, crushed

Method:

1. Mash egg yolks with a fork.
2. Add oil little by little.
3. Add mustard powder and the rest of the ingredients.

SAUCE FOR COLD TURKEY

This is a very good way of using up a Christmas turkey.

<u>Ingredients:</u>

1 pint white sauce (made with 1 pint milk and 2 tbs. flour and 2 oz butter)
½ to ¾ bottle of Green label Mango chutney
½ pint double cream
2 heaped tsp. Madras curry powder
breadcrumbs
seasoning

<u>Method:</u>

1. Mix chutney and cream into white sauce.
2. Add white pepper, 2 heaped teaspoons of Madras curry powder and salt to give a strong taste. Mix with slices of turkey.
3. Place turkey in an oven proof dish.
4. Dot with breadcrumbs.
5. Bake for 30 to 40 minutes at 200° C.
6. Serve with boiled rice.

Note:
Can be eaten hot or cold (if cold, omit breadcrumbs and only use 1½ tbs. of flour. Then it is not so heavy. Double the amount of sauce if you have much turkey to cover.

FRENCH DRESSING WITH OLIVE OIL

Serves 4 to 6

Ingredients:

¾ cup of olive oil
¼ cup of white wine vinegar
2 crushed cloves of garlic (omit if you do not like garlic)
¼ tsp. of English mustard
salt and freshly milled black pepper

Method:

1. Put all the ingredients into a screwtop jar and shake well.
2. Taste for seasoning. (The blend of oil and vinegar should be to your taste and the dressing needs a fair amount of salt.)

ORIENTAL DRESSING

Ingredients:

¾ cup of vegetable oil
¼ cup of white wine vinegar
2 dsp. light soy sauce
a few shakes of Tabasco sauce
2 tsp. finely chopped fresh ginger root, or ⅓ teaspoon ground ginger
2 cloves of crushed garlic
1 tsp. of sesame oil
salt and freshly milled black pepper

Method:

1. Put all the ingredients into a screwtop jar and shake well.
2. Check seasoning carefully. (Add more salt if necessary.)

MUSTARD DRESSING FOR SMOKED SALMON

Serves 6

Smoked salmon is a very delicious starter. Here is a dressing which makes it extra special.

Allow 2 oz of smoked salmon, or smoked salmon trimmings per person. If using trimmings chop coarsely and serve a small heap on each plate garnished with lemon and brown and butter.

Ingredients:

7 tbs. of vegetable oil, (*never* olive oil)
3 dsp. white wine vinegar
2 tsp. English mustard or 1 English and 1 French
1 tbs. of caster sugar
1 tsp. salt
black pepper
1 egg yolk
1 dsp. fresh or dried dill, chopped
(It is easier to make double quantity of the sauce.)

Accompaniments:

thin brown bread and butter and slices of lemon and mustard sauce.

Method for Mustard Sauce:

1. Place egg yolk in a bowl.
2. Add oil a few drops at a time while whisking hard (as for mayonnaise).
3. Add the rest of the ingredients.
4. Taste for flavour. The dressing should be fairly sharp but have sweet undertones. (Add a little more mustard if necessary.)
5. Keep in screwtop jar and shake well before serving to emulsify sauce.

Keeps for a week in the fridge.

To serve:

Prepare brown bread and butter and some slices of lemon. Spread the smoked salmon out on individual plates. Garnish with a little fennel or dill and a slice of lemon. Serve with the mustard sauce for guests to add as they wish, dribbling it over the smoked salmon.

SOUR CREAM DRESSING FOR SALMON

Serves 8

Ingredients:

2 small tubs of sour cream
2 spring onions, chopped
2 tbs. chopped chives
2 tbs. chopped parsley
a few drops of Tabasco
salt and pepper

Method:

Stir the herbs into the sour cream and add seasoning. Do not stir much as the cream goes thin.

Note:

Different ways of cooking salmon fillets:

1. Poach in a court bouillon (water flavoured with onion, vinegar, bay leaf, salt and peppercorns.)
2. Turned in seasoned flour and fried in a mixture of butter and oil.
3. Baked in foil with butter and herbs and cooked for about 25 minutes or until done. (180° C)
4. Microwave with herbs and seasoning covered by cling film, a very good way to cook fish (3-4 minutes).

SALADS

Here are a few ideas: the recipes are not exact.

1. **Salad Niçoise** – A classic salad starter. It consists of lettuce, cooked French beans, tuna, tomatoes, onion and olives. Hard boiled eggs as a garnish is also common. Use French dressing with garlic in it.
Serve on its own as a starter or as a lunch dish.

2. **Green salad** – I rather prefer a plain salad of this type, which includes only 2 or 3 different kinds of lettuce. Perhaps two varieties such as Cos lettuce and Little Gem, with a bit of parsley is sufficient. French dressing is essential.
Used as an accompaniment to the main course.

3. **Round lettuce salad** – Can be used as above but ideal for lining dishes and bowls which carry other cold foods.

4. **Tomato salad** – Thinly slice beef or plum tomatoes, with the core removed. Thinly slice sweet Spanish onion, which is mild. Parsley and French Olive Oil dressing. Garnish of black olives.
Serve on its own, as a starter, with French bread, or to accompany other dishes, such as cold meat.

5. **Cucumber salad** – Washed, thinly sliced cucumber with peel on is dressed with a mixture of water, vinegar and sugar, (as you make mint sauce). Improves with standing for a few hours. Dried or fresh dill can be added, but not parsley, the texture is too coarse. (Dressing: 1½ tbsp. white wine vinegar + 1½ tbsp. hot water, salt, pepper and teaspoon of sugar.)
Serve with rich pies or dishes with mayonnaise, or fried fish.

6. **Beetroot salad** – Cooked beetroot (NOT in vinegar) sliced and mixed with chopped spring onion and parsley and a dressing of mayonnaise and yoghurt. You can use vinaigrette sauce as an alternative, in which case finely sliced onion would be a pleasant change from the spring onions.
Goes well with meat or meat pie.

7. **Sweetcorn and beansprout salad** – with some tomato, spring onion and parsley.
Nice with baked potatoes.

8. **Grated carrot** – with a few sultanas and grated cheese. Mix with a light oil and vinegar dressing (no garlic), diluted with a little water.
Use as part of a cold salad table. A good vegetarian dish.

(Continued)

9. **Potato salad** – Waxy new potatoes, boiled and sliced. Mix with finely chopped red onion and a dressing of half mayonnaise mixed with half yoghurt, salt and pepper.
Excellent with hot or cold sausages.

10. **Red cabbage salad** – Chop red cabbage and courgettes, finely, Use twice as much cabbage as courgettes. Add a little onion, a few hazelnuts and French dressing. Nice with cold turkey.

11. **Greek salad** – Chunks of tomato, unpeeled cucumber, mixed with lettuce and slivers of raw onion. Dress with garlicky French dressing. Decorate with black olives and cubes of feta cheese.
Use as a starter or with a moussaka or a rich stew.

12. **Bean salad** – Mixed, tinned beans such as borlotti, red kidney beans and chickpeas. Add some chopped celery, onion, tomato and parsley. Use plenty of French dressing and some extra vinegar or lemon. A few drops of Tabasco also gives the salad a lift.
Good with meat and also with tuna.

13. **Coleslaw** – Mix freshly grated carrot or fine carrot sticks with finely sliced white cabbage. Add touch of onion, chopped, and salt and pepper. Toss in a dressing of part mayonnaise and part yoghurt. Best eaten soon after it is made.
Excellent with cold meat, especially turkey or baked potatoes. You can dress this salad with French dressing but I would then suggest adding a few fresh, chopped tomatoes to it for moisture and some chopped parsley.

14. **Rice salad** – Boil brown or white long grain rice until just tender. Mix with drained, tinned sweetcorn, chopped spring onion, some fresh, chopped tomatoes, parsley and sultanas. Use a light French dressing with no garlic in it. Nuts and chopped, dried apricots could be added if liked. (Cut apricots into strips.)
Good with chicken mayonnaise or frankfurter sausages, medallions of pork tenderloin covered in egg and breadcrumbs, fried and cooled, also cold breaded chicken portions. A good FOIL to other things. Mango chutney goes especially well with it.

15. **Lentil salad** – Mix tinned, drained, cooked brown lentils with vinaigrette dressing, a little sliced onion and tomato and chopped parsley. Garnish with quarters of hard boiled eggs and some drained tuna (in oil), and possibly some salami or garlic sausage, which would make it a good summer luncheon dish.
This can turn into a main course salad, especially good for vegetarians.

16. **Pasta salad** – Boil shell-shaped pasta until cooled. Drain well and mix when cold with cooked peas, some chopped celery, a little tinned sweetcorn, some chopped red pepper, and dress with a mixture of mayonnaise and yoghurt.

17. **Raw mushroom salad** – Rinse small button mushrooms well. They must be very fresh. Cut off some of the stalk and slice thinly. Add a little chopped pepper,

chopped parsley and chives and a vinaigrette dressing. Leave it fairly plain, it does spoil it to add too many other things. It must be eaten within 10 to 15 minutes of preparation or it will go brown. Decorate with a little mustard cress.

HAM WITH GRAPE SALAD

Serves 6

A good buffet dish and suitable for a simple lunch dish in the garden.

Ingredients:

6 slices of ham. (Large slices of boiled ham, not too thin.)

GRAPE SALAD

Ingredients:

¼ lb. black grapes, halved and de-seeded
¼ lb. green seedless grapes
½ pt. mayonnaise
¼ pt. sour cream
salt and white pepper
finely chopped parsley

Method:

1. Prepare grapes, wash and remove stalks.
2. Mix mayonnaise and sour cream.
3. Add mayonnaise to grapes and season.
4. Taste for flavour.
5. Add more salt and some lemon juice, if necessary.
6. Serve ham folded with some salad inside each slice.

Serve salad separately.

Accompaniments:

Hot new potatoes, green salad, fresh bread.

WEST COAST SALAD

Serves 4 to 6

A very nice Swedish first course served with white wine.

Ingredients:

½ lb. shelled prawns (frozen will be fine, defrosted and drained)
1 tin green asparagus spears or pieces
1 tin smoked mussels or oysters
1 small tin peas (petit pois)
4 oz fresh mushrooms, sliced
2 tbs. chopped parsley
1 tbs. chopped dill (or fennel)
vinaigrette, dressing

Garnish:

2 hard boiled eggs
1 lemon
1 lettuce

Method:

1. Drain asparagus and, if not cut already, cut into small 1 inch pieces.
2. Clean and slice mushrooms and marinade in some vinaigrette dressing.
3. Mix together mussels, (including oil), prawns and peas (drained) and add most of the asparagus pieces.
4. Add mushrooms with parsley, very carefully, so as not to break up the asparagus pieces.
5. Stir in dill and dressing, also extra salt, pepper and lemon juice to taste.
6. Line dish with lettuce leaves. Fill with salad.
7. Decorate with hard-boiled egg wedges, slices of lemon and the rest of the asparagus spears. Serve cold with toast and butter.

Note:

My Husband's favourite starter. Of course, it should be made with freshly cooked prawns from the Swedish West Coast, that gives the dish its name. However, it is surprising how well the combination of tinned asparagus, frozen prawns and tinned peas works with vinaigrette dressing flavoured with dill! I always add freshly sliced mushrooms and smoked oysters or mussels with their oil for texture and more flavour.
I first had this dish in a famous restaurant in Stockholm. It was a very elegant place and this salad was served in a glass bowl on a bed of ice and topped with fresh dill fronds. The string orchestra was playing and we were entertained afterwards by the incomparable Danish musician and funny man, the late Victor Borge: an experience that impressed me as a teenager and I would love to repeat.

HERRING SALAD WITH BEETROOT DRESSING

Serves 6

'Salma-gundi' is the ancient name of this dish, found in many different parts of Europe. It is really a way of using up leftovers. It is a very popular dish on any Finnish Smörgåsbord, (cold table). I cannot think of a Finnish Wedding or Funeral that I have attended when this dish has not been served.

To facilitate the making of this salad, we have a special wooden box in Finland, in which you chop the vegetables by means of a 'D' shaped blade with a handle. This exactly fits the box, so that no vegetables escape the chopping process.

Ingredients:

1 cup pickled herring (available from stores)	cubed (1 cm)
2½ cups of carrots, cooked	cubed (1 cm)
2 cups potatoes, boiled, peeled	cubed (1 cm)
2 cups cold meat	cubed (1 cm)
2 sweet and sour gherkins	cubed (1 cm)
2 sharp apples	cubed (1 cm)
2 tbs chopped onions	
white pepper and salt	

3 boiled, peeled beetroots (keep some of their juices) cubed (1 cm)

Garnish:

2 hard-boiled eggs, finely chopped
2 tbs. chopped parsley

Dressing:

½ pt. whipping cream
beetroot juice for colouring
vinegar or lemon juice to taste

Method for Dressing:

1. Whip the cream, add 2 tbs. beetroot juice (from preserved beetroot or cooked beetroot).
2. Add vinegar, salt, pepper and 1 tsp. sugar to make a sharp sauce.

Use as described above.

Method:

1. Toss all the ingredients together.
2. Check and season.
3. Rinse a round pudding bowl or Pyrex dish with cold water.
4. Pack the salad into it and leave for a couple of hours in the fridge.
5. Then turn out on a large serving dish. Garnish with egg slices.
6. Before serving, dribble dressing from the top of the salad, down the sides. Serve the rest of the dressing separately. (The whipped cream dressing is coloured with the beetroot juice.)

Ingredients for alternative sauce piquant:

2 yolks of hard-boiled eggs
1/4 tsp. salt
1 tsp. mustard
¾ tsp. sugar
white pepper
2 tbs. vinegar
1½ cups cream

Method:

1. Rub all ingredients together.
2. Whip cream until soft peaks and fold in gradually.
3. Check seasoning.

KALAMARES SALAD
Serves 6

A delicious Sicilian starter, eaten cold.

Ingredients:

4 squid (the size of a hand) or 1½ lbs. of baby squid or prepared squid rings
½ bottle red wine
1 onion chopped
1 x 14 oz tin of chopped tomatoes or 4 large tomatoes, skinned and chopped
3 cloves garlic, crushed
4 tbs. olive oil
salt, freshly milled black pepper
thyme, parsley and bay leaf

Garnish:

a few black olives
more chopped parsley

Method:

1. Remove the head from squid.
2. Cut off the tentacles from the head. Keep them to one side. Discard head.
3. Split open the main body and remove sack, etc. including long blade-like back bone.
4. Cut body into strips, about ¼" wide.
5. Fry onion in some olive oil.
6. Add garlic and tomatoes.
7. Cook for 10 minutes.
8. Add herbs, seasoning and squid.
9. Add the rest of the olive oil and the wine.
10. Simmer for 20 to 30 minutes, until squid is tender. It will always have a firm texture. Do not cook longer than necessary, or squid may become tough. Baby squid cooks in a shorter time.
11. Leave to get cold.
12. Add some more olive oil and herbs for garnish.
13. Check for seasoning.
14. Sprinkle on parsley.
15. Serve with pitta or Italian country bread.

Note:

If you like garlic a lot, cut up 3 cloves very small and scatter them with the parsley on the finished dish.

AUBERGINE SALAD

Serves 4

A Middle Eastern dish, suitable for the salad table.

Ingredients:

2 aubergines
½ pint plain yoghurt
3 garlic cloves, crushed
olive oil for frying
salt and freshly milled black pepper

Garnish:

Mint leaves, chopped parsley

Method:

1. Prepare aubergines by cutting into slices, sprinkling with salt and leaving for 20 minutes.
2. Rinse in clean water and dry well.
3. Fry in hot olive oil on each side until soft.
4. Arrange, neatly on a plate.
5. Mix yoghurt with garlic and seasoning.
6. Spread over most of the aubergines, without covering them all.
7. Scatter mint and parsley on top.
8. Eat with chunky bread or pitta bread.

Note:

This dish goes well with meat balls or roast lamb.

SEAFOOD SALAD

Serves 6 to 8

An expensive but delicious starter.

Ingredients:

2 doz mussels or clams, ready cooked, no shells
6 tbs. olive oil
2 tbs. lemon juice
1 lb. squid rings
1 lb. fillet of cod, steamed
3 doz. large, shelled prawns
6 scallops, baked
Chopped parsley and fennel or dill
Salt and pepper
Lemon wedges

Method:

1. Cook squid in olive oil and lemon juice for 20 minutes and allow to cool.
2. Bake the scallops for about 4 minutes.
3. Steam the cod until barely cooked – about 10 to 15 minutes depending on thickness.
4. Skin and flake it removing all the bones.
5. Combine these with the mussels out of their shells or clams and prawns.
6. Toss with an oil and lemon juice dressing.
7. Season with salt and pepper.
8. Sprinkle with parsley.
9. Decorate with lemon wedges.

Serve with brown bread and butter.

BEAN SALAD

Serves 10 to 15

Ingredients:

4 cans Borlotti beans
½ lb. fresh French beans, lightly poached
4 cloves of garlic, crushed
1 large cup of French dressing, made with olive oil and wine vinegar (3 to 1), and seasoning
1 bunch of spring onions, chopped
juice of 2 lemons
10 drops of Tabasco
1 tbs. fresh tarragon
1 tbs. fresh basil
½ cup of chopped parsley
salt and freshly ground black pepper

Garnish:

6 hard boiled eggs, peeled and quartered
10 black olives

Method:

1. Empty the cans of beans into a sieve and rinse with cold water, draining well.
2. Add chopped French beans. (1" pieces)
3. Add herbs, dressing, onions, garlic, lemon juice, Tabasco and seasoning.
4. Toss well. Taste and adjust seasoning.

Note:

OLIVES. I prefer olives with stones as the flavour seems to leech out otherwise, into the brine. Some stoned olives are stuffed with garlic and herbs in an oil marinade and they are excellent. One of my favourite stuffings for olives is anchovies.

To serve this dish as a main course display on a large dish surrounded by cooked ham and charcuterie and serve a plain green salad and crusty bread with it.

A very useful and easy buffet dish.

EASY LENTIL SALAD

Serves 4

Ingredients:

1 14 oz tin cooked brown lentils
4 tbs. mayonnaise
1 small onion, finely chopped
3 tbs. chopped parsley (keep some back for decoration)
1 tbs. lemon juice
salt and pepper
2 cloves of garlic, squeezed

Garnish:

4 hard boiled eggs, cut into wedges
some parsley

Method:

1. Drain lentils and rinse lightly under the tap.
2. Mix with mayonnaise, onion and seasoning.
3. Add some parsley and lemon juice and garlic.
4. Check seasoning.
5. To serve: spread on a shallow dish.
6. Garnish the edges with hard boiled eggs and scatter with parsley.

An interesting addition to the salad table, perhaps served with cooked ham, in which case add 1 tsp of English mustard to the mayonnaise.

MIXED BEAN SALAD

Serves 6

Ingredients:

1 tin Borlotti beans or Cannelloni beans
1 tin butter beans
8 oz fresh haricot verts
4 stalks celery
3 cloves garlic
6 tbs. olive oil
3 tbs. lemon juice
4 spring onions chopped
1 tsp. dried thyme
6 drops Tabasco sauce
salt and freshly milled black pepper
4 tbs. chopped parsley (keep some for garnish)
4 tomatoes chopped

Garnish:

2 hard-boiled eggs
2 tomatoes
some of the chopped parsley

Optional:

1 tin tuna in oil, drained, and 3 sweet and sour gherkins, chopped

Method:

1. Drain the tinned beans.
2. Boil the fresh beans until barely tender, rinse in cold water.
3. Slice celery thinly.
4. Chop spring onions.
5. Combine all the ingredients, except for half the oil.
6. Toss and taste for flavour. You may wish to add more lemon juice, Tabasco or seasoning.
7. Add more olive oil as it is absorbed.
8. To make the salad more filling flake in a tin of tuna fish and gherkins for flavour.
9. Garnish with wedges of hard-boiled eggs, slices of tomato and more parsley.

Notes:

Eat with crusty brown bread.
Better made a few hours in advance.
Keeps 2-3 days in the refrigerator, but serve at room temperature.
A useful dish for the salad table. Stir before serving. The salad must have plenty of dressing as it is so quickly absorbed by the beans.

PUDDING DISHES

CHOCOLATE & CHESTNUT LOAF

Serves 12

A very rich chocolate loaf, which I first had in Belgium at Christmas time.

Ingredients:

2 tins unsweetened chestnut purée
4 bars Meunier chocolate, about 4 oz each (any dark chocolate will do)
3 heaped tbs. caster sugar
1½ tsp. vanilla essence
8 oz unsalted butter
6 egg yolks
1 sherry glass of brandy
½ pint of double cream

Method:

In four separate bowls:
1. Melt chocolate in a microwave or over a pan of steaming water.
2. Melt butter.
3. Whisk egg yolks slightly to mix.
4. Break up chestnut purée.
5. Add a little hot chocolate to the egg, then add the rest gradually, stirring all the time.
6. Add brandy and vanilla.
7. Stir in the melted butter.
8. Add sugar, then chestnut purée and mix well.
9. Line a tin with oiled foil.
10. Fill with mixture.
11. Refrigerate.

To serve:

1. Remove from the tin.
2. Peel off the foil.
3. Slice and place slices on plates.
4. Decorate with a dollop of whipped cream on the side.

SALLY'S CHEESECAKE
Serves 15

A cooked cheesecake which does not look very pretty but tastes *gorgeous*.
Cook the day before.

Ingredients:

crumb base:
7 oz digestive biscuits, crushed
2 oz of butter, melted

Cake:
1 lb. curd cheese
8 oz philadelphia cream cheese
5 eggs, whisked together
½ tsp. vanilla essence
5 oz caster sugar
grated rind of a lemon

Method:

1. Mix the biscuit crumbs with the butter and press them into a deep, loose bottomed cake tin, previously buttered.
2. Mix the two kinds of cheese together by hand – NOT in a food processor.
3. Gradually add the rest of the ingredients for the cake.
4. Put mixture on biscuit crumb base in the cake tin.
5. Bake in a medium heat, oven 180° C for 1 hour.
6. The cake will rise as it cooks.
7. Turn oven off, but leave the cheesecake in oven.
8. It will sink down and crack a little.
9. Lift out when cold.
10. Can be decorated with a cherry pie filling, or dusted with icing sugar or topped with whipped cream.

Keeps for 4 days.

PEARS IN WINE &
REDCURRANT SAUCE

Serves 8

Ingredients:

8 large slightly under ripe pears (comice for preference)
½ bottle red wine
6 cloves
4 oz sugar
½ jar redcurrant jelly
½ pint water

Method:

1. Peel pears.
2. Boil wine, cloves, sugar and water and simmer pears in liquid until soft.
3. Remove pears.
4. Continue simmering liquid for 15 minutes without lid to concentrate flavours.
5. Halve pears and remove core with a teaspoon.
6. Place on a serving dish, cut side down.
7. Take ½ pint of the wine syrup.
8. Bring to boil in separate pan with redcurrant jelly.
9. When jelly has dissolved, taste syrup and add some sugar or some lemon juice, if liked.
10. Pour over the pears and leave to cool.
11. Serve chilled with cream.

Variation:

Cook pears in white wine syrup and serve as above covered with a butterscotch sauce.

Butterscotch Sauce:
2 oz butter
6 oz brown soft sugar
2 tbs. golden syrup
3 tbs. cream

Method:

1. Melt butter, sugar and syrup in a saucepan.
2. Add cream and bring to boil.
3. Ready to serve with fried bananas, on ice cream, or poured over a cake. If used in the latter way, scatter with toasted almonds for decoration.

FINNISH OVEN PANCAKE

Serves 6 to 8

A favourite dish with children. Serve hot or cold with jam as a simple dessert.

Ingredients:

3 pints milk
1 oz butter
2 tsp. caster sugar
3 cups flour
3 eggs

Method:

1. Pre-heat the oven to 200° C.
2. Butter an ovenproof dish, generously.
3. Whisk eggs.
4. Gradually add flour and milk to make a smooth batter.
5. Place in the buttered dish and bake for about 50 minutes, until risen and brown in places.
6. Slice into wedges.

Serve hot with jam.

For a luxury version of this dish see this recipe on the next page.

OVEN PANCAKE SUPRÊME
Serves 6

Ingredients:

4 eggs
½ cup caster sugar
2 cups creme fraiche
2 cups of milk
1 cup flour
1 oz butter

Method:

Proceed as for previous recipe.

Note:

This will rise like a soufflé and is very light and delicious.

ORANGE PARFAIT
Serves 8

This makes a seductive, semi-hard sorbet. Very good after a rich meal or for a summer lunch.

Ingredients:

3 egg whites
pinch of salt
8 oz granulated sugar
¼ pint water
6½ oz can frozen concentrated orange juice
½ pint whipping cream

Method:

1. Whisk egg whites with the salt until they are in soft peaks.
2. Dissolve the sugar in the water and boil fiercely for a few minutes.
3. Pour onto the egg whites while whisking.
4. Continue until you have a stiff meringue mixture.
5. Add the orange juice, defrosted.
6. Whisk cream separately and stir into orange mixture.
7. Pour into a bowl and put in freezer for at least 5 hours.
8. Decorate with orange segments and whipped cream if you like.

Note:

It will not go really hard.

HAZELNUT MERINGUE
Serves 6

A firm favourite at parties.

Ingredients:

4 egg whites
9 oz caster sugar
a few drops vanilla essence
1 tsp. vinegar
4 oz ground hazelnuts

Filling:

½ pint whipping cream (save some for the top)
½ lb. fresh or frozen raspberries. – (If you use frozen ones, defrost on a plate and drain well before adding)
1 oz sugar

Topping:

Sifted icing sugar and a few whole hazelnuts

Method:

1. Line two x 8" flan tins with oiled greaseproof paper or baking paper.
2. Heat oven to 200° C.
3. Whisk egg whites until stiff.
4. Add the sugar and continue whisking until meringue is very stiff, until you get 'peaks'.
5. Fold in vanilla, vinegar and hazelnuts gently.
6. Divide the mixture between two tins.
7. Bake 40-45 minutes.
8. Loosen with a sharp knife.
9. Turn out very carefully and cool on a wire rack.
10. Peel off any paper that adheres to the meringue bases.
11. Sandwich meringues with raspberries and whipped cream.
12. Decorate top with icing sugar, whirls of cream and whole hazelnuts.

Warning! Do not put raspberries on top as they discolour the meringue.

COFFEE MOUSSE

Serves 4 to 6

Ingredients:

3 oz caster sugar
½ oz gelatine soaked in 3 tbs. water
3 eggs +2 egg yolks
½ pint whipping cream

To decorate:

¼ pt. double cream
2 oz plain chocolate

To make caramel:

4 oz sugar
4 tbs. water
4 tbs. strong black coffee

Method:

1. Cook sugar with water to make caramel until sugar turns a rich brown.
2. Add coffee all at once and melt the caramel to get a syrup by heating gently and shaking the pan.
3. Place the eggs, egg yolks and sugar in a pan over hot water and whisk until thick and mousse like.
4. Dissolve gelatine in water over gentle heat and fold into mousse with the caramel.
5. Place in a bowl over cold water and stir from time to time until beginning to set.
6. Whip cream and add, folding in gradually with a spoon.
7. Pour into a glass bowl and leave to set in the fridge.
8. Decorate with whipped cream and grated chocolate.

APPLE CHEESECAKE (Judy Clark's)

Serves 6

A homely cheesecake, not rich but delicious.

Ingredients:

plain pastry made with:
8 oz flour
2 oz butter
2 oz lard
pinch of salt
water to mix

Filling:

½ lb. cottage cheese
3-4 oz caster sugar
a few drops vanilla essence
2 eggs
1 lb. cooking apples, peeled and sliced, 2 oz extra sugar, if apples are sharp.
2 tbs. sultanas, 2 tbs. rum or whisky, (optional)

Method:

1. Line a loose-bottomed cake tin with the pastry covering the bottom and sides within 1" from the top rim.
2. Mix sugar with apples.
3. Mix the rest of the filling ingredients.
4. Fold apples into it.
5. Put filling into the pastry-lined tin.
6. If any pastry is left, decorate cake with a lattice work of pastry strips.
7. Brush with egg.
8. Cover loosely with foil.
9. Bake for 1½ – 2 hours in a slow oven (160 C) until the cake is well risen.
10. Cool in tin.
11. Loosen sides with sharp knife to prevent pastry sticking to the tin.
12. Push up by the bottom of the tin, but leave cake on this base.
13. Before serving sprinkle with castor sugar and serve, preferably slightly warm, with single cream.

BUTTERSCOTCH FLAN

Serves 4 to 6

Ingredients:

shortcrust pastry made with:
6 oz flour
3 oz butter
pinch of salt
water to mix

Filling:

½ pint milk
1½ oz cornflour
3-4 oz brown sugar
1½ oz butter
pinch of salt
1 egg yolk

Meringue:

1 egg white
2 oz caster sugar

Method:

1. Line a 6-8" flan dish with pastry and prick with a fork. (Use a pretty china flan container, as you cannot easily remove the dessert before cutting it to serve.)
2. Bake in pre-heated oven at 200° C for 15 minutes until done.
3. Blend sugar, cornflour and salt.
4. Add milk, bring to boil and cook 3-5 minutes, stirring continuously. (You will have a thick sauce.)
5. Remove mixture from the heat.
6. Stir in the butter in small pieces.
7. Add yolk of egg.
8. Turn into flan case.
9. Whip egg white until stiff.
10. Fold in the sugar.
11. Pile meringue on top of the flan and cook in cool oven (150° C) until firm, about 30 minutes.

You can now buy finished, rolled out pastry to line your tin.

PAM BAKER'S PAVLOVA
Serves 8

This meringue was most impressive like a high iceberg. Pam is an Australian so she is a real Pavlova expert.

Ingredients:

4 large egg whites (not too cold)
8 oz caster sugar
½ tsp. vanilla essence
1 tsp. vinegar, preferably wine vinegar
1 tsp. cornflour

Method:

1. Preheat oven to 200 C. (As you put the meringue in, reduce heat to 130°.)
2. Wet a large ovenproof dish or plate.
3. Beat the egg whites a little.
4. Add 4 tbs. sugar.
5. Add the vanilla and vinegar.
6. Beat until stiff, but not too dry.
7. Then tip in the rest of the sugar and beat a little more.
8. Sprinkle cornflour on top and fold in.
9. Pile the meringue in a high round heap on the oven tray.
10. Put in the middle of the oven.
11. Bake at 130° C 1½ hours.
12. Leave in the oven after turning the heat off, if possible.

To serve:

Transfer meringue to serving dish.
When cool top with whipped cream and decorate with fresh fruit (kiwi fruit, fresh strawberries, raspberries, grapes, bananas, etc.).

Note:

Can be made 2 days in advance, but put the cream and fruit on 1 hour before the meal.

FINNISH CHRISTMAS TART

Serves 12 to 15

Ingredients:

2 lb. prunes
6 oz granulated sugar
2 lb. frozen puff pastry (each pound of pastry can be bought as 2 pieces, ready rolled out)
flour
icing sugar
egg and milk to brush pastry

Method:

1. Soak prunes, if necessary, for 3-4 hours, or overnight.
2. Boil in sugar just covered with water until really soft.
3. Cool. Remove stones. Taste them. They should be soft and sweet.
4. Roll out each pack of pastry into two rectangles, 12" long and 4" wide. (If pastry is ready rolled out use as in pack.)
5. Place a quarter of the prunes in the middle of each pastry rectangle, reaching almost to both ends.
6. Now fold over each long side of the pastry over the prunes, but leave 1" of the prunes exposed.
7. Pinch the edge next to the prunes at intervals to gather the pastry.
8. Turn the short ends of the pastry up over the prunes to stop the juices running out.
9. Brush pastry with egg and milk and bake in a hot oven for 30-35 minutes.
10. Repeat, so you have 2 lengths of tart.
11. When cooked slice and serve warm dusted with icing sugar.
12. Serve pouring cream with it, if liked.

Note:

This idea of prunes and puff pastry can also be made as the more traditional Christmas stars with the prunes in the middle. However, the legs of the stars break off so easily, so I think it is more practical to make the long tarts.
Simply cut each 'log' into 1" slices.
Reheats well.

APRICOT PANCAKES
Serves 6 to 8

Ingredients:

Pancake batter:

1½ pts. milk
3 cups of plain flour
2 eggs
¼ tsp. salt
2 tsp. sugar
1 tbs. oil
butter for frying

Filling:

apricot jam

Decoration:

Icing sugar

Accompaniment:

½ pt. whipped cream
1 dsp. caster sugar
1-2 tbs. apricot liqueur

Method:

1. Make up the batter by whisking eggs with a little milk.
2. Gradually add the flour and the rest of the milk.
3. Season, add oil and leave to stand for 1 hour in a jug.
4. Whisk mixture between each pancake.
5. Heat a dsp of butter in a frying pan (you need less for each subsequent pancake).
6. Pour just enough batter to cover the base of the pan thinly.
7. Cook for a minute or two until the underside looks cooked. No need to turn it.
8. Put on 1 tbs. of apricot jam on one half of the pancake.
9. Start rolling the pancake up round the jam and tilt the pan to remove the pancake onto a buttered oven dish.
10. Repeat until all the batter is used up.
11. Sprinkle pancakes with sugar, cover with loose foil and keep warm in the oven.
12. Before serving, sprinkle with icing sugar.
13. To gild the lily, serve some whipped cream with the pancakes, slightly sweetened and perhaps flavoured with a spoonful or two of apricot liqueur.

Variations:

This batter and method can also be used for savoury pancakes, (omitting the sugar) such as seafood, ratatouille and creamed spinach pancakes.

Note:

Do not re-heat pancakes in a microwave, but keep hot in an ordinary oven.

AMERICAN CHOCOLATE CHEESECAKE

Serves 6 to 8

Ingredients:

6 oz flour
3 oz butter
½ oz sugar
salt
water

For the filling:

8 oz pack cream cheese
3 oz plain chocolate
1 tsp. cocoa dissolved in boiling water
2 eggs
1 tbs. whisky (optional)
3 oz caster sugar

Method:

1. Prepare the pastry base and press into a decorative flan tin.
2. Prick it and bake for about 25 minutes at 200° C.
3. Remove from oven and cool.
4. Melt the chocolate in the microwave or in a double saucepan.
5. Separate eggs.
6. Add sugar, yolks, and dissolved cocoa into cream cheese and mix well by hand into a smooth paste.
7. Mix in melted chocolate.
8. Whip egg whites and fold in gently with the whisky (if used).
9. Pour into the prepared flan case.
10. Leave in the refrigerator for at least 2 hours.
11. Decorate with some whipped cream.

Note:

You can also use the filling on its own, served in small ramekins decorated with whipped cream and with a dusting of cocoa powder as decoration.

An American professor entertained me, with over 20 other English students, to coffee with this cheesecake at his home. It was a huge cartwheel of a tart and it seemed like food for the Gods!

BAKED ORANGE SOUFFLÉ

Serves 8

This recipe comes from the Iberian peninsula and I first had it in the home of a great cook and friend of mine who always discovers interesting recipes.

Ingredients:

¾ pt. orange juice
6 eggs
3 oz caster sugar
grated rind of one orange. Keep fruit for decoration
pinch of salt
¼ pt. whipping cream, for decoration.

Method:

1. Separate eggs.
2. Whisk yolks with sugar until fluffy.
3. Add orange juice.
4. Whisk whites with a pinch of salt.
5. Fold into orange mixture.
6. Pour into ramekin dishes.
7. Decorate with orange rind.
8. Bake in a bain marie (see note) at 170° C until set – about 40 minutes.
9. Leave to get cold.
10. Decorate with a little swirl of whipped cream and a slice of orange.

Note:

Bake in an oven tray filled with water.

RICH ORANGE CUSTARD

Serves 6

Ingredients:

¾ pt. single cream
3 tbs. Grand Marnier or other liqueur
4 eggs + 4 yolks
4 tbs. sugar

Method:

1. Scald cream and liqueur.
2. Add a little at a time into the beaten eggs and yolks.
3. Add sugar.
4. Pour into buttered baking dish.
5. Bake in bain marie at 170° C for 35 to 45 minutes or until set.
6. Leave to get cold.

Note:

This is a super-rich custard. You might consider serving a fruit compôte with it, such as sliced oranges and grapes.

HEAVENLY RICE &
APRICOT SAUCE

Serves 6

A sweet that we often had on Sundays in my childhood.

<u>Ingredients</u>:

4 oz pudding rice
¾ pint of milk
3 oz caster sugar
1 tsp. vanilla essence
¾ pt. whipped cream
optional: grated rind of 1 lemon

<u>Apricot Sauce</u>:

½ lb. dried apricots
½ pt. water
3 oz caster sugar

<u>Method</u>:

1. Cook rice in milk and sugar until soft (about 30-40 minutes). Add more milk if porridge gets too thick.
2. Add vanilla essence and lemon rind and leave to get cold, but not set.
3. Whisk cream and fold into porridge.
4. Put in a glass bowl in the fridge.
5. Stew apricots in sugar and water until really soft and liquidise.
6. When rice and apricots are cold, cover the rice with apricot sauce.

RED FRUIT SALAD

Serves 8

Only fresh fruit will do for this recipe.

Ingredients:

2 lb. fresh strawberries, hulled
½ fresh cherries, stoned
1 lb. fresh raspberries
3 tbs. caster sugar

Method:

1. Place all in a saucepan and boil up for 3 minutes.
2. Taste for flavour.
3. Leave to cool.
4. Serve chilled with creme fraiche or Greek yoghurt.

Note:

This can be thickened slightly by 2 tsp. arrowroot (or cornflour) in half a cup of cold water at the end of boiling.

Serve with pouring cream, or as above.

OLD-FASHIONED TRIFLE

Serves 10

Ingredients:

12 sponge cakes, split and spread with jam
2 small glasses of sherry
fresh soft fruit or de-frosted raspberries
custard – (see below)
½ pint whipping cream
glace cherries, angelica and split almonds toasted to decorate

Custard:

2 tbs. cornflour
2 tbs. sugar
½ pt. milk
3 eggs
1 tsp. vanilla essence

Method:

1. Mix cornflour with sugar and a little milk.
2. Heat the rest of the milk.
3. Add the cornflour mixture and transfer into a double boiler.
4. Stir custard until it thickens.
5. Take off the heat.
6. Add eggs one-by-one.
7. Re-heat without boiling, but cook, while stirring, for about 10 minutes until custard thickens again.
8. Leave to cool and add the vanilla essence.

To assemble the trifle:

1. Line a glass bowl with the sponge cakes, soak with sherry.
2. Cover with raspberries.
3. Pour on the custard and leave until set in the refrigerator.
4. Whip the cream and add 2 tbs. caster sugar.
5. Smother the custard with the cream, once the custard is set.
6. Decorate with glacé cherry halves, sticks of angelica and lightly toasted almonds or macaroon biscuits (made with almonds).

PEAR & ALMOND TART
Serves 8

A very popular tart: it is rich and light at the same time.

Ingredients:

Pastry:

6 oz plain flour
3 oz butter
1 tbs. sugar
pinch of salt

Filling:

1 large tin of pear halves or fresh pears peeled, cored, halved and poached in a light syrup
2 oz caster sugar
2 oz ground almonds
2 eggs
1/4 pt. cream
1 tsp. almond essence
3 tbs. apricot jam, slightly warmed if it is very stiff.

Method:

1. Make pastry in a Magimix or by hand in the usual way.
2. Line an attractive flan dish with the pastry.
3. Prick and bake for 15-20 minutes at 200° C.
4. When cool, spread base with apricot jam.
5. Place 8 drained pear halves on top in a circle, flat side down.
6. Mix cream, sugar, eggs and almond essence and pour around the pears.
7. Bake at 180° C for 35-40 minutes or until risen and lightly brown.
8. Serve lukewarm with cream.

CHOCOLATE ROULADE

Serves 10 slices

This cake has no flour in it!

Ingredients:

6 eggs
8 oz caster sugar
2 oz cocoa
¾ pint whipping cream
8 oz melted chocolate or jam

For decoration:

Slivered or chopped nuts (optional)

Method:

1. Line a Swiss roll tin (a shallow, rectangular oven tin) with an oiled sheet of greaseproof paper.
2. Separate eggs, whip yolks with sugar until white.
3. Add cocoa folding it in gently with a spoon.
4. Whip whites until stiff and fold into yolks.
5. Pour mixture into the tin and cook about 25 minutes at 180° C, until the top is firm to the touch.
6. Leave to cool.
7. Place a sheet of greaseproof paper on the table, sprinkle it with caster sugar.
8. Turn out the cake onto the sugared sheet *very quickly*, having first loosened the edges with a knife.
9. Gently pull off the greaseproof paper that is attached to the cake.
10. Melt some plain chocolate or jam and spread over cake when it has cooled.
11. Whip cream and spread ⅔ of it over the cake.
12. Roll the cake up gently with the help of the greaseproof sheet under it and press cake gently down with the seam edge underneath. Cut off the uneven ends.
13. Now transfer the cake, by means of the greaseproof paper, onto a serving plate.
14. Gently remove the sugared greaseproof paper.
15. Pipe the rest of the cream on the roulade.
16. Decorate with some toasted slivered almonds or chopped walnuts.

Variation:

Victoria Cooks Strawberry Roulade: see next recipe.

VICTORIA COOKS
STRAWBERRY ROULADE
Serves 10

Ingredients:

6 eggs, separated
8 oz caster sugar
2 oz plain flour, 1 tsp. vanilla essence

Filling:

1 cup of strawberry jam, heated
½ lb. sliced strawberries
1 dsp caster sugar
¾ pint whipping cream

Method:

1. Whip egg yolks with sugar.
2. Whip whites, separately.
3. Fold the plain flour and vanilla essence into the yolks.
4. Finally fold in the whipped whites.
5. Line a Swiss roll tin with oiled greaseproof paper.
6. Fill with the cake mixture.
7. Bake at 180° C for about 25 minutes, until the cake feels firm when touched.
8. Cool on wire rack.

To assemble:

1. Spread a piece of greaseproof paper on the table and cover with about 2 oz caster sugar.
2. Turn out the cake onto the sugared paper, after loosening the edges first.
3. Peel off the greaseproof paper.
4. Warm the jam and spread over the cake.
5. Scatter the sliced strawberries over the top.
6. Roll the cake up using the greaseproof paper to move the cake.
7. Leave the seam side facing down and trim the two ends of the cake.
8. At this stage, transfer the cake onto a serving dish and gently pull out the sugared greaseproof paper from under it.
9. Decorate with piped, whipped cream, and (just before serving) with a few strawberry pieces.

PAVLOVA GATEAUX

Serves 6

Ingredients:

3 egg whites
6 oz caster sugar
l tsp. cornflour
l tsp. white wine vinegar
pinch of salt
½ pint of whipping cream
fresh fruit to garnish: strawberries, raspberries, Kiwi fruit, bananas and seedless grapes (halved) are all suitable.

Method:

1. Whip egg whites with pinch of salt.
2. Add half the sugar when the mixture is becoming stiff.
3. Add the rest of the sugar and whip a little longer until stiff.
4. Fold in the cornflour and vinegar.
5. Oil greaseproof paper and place on baking sheet.
6. Spread meringue mixture over it, in one or two circles.
7. Bake for l¼ hours at 140° C until pale cream colour and firm.
8. Leave to cool and move the meringue very gently onto plates.
9. An hour before the meal, whip the cream and slice the fruit if used.
10. Spread half the cream between the meringue sheets, if you have made two, and the rest on top.
11. At the last minute, decorate the top with plenty of fresh fruit.

APPLES IN PASTRY

Serves 4

Ingredients:

4 medium sized apples, peeled and cored
½ lb. of shortcrust pastry
Egg or milk to brush the pastry with

Optional fillings:

Jam, mince meat or dried fruit mixed with sugar and cinnamon

Method:

1. Divide the pastry into 4 and roll out each piece and cut into a square.
2. Place an apple on top of each square.
3. Fill centre cavity with any of the optional fillings.
4. Cover apples with pastry, keeping the pastry corners underneath the apples.
5. Place on an oiled baking sheet.
6. Brush with beaten egg or milk and cook at 200° C for about 1 hour.
7. Turn down the heat if the apples brown too much.
8. Serve with custard.

RHUBARB & DATE COMPÔTE

Serves 6 to 8

Ingredients:

1 lb. of rhubarb, washed and cut into 1" pieces
½ lb. of stoned dates. If you are using a packet of stoned dates, cut up the date 'brick' into cubes
sugar to taste

Method:

1. Stew dates and rhubarb gently until soft.
2. Add sugar to taste.
3. Leave to get cold.
4. Serve in small glass dishes with cream or custard.

APPLE PUDDING

Serves 4

This recipe was given by Emmy Woolf of 'Ellesmere' old peoples' home.

Ingredients:

1 lb. of cooking apples, peeled, cored and in pieces cooked for a few minutes with sugar to taste
2 oz butter
2 oz sugar
2 oz plain flour
pinch of salt
2 eggs
1/3 pint of milk
rind and juice of a lemon

Method:

1. Cream butter and sugar until fluffy.
2. Add the flour and salt with the grated lemon rind and juice.
3. Beat in the egg yolks with the milk.
4. Whisk the whites until stiff and fold in.
5. Pour apples into a baking dish and cover with the sponge mixture.
6. Cook for 40-45 minutes in the oven set at 180°C.
7. Dredge with sugar before serving.

BAKED APRICOT CUSTARD

Serves 6

Ingredients:

3-4 tbs. apricot jam
6 eggs or 4 eggs + 2 yolks
1½ pts. full cream milk (or milk with ¼ pt. double cream)
1 tsp. vanilla essence
3 dsp. caster sugar

Method:

1. Heat milk almost to boiling point.
2. Whisk eggs in a bowl.
3. Pour on the hot milk while whisking.
4. Add sugar and vanilla.
5. Spread jam over base of Pyrex dish.
6. Pour on the custard mixture.
7. Place bowl in a dish of hot water in the oven (bain marie) and cook in a cool oven 150° C until set. About 45 minutes to 1 hour.
8. Leave to cool and then put in fridge for 1 hour.
9. Decorate with piped cream and slivers of ready to eat apricots.

Delicious with pouring cream, (optional).

Note:

The time it takes for the custard to set varies according to the depth of your dish, so keep an eye on the custard. When it feels firm when you test it with a skewer or knife, take it out of the oven. If the custard develops little bubbles, the oven is too hot. You can see if this is happening through the sides of a Pyrex dish. If it does, lower heat to 100° C. The mark of a really well baked custard is that it should be silky smooth, with no bubbles.

FRUIT PIES
Serves 6

Ingredients:

Pastry:

5 oz butter
3 tbs. sugar
½ tsp. vanilla essence
1 egg
9 oz plain flour
1 tsp. baking powder
sugar to go with berries used

Method:

1. Cream butter and sugar.
2. Add egg and vanilla essence.
3. Add flour mixed with baking powder.
4. Spread pastry in a flan tin and push up the side of the tin with your fingers.
5. Mix the berries used with sugar.
6. Fill the flan base.
7. Bake at 175° C for 45 minutes.

Note:

The fruit used could be blackcurrants, raspberries, bilberries or rhubarb.
One or two egg yolks mixed with ¼ pint single cream poured over the fruit before baking, makes a pleasant addition to the dish.

Tip:

If you spread 1 to 2 tsp. cornflour on the pastry before adding the fruit, it will thicken the juices that come out of the berries. In this case, it is not necessary to add the egg and cream mixture.

Serve warm, with cream.

SIMPLE CHOCOLATE MOUSSE

Serves 6

Ingredients:

6 oz plain chocolate
3 eggs
½ oz butter
1½ oz caster sugar

Optional:

1 dsp. orange liqueur such as Grand Marnier

Decorate with a swirl of whipped cream and a pinch of cocoa

Method:

1. Melt chocolate in a double boiler. You can put your small pan in the water of a larger pan.
2. Add sugar.
3. Separate eggs and add yolks to the saucepan.
4. Cut butter into little squares and add one at a time stirring all the time.
5. Remove from heat and transfer into a bowl.
6. Whisk egg whites until stiff and fold into chocolate mixture.
7. Fill ramekins and leave to set overnight.

Note:

It can be hard to get the white into the chocolate mixture, but persevere!

EXTREMELY RICH
CHOCOLATE MOUSSE
Serves 6 to 8

My husband's favourite.

Ingredients:

6 oz plain chocolate
6 oz unsalted butter
6 oz sugar
6 egg yolks
¼ pint whipping cream

Method:

1. Melt chocolate in a double pan over steaming water.
2. Cut butter into lumps.
3. Add sugar and egg yolks, one by one, making sure the mixture does not get too hot so the eggs curdle.
4. Finally stir in a few lumps of butter at a time until all are absorbed.
5. Remove chocolate mixture from heat and transfer into a bowl.
6. Whisk egg whites until stiff.
7. Fold whites into the chocolate mixture.
8. Fill some small ramekins (i.e. small china pots), and leave to set overnight.
9. Pipe some cream on top of each ramekin.

Variation:

Place stoned, stewed prune pieces or apricot pieces with a teaspoon of brandy at the bottom of each ramekin before you fill them.

Note:

The French have delightful little 'pots au chocolate' – delicate little china pots with lids, especially for chocolate mousse. They would make a useful gift for a wedding.

POOR KNIGHTS
Serves 2 to 4

Ingredients:

4 slices white bread (remove crust and don't cut the bread too thinly, about ⅓")

Batter:

1 egg
1 ½ cup milk
1 tbs. flour
pinch salt
2 tbs. melted butter

Accompaniment:

Jam
¼ pint whipped cream

Method:

1. Whisk egg and milk.
2. Sprinkle on flour, while whisking.
3. Add salt.
4. Dip each slice of bread in the batter. Use a spatula.
5. Fry in butter, (not oil), on both sides in a frying pan until slightly brown.
6. Keep hot while you fry the rest of the slices.
7. Spread jam on each slice, if you heat the jam it is easier to spread.
8. Decorate with a dollop of whipped cream.

Note:

This dish exists all over Europe. It can be used as a breakfast dish, served with bacon instead of jam and cream. It is a very economical dish and a good way to use up stale bread.

CLARET JELLY
Serves 8 to 10

Ingredients:

1 bottle of ordinary claret
1 packet of blackcurrant jelly + 1 sachet gelatine, (3 tsp.)
¼ pt. hot water
3 oz caster sugar
¼ pt. whipping cream, for decoration

Decorate with real flowers or crystallized violets

Method:

1. Put gelatine in a few tablespoons of hot water to dissolve. Shake pan while the gelatine melts.
2. Cut up jelly into pieces and dissolve in the ¼ pt. of hot water.
3. Combine gelatine and jelly and add the sugar.
4. When all is dissolved add the wine, slightly warmed.
5. Finally taste for sweetness (add more sugar if necessary as wine varies in sweetness).
6. Pour into 8 glasses or into a glass bowl.
7. Leave to set in the fridge.
8. When set, decorate with whipped cream.
9. Just before serving, decorate each portion with crystallized violets or with real flowers e.g. nasturtiums. Real violets are especially nice, if you can get them!

Note:

This is a very elegant Victorian dish, especially good after a large rich main course, perhaps followed by an old fashioned savoury, instead of cheese, for instance:-

Savouries:

Scrambled eggs on toast with capers decorated with anchovies.
Welsh Rarebit – melted cheese with mustard and Worcester sauce on toast.
Stewed, stoned prunes, rolled in bacon and baked and served on toast.
Tinned oysters wrapped in bacon, grilled and served on toast.

In Scandinavia, hot open sandwiches, which are often 'gratinée', are very popular supper dishes.

PORT & PRUNE FOOL

Serves 6 to 8

Ingredients:

1 lb. dried prunes
4 fl. oz (wine glass) of Ruby Port
6 oz caster sugar
½ pt. double cream (or ¼ pt. cream + ¼ pt. Greek yoghurt)

Method:

1. Soak prunes for 2-3 hours (if necessary) and stew them gently just covered by water and 4 oz sugar.
2. When really soft (30 minutes), cool.
3. Remove stones and Magimix with about 4 tbs. of their cooking juice.
4. Taste the purée, you may not need to add any more sugar.
5. Add port.
6. Finally fold in whipped cream.
7. Pour into individual glasses or ramekins and leave to thicken in the fridge for 2-3 hours.
8. Serve with almond biscuits.

BAKLAVA
Serves 10 to 12 people – makes 2 dozen squares

This is a Greek, sweet pastry, suitable to serve with the coffee as a dessert.

Ingredients:

1 lb. filo pastry
12 oz melted butter
1 lb. chopped walnuts or almonds
4 oz sugar
1 tsp. cinnamon

For the syrup:

juice of 1 lemon
1 lb. runny honey
3 cloves
1 tsp. cinnamon
½ pint water

Method:

1. Divide filo pastry sheets very gently into 2 piles for the two tins. Also divide up filling into 2.
2. Butter two Swiss roll trays, 12" x 8".
3. Lay 2 sheets of filo on one of the baking sheets, one on top of the other and brushing each with melted butter.
4. Sprinkle half the nuts, sugar and spice over the pastry.
5. Arrange the next 3 layers of filo over the top, again brushing each layer with melted butter.
6. Repeat the above with the rest of the filo on the second baking sheet.
7. Press edges of pastry down, and with a very sharp knife, cut the pastry in each tray into 12 diamond shapes.
8. Boil the syrup ingredients for 10 minutes.
9. Bake pastries at 180° C for 1 hour, until golden.
10. Pour hot syrup over the Baklava and allow to stand for ½ a day before eating.

FRIED BANANAS WITH
BUTTERSCOTCH SAUCE

Serves 6

For vanilla ice-cream or fried bananas.

Ingredients:

2 oz butter
6 oz dark brown soft sugar
2 tbs. golden syrup
3 tbs. cream or evaporated milk

Method:

1. Melt butter, sugar and syrup in a saucepan.
2. Add cream and bring to boil. Boil gently for 2-3 minutes.
3. Ready to serve hot on ice cream or poured over a cake.
4. If used in the latter way, scatter with almond slivers for decoration.

RECIPE WITH BANANAS

Method:

1. Pour the butterscotch sauce into a frying pan.
2. Add 1 small, peeled banana per person.
3. Cook gently in the sauce until the bananas are soft. If sauce browns a little bit too much, take off the heat and cool with a little milk.
4. Serve scattered with slivers of almond.

Scrumptious!

LINZER TORTE
Serves 12

Ingredients:

For the pastry:

6 oz plain flour
8 oz butter
6 oz ground almonds
5 oz caster sugar
2 egg yolks
½ tsp. each of ground cinnamon and cloves
grated rind of 1 lemon
1 tsp. vanilla essence

Filling:

1 jar raspberry jam

milk and egg to brush the pastry
icing sugar for decoration after the pastry has been baked

Method:

1. Mix flour and spices with almonds.
2. Cream butter and sugar until soft and fluffy.
3. Add the flour and beat until smooth.
4. Add yolks, vanilla and lemon rind and mix well.
5. Put on a plate and place pastry, covered, in the fridge to cool for one hour.
6. Use a 9" flan tin, preferably with a loose base, or use a pretty china quiche dish.
7. Press ¾ of the dough into the flan tin.
8. Spread with jam, (warmed if necessary, it spreads more easily).
9. Roll out the rest of the pastry into long thin sausage shapes.
10. Place them like the spokes on a wheel over the jam securing them to the sides. (Do not put pastry over the sides of the tin as you cannot then remove the pastry from the tin.)
11. Brush pastry with milk and egg.
12. Bake in a medium oven (180° C) for 45-55 minutes.
13. Cool before attempting to loosen cake from tin. It is easier to serve straight from the tin.
14. Sprinkle with icing sugar before serving.

Note:
Keeps for several days in the fridge. Makes a fairly solid rich cake, so serve in thin wedges only. My Austrian friend gave me a present of a real Linzer torte as she lives near the town of Linz. I was amazed to find that the commercial version was not quite as nice as the one above.

SOUFFLÉ GRAND MARNIER WITH CARAMELIZED ORANGES

Serves 6 to 8

This is a grand finale to a meal.

Ingredients:

3 eggs
6 oz caster sugar
2½ tsp. gelatine
½ pt. double cream
2 tbs. Grand Marnier

Method:

1. Put gelatine in a saucepan with a little water.
2. Warm slowly and shake pan from time to time until liquid is clear.
3. Separate eggs and whisk yolks with sugar over simmering water until white and foaming.
4. Add Grand Marnier and gelatine dissolved in a little hot water and whisk again in a bowl over cold water.
5. Place in the fridge until *almost* set.
6. Beat whites with a pinch of salt.
7. Beat the cream.
8. When the mousse is beginning to set, first fold in the whipped cream.
9. Then fold in the whipped whites.
10. Place in a large glass bowl and leave to set in the fridge.

Serve with: **CARAMELIZED ORANGES**

Ingredients:

6 oranges
4 oz caster sugar
2 tbs. brandy – optional

Method:

1. Peel oranges and remove pith.
2. Slice them fairly thinly and arrange in a heat-proof dish.
3. Keep juice.
4. Melt sugar in 4 tbs. water, until beginning to brown.
5. Sprinkle orange juice and brandy over the oranges.
6. Pour the caramel over the oranges.
7. Serve with orange soufflé.

SOUFFLÉ WITH ORANGES & LYCHEES

Serves 6

Ingredients:

3 eggs
6 oz caster sugar
3 tsp. gelatine
¼ pt. orange juice
1 tin of lychees, keep ¼ pt. lychee juice
pinch of salt
½ pt. double cream
1 orange
lemon juice to taste

Method:

1. Dissolve gelatine by placing in a little water in a saucepan.
2. Warm slowly shaking the pan until the heat melts the gelatine. It should be clear.
3. Separate eggs and whisk yolks with sugar.
4. Add orange juice, lychee juice and half the lychees pureed in the blender.
5. Add the gelatine and little lemon juice to taste.
6. Place in the refrigerator until almost set.
7. Whip cream, – keep a little back for decoration.
8. Fold cream into the mousse, and then the whipped whites.

To serve:

Put in individual glass dishes, leave to set.
Pipe a little rosette of cream onto each mousse.
Decorate with a slice of orange and a lychee.

HILDA'S FRUIT SALAD
Serves 12

This is an interesting rich mixture of fruit, dried, tinned and fresh. You can add a touch of freshness by adding apple slices.

Ingredients:

1 lb. large prunes – pre soaked
½ lb. dried apricots – pre soaked
½ lb. dried peaches – pre soaked
½ lb. dried pears – pre soaked
1 tin guavas
1 tin lychees
½ pt. orange juice
grated rind of 1 orange
4 tbs. orange liqueur, or a glass of sherry, (optional)
vanilla pod

Method:

1. Cook prunes, pears and peaches in water until soft.
2. Cook apricots with a vanilla pod, in orange juice until barely soft.
3. Cut pears and peaches into strips.
4. Drain the tinned fruit (reserve these juices).
5. Mix together with orange juice.
6. Remove vanilla pod.
7. Stir in Grand Marnier or sweet sherry (4tbsp).
8. Add some of the reserved juices from the tinned fruit if necessary.
9. Leave to mature for several hours.
10. Serve with cream.

Note:

If you have any of this fruit salad left after the party, eat it for breakfast with yoghurt and muesli.

PASKA

a Russian Easter pudding
Serves 10

This is a very rich pudding to celebrate the end of the fast.

Ingredients:

1 lb. curd cheese
8 oz cottage cheese
8 oz cream cheese
4 oz unsalted butter
1 tsp. vanilla essence
3 egg yolks
1 oz mixed glacé fruits
2 oz chopped almonds
½ pt. double cream
6 oz caster sugar
grated peel of 1 lemon
1 tbs. lemon juice
¼ pt. single cream

Method:

1. Magimix cottage cheese and mix with curd and cream cheeses.
2. Beat in softened butter, with egg yolks, sugar, vanilla, lemon peel and juice.
3. Whisk cream and fold in with the almonds and glace fruits, chopped.
4. Line a 2 pint pudding basin with wet muslin. (See note below).
5. Fill with mixture and cover with muslin.
6. Leave overnight in fridge.
7. Turn out on a plate.
8. Remove muslin.
9. Place on a serving dish and pour over the single cream.
10. The pudding can be decorated with some glace fruit, including cherries and some almonds.
11. Serve in very small helpings, to be eaten with a teaspoon.

Accompaniment:

Thin almond biscuits.

Note:

I have been told that you can make this pudding by lining a plastic flower pot which has a hole (for drainage) in the bottom with muslin and packing the curd mixture into it.

319

SLICE NAPOLEON
Serves 6

Ingredients:

2 packs frozen Puff Pastry (I recommend Jus-rol pastry, 375g, 2 sheets ready rolled out)

Pastry cream: (a thick kind of custard)

4 egg yolks
2 dsp. sugar
2 tsp. cornflour
½ pt. warm milk
½ tsp. vanilla essence

Other ingredients:

½ pt. double cream, whipped
strawberry jam
icing sugar for icing the top of the cake
4 oz caster sugar
1 tbs. flaked almonds

Method: to make custard (creme patisserie)

1. Mix egg yolks and sugar and milk in a saucepan over steaming water.
2. Mix cornflour with a little cold water and add to the milk mixture.
3. Heat gently almost to boiling point, stirring continuously to stop eggs from curdling.
4. Lastly, add vanilla essence.

You now have a very thick custard which gets even thicker when it gets cold.

While the custard is cooling, bake the pastry as follows:

Method:

1. Roll out puff pastry into three rectangular sheets 12" x 3".
2. Bake at 200° C on oven trays for 20-25 minutes, until well risen and golden.
3. When cool, place one of the sheets on a long serving tray.

Method: to make icing

1. Sieve 1 cup of icing sugar.
2. Mix with 1 to 2 tbs. of cold water, until you have a smooth paste.
3. Brush this glaze over the top of the cake.

4. Decorate top with flaked almonds, before icing is set.

To assemble cake:

1. Cover base of the first pastry sheet with jam and then pastry cream.
2. Put a second sheet of pastry on top of the first.
3. Cover this top sheet with the whipped cream.
4. Finally place last pastry sheet on top and brush some icing on it.
5. With a sharp serrated knife cut cake into 6 slices each 2" or more wide.

BREAD & BUTTER PUDDING

Serves 4

Ingredients:

6 slices of currant bread
1 oz sultanas
3 whole eggs + 1 extra yolk
2 oz caster sugar
1 pt. milk
½ tsp. vanilla essence
butter

Method:

1. Butter shallow porcelain or Pyrex baking dish.
2. Soften butter slightly in microwave and spread on slices of currant bread.
3. Cut each slice into 4.
4. Arrange squares in lines in the buttered dish.
5. Sprinkle with sultanas.
6. Heat milk.
7. Add sugar.
8. Cool slightly.
9. Add vanilla.
10. Pour milk over bread.
11. Leave to stand for 1 hour.
12. Bake at 200° C until risen and set, about 40 minutes.

Serve warm with cream or custard.
Decorate with caster sugar sprinkled on top.

TOSCA APPLES
Serves 4 to 6

Any recipe that involves the word 'Tosca' has toffee with it, in some form.

Ingredients:

5-7 sour apples – e.g. Granny Smiths
2 oz flaked almonds
50 g. butter
3 oz brown sugar
1 tbs. flour
2 tbs. milk or cream

Method:

1. Peel and core apples and cut them in half.
2. Place flat side down in a buttered oven dish.
3. Mix butter, sugar, flour with milk or cream and simmer until you have a glossy sauce.
4. Pour over the apples.
5. Bake at 200° C for about 30 minutes. (Watch that they don't brown too much.)

Serve warm, scattered with flaked almonds. Vanilla ice cream is good with this dish.

RHUBARB CRUMBLE

Serves 4

Ingredients:

4 to 6 sticks of rhubarb
3 tbs. sugar – or to taste
1 tbs. cornflour

Crumble:

4 oz plain flour
2 oz sugar
4 oz butter

Optional: 1 oz of chopped nuts

Method:

1. Wash rhubarb and cut into 1" pieces.
2. Place in a greased oven dish.
3. Mix cornflour and sugar and sprinkle on top.

For the crumble:

1. Mix flour, sugar and nuts if used.
2. Cut butter into cubes and crumble into the flour with your finger tips.
3. Spread over fruit.
4. Bake at 225° C for about 20 minutes until rhubarb is tender and the crumble has coloured slightly.

Note:

Sometimes I stew the rhubarb, gently, with sugar to soften it before I put it in the oven dish.
You could add 3 tbs. of porridge oats to the crumble mix to give extra texture.

REAL VANILLA SAUCE (Custard)

Serves 6

Note:

Ideally this sauce is made with vanilla sugar, which is 4 tbs. of sugar which has had a vanilla pod steeped in it for a couple of weeks. Alternatively you could boil the milk without the eggs in it, but with a vanilla pod in it for a little while. You then add the eggs while whisking.

Ingredients:

1¼ pints milk
2 eggs
3 tsp. cornflour
2 tbs. sugar
1 tsp. vanilla essence
¼ pt. cream, whipped (optional)

Method:

1. Mix milk, eggs, cornflour and sugar in a pan.
2. Bring almost to the boil whilst stirring continuously. DO NOT boil as the egg will curdle.
3. When cool add vanilla and softly whipped cream.

Note:

This makes a fairly runny custard but if you like it thicker, increase the amount of cornflour by 2 to 3 teaspoons.

BANOFFI PIE
Serves 8

Note:

This fairly modern recipe has become universally popular. It is a very funny but a delicious sweet; all the skill you need is to boil some tins!

Ingredients:

3 small tins of sweetened condensed milk
2 bananas
½ pt. cream

Pastry:

6 oz flour
3 oz butter
1 dsp. sugar
a little water to mix

Method:

1. Boil tins unopened and covered in water for 3 hours.
2. Cool the tins and open them and pour the toffee-like substance into a bowl.
3. Meanwhile, make the pastry and bake it blind in a china baking dish, in the oven for about 15 minutes at 200° C.
4. Slice bananas.
5. Whip cream.
6. Pour the toffee mixture into the flan.
7. Arrange bananas on top.
8. Pipe the cream on top.

Note:

As an alternative to the pastry case, you can do a simple biscuit base consisting of 6 oz of crushed digestive biscuits, (a rolling pin does the job well), mixed well with 2 oz melted butter. Press the mixture into the flan and leave to cool in the fridge.
Then fill flan as above.

BANANA SOUFFLÉ
Serves 4 to 6

Ingredients:

2 eggs – separated
1 sachet gelatine – about 3 tsp.
3 tbs. caster sugar
4 ripe bananas
¼ pt. whipping cream
1 dsp. lemon juice

For decoration:

Flaked, toasted almonds

Method:

1. Whip egg yolks and sugar until white and thick.
2. Dissolve gelatin in ½ cup of hot water over a low heat and shaking the pan all the time until the liquid is clear.
3. Crush the bananas really well with a fork and mix with the egg mixture.
4. Whisk the whites until stiff.
5. Whisk the cream until fairly stiff.
6. Fold in first the cream and then the whites, into the banana mixture.
7. Put it in a nice glass serving bowl.
8. Leave to set in the refrigerator for 2 to 3 hours.

BAKED ÅLAND PANCAKE
Serves 8

This is a rather solid pancake, traditionally made on the beautiful Åland islands between Sweden and Finland. It is delicious eaten hot or cold with jam and perhaps some whipped cream. The pancake has a special texture because it incorporates rice porridge. Anything with this number of eggs in it and rice, which had to come all the way from China, used to be considered as a great treat.
Åland is a group of islands. Their inhabitants sailed all around the world in their sailing boat.

Ingredients:

6 eggs
4 oz sugar
2 cups of half-cooked (20 minutes) rice porridge made with 3 tbs. pudding rice and ½ pt. milk
6 oz plain flour
2 tsp. ground cardamom, if not available, use cinnamon
3 pints milk
pinch of salt

Method:

1. Make the rice porridge.
2. Boil rice in a little water for 20 minutes and then add just enough milk, a little at a time to achieve a thick porridge which is almost cooked.
3. Whisk the eggs, salt and spice together.
4. Add the flour and some milk.
5. Add the porridge.
6. Add the rest of the milk.
7. Place in a large, shallow oven dish, well buttered.
8. Cook for 45 minutes to 1 hour at 200° C until golden and slightly brown.
9. Serve warm or cold, with jam and whipped cream.

Note:

This can be served as a cake as well as a dessert.

STRAWBERRY SHORTCAKE

Serves 8

Ideal for a summer lunch or garden party.

Ingredients:

8 oz plain flour
2 tsp. baking powder
½ tsp. salt
3 tbs. caster sugar
6 oz butter
3 tbs. milk

Filling:

½ pt. double cream
1 lb. strawberries

Method:

1. Mix flour, baking powder and salt.
2. Cut butter into cubes and rub in.
3. Finally add the milk, to form a stiff dough.
4. Cut the dough in half.
5. Roll out each half into a circle to fit two identical tart tins which have been well oiled or lined with greaseproof paper.
6. Bake the shortbread bases at 160° C for 30 to 40 minutes.
7. Cut each round disk into 8 pieces while still warm.
8. Cool on a wire rack.

How to assemble the cake:

1. Beat the cream until stiff.
2. Rinse and hull the strawberries and cut the biggest ones in half.
3. Assemble one disk of shortbread to form the base.
4. Spread cream over the top.
5. Place the other 8 segments of shortbread on their edge like the blades of a turbine.
6. Decorate with strawberries between these shortbread 'blades'.

QUEEN VICTORIA'S
FAVOURITE PUDDING
Serves 6 to 8

Ingredients:

½ pint milk
2 egg whites
½ oz (3 tsp.) gelatine
2 tbs. caster sugar
2 tbs. water
3 tsp. orange flower water
½ pint double cream
4 oz ratafia biscuits (almond macaroons)

Decoration:

glacé cherries
angelica

Method:

1. Add gelatine to water and heat gently until it is dissolved.
2. Heat the milk.
3. Add gelatine, sugar and orange flower water to the milk.
4. Leave to cool.
5. Beat cream.
6. Beat egg whites.
7. Crush 3 oz Ratafia biscuits. Keep some whole for decoration.
8. Add cream to the milk (keep some back for decoration). Make sure it is well distributed.
9. Fold in egg whites and Ratafia biscuits.
10. Put in a nice glass dish and leave to set.

To decorate:

Halve the cherries and cut the angelica into sticks.
Pipe the remaining cream onto the pudding.
Decorate with cherries, angelica and the remaining Ratafia biscuits.

Note:

Do not worry if the pudding separates a little, leaving the milk at the bottom. It will still all be delicious, very light, with a delicate, old fashioned flavour.

SOUTH AFRICAN BRANDY TART

Serves 8

This is a luscious, moist gateau which can be served either as a pudding or for tea. It was given to me by my South African friend Dr. Odie Robey.

Ingredients:

1 cup finely chopped dates
1 cup boiling water
1 tsp. bicarbonate of soda
2 oz butter
pinch of salt
1 egg
2 oz sugar
1 cup plain flour
1 tsp. baking powder
½ pint cream
2 oz walnuts

For the syrup:

1 cup sugar
¾ cup water
1 tsp. vanilla
½ oz butter
¼ cup brandy

Method to make the cake:

1. Prepare 2 x 8" sandwich tins.
2. Cream butter, sugar and egg.
3. Pour boiling water and soda over dates.
4. Sieve the dry ingredients together.
5. Add dates to creamed butter.
6. Add dry ingredients and mix well.
7. Divide cake batter between the two flan tins. (7-8")
8. Bake for approximately 20 minutes at 200° C.
9. Leave to cool on a wire rack.

Method to make the syrup:

1. Simmer water and sugar gently for 5 minutes. (It is best to dissolve the sugar before boiling it.)
2. When sugar is dissolved, boil it to thicken it.
3. Add butter and continue simmering until the mixture begins to thicken.
4. Add brandy and vanilla.

To assemble:

1. Place one of the cakes on a plate and, while the cake is still warm, pour ½ the syrup over it.
2. Place the other cake on a separate plate and pour the rest of the syrup over it.
3. Whip the cream.
4. Chop the nuts.
5. When cakes and syrup are cool put half the cream on one of the cakes and spread it evenly.
6. Place the other cake on top.
7. Decorate with the rest of the cream and the nuts.

CHOCOLATE CHESTNUT CHARLOTTE RUSSE
Serves 10

This is a sumptuous rich dessert suitable for Christmas time. Note: You need a cake tin with detachable sides and base.

Ingredients:

2 packets boudoir biscuits
1 x 15oz can of sweetened chestnut purée
½ oz gelatine
4 tbs. rum or brandy
½ pt. double cream
¼ pt. single cream
3 egg whites
grated rind of 1 orange
8 oz dark chocolate
3 oz butter
flaked almonds or chopped walnuts for decoration

Method:

1. Grease and line the base of a 7" cake tin, with detachable sides and base.
2. Trim the boudoir biscuits to fit the depth of the tin.
3. Beat the chestnut spread in a bowl until smooth.
4. Dissolve the gelatine by heating gently in the rum or brandy.
5. Beat thoroughly into the chestnut purée.
6. Combine the two sorts of cream and whisk into soft peaks and fold into the chestnut purée.
7. Whisk the egg whites until very stiff and fold into the mixture.
8. Pour about 1" of this mixture into the tin.
9. Arrange the Boudoir biscuits around the edge of the tin with the sugar-coated side outwards.
10. Pour in the rest of the chestnut mixture and leave to set in fridge for 6 hours or overnight.

For the sauce:

1. Melt the chocolate with the butter and orange rind over a low heat.
2. Beat until smooth.
3. Leave to cool slightly.
4. Turn out the cake onto a dish, by loosening the sides of the tin.
5. Pour the chocolate sauce over it.
6. Decorate with flaked almonds or chopped walnuts.

SOLEIKA
Serves 6 to 8

A very rich, festive dessert with Russian origins.

Ingredients:

For the cake:

4 large egg whites
6 oz caster sugar
4 oz ground almonds
1 heaped tsp. plain flour
1 pinch baking powder

For the sauce:

4 large egg yolks
3 oz single cream
2 oz butter
1 tsp. vanilla essence
1 oz split almonds
1 tsp. cornflour
a little green vegetable colouring (optional)

Method for the cake:

1. Heat the oven to 150° C.
2. Prepare a 9" sandwich tin by greasing it with butter and sprinkling it with equal quantities of fine breadcrumbs and flour.
3. Whip egg whites until stiff.
4. Fold in the sugar.
5. Mix ground almonds with the flour and baking powder and fold into the egg whites.
6. Bake for 30 to 40 minutes till golden brown.
7. Leave to cool slightly before turning out onto a serving dish. (If too hot when turned out it may break and if too cold it will stick!)

Method for the sauce:

1. Bring single cream almost to boiling point in the top of a double saucepan. You can use a small saucepan placed in a larger one containing simmering water.
2. Whip egg yolks in a basin with cornflour.
3. Pour on scalded cream while whisking continuously.
4. Return to the double saucepan.
5. Cook, stirring, until the custard begins to thicken.
6. Remove from the stove.

7. Add vanilla and the butter gradually, in small pieces, stirring all the time.
8. Leave sauce to cool, stirring it from time to time.
9. Rub the split almonds in a very small amount of green colouring.
10. Finally assemble cake by pouring the sauce over the cake and decorate it with the green almonds.

Note:

Do not put the gateau in the refrigerator. It needs to be served at room temperature.

PECAN PIE
Serves 6

This pie can also be made with walnuts.

Ingredients:

Shortcrust pastry made with 6 oz flour and 3 oz butter in the usual way, by rubbing fat into flour and adding a little water to hold the dough together

For the filling:

2 oz butter
4 oz demerara sugar
4 eggs
½ small tin golden syrup
4 oz pecans or walnuts (whole)
1 tsp. vanilla essence
½ tsp. salt

Method:

1. Cream the butter and sugar.
2. Beat in the eggs, one at a time.
3. Stir in the golden syrup, vanilla and salt.
4. Finally, fold in the pecans or walnuts.
5. Line a 9" sandwich tin with the pastry.
6. Bake it 'blind' for about 15 minutes until cooked.
7. Leave to cool.
8. Fill with the pecan/walnut mixture.
9. Bake pie for about half an hour at 180° C, or until a knife inserted in the filling comes out clean.
10. Keep an eye on the tart so the nuts do not get too brown.
11. Serve warm or cold.

ENGLISH CHOCOLATE CHEESECAKE

Serves 6

Ingredients:

For the base:

6 oz digestive biscuits
1½ oz melted butter
1 tsp. cinnamon

Method:

1. Crush the biscuits with a rolling pin.
2. Mix with melted butter and cinnamon.
3. Pack into a china flan dish.
4. Chill for 30 minutes.

Filling:

8 oz cream cheese
2 eggs, separated
4 oz plain chocolate
½ pint double cream
3 oz caster sugar
½ oz gelatine
1 tbs. brandy (optional)

Method:

1. Beat cream cheese with sugar.
2. Add yolks to the mixture.
3. Dissolve gelatine in water at low heat.
4. Melt chocolate in a pan over boiling water, or in the microwave.
5. Add gelatine and chocolate to the cream cheese with the brandy, if used.
6. Whip cream and fold in.
7. Whisk egg whites until stiff and fold in.
8. Fill base with the cream cheese mixture. Chill and decorate with a little grated chocolate. (A Flake bar is good for this, slightly crumbled.)

EASY RHUBARB FOOL

Serves 6

Make a rhubarb compôte or buy it ready made. The French have a good version of it, and can be found in English supermarkets.

Ingredients:

6 oz rhubarb purée (home made or bought)
approx. 6 fl. oz ready made custard
6-8 fl. oz double cream

Method:

1. Stew ½ lb. of washed and chopped rhubarb with 3 to 4 oz sugar. Add hardly any water. Cool and break down the rhubarb by stirring.
2. Whip the cream.
3. Add custard to rhubarb, followed by the whipped cream.
4. Stir gently.
5. Taste for correct amount of sweetness.
6. Fill 6 dessert bowls with this mixture.
7. Leave to set, preferably over night.
8. Decorate with a few halved green grapes.

Serve with some delicate biscuits or shortbread.

COEUR À LA CREME
Serves 10 to 12

Ideally this should be made in a heart-shaped mould and preferably one with holes in it so that any excess whey can drain away, but this is not strictly necessary. It is served in the Summer time with fresh red fruit.

Make the cream cheese pudding the day before you are going to use it and keep it chilled in the fridge.

Ingredients:

½ lb. cream cheese
¼ lb. curd cheese
¼ lb. cottage cheese
¾ pint double cream
2 egg whites
1 tsp. vanilla essence
a pinch of salt
3 tbs. caster sugar

Method:

1. Magimix cottage cheese to get rid of granular texture.
2. Mix in with the other cheeses.
3. Add vanilla and sugar and mix in well.
4. Whip cream until in soft peaks and fold into the cheese mixture.
5. Whip egg whites until stiff, with a pinch of salt, and fold in gently.
6. Use a 9" cake tin lined with cling film and fill the tin with the cheese mixture.
7. Cover with cling film.
8. Place in the refrigerator till the following day.
9. To turn out, remove cling film and invert onto a plate.
10. Serve in small portions with fresh or stewed red fruit or plain, covered with single cream and sprinkled with caster sugar.
11. 'Langue de chat' biscuits are also very nice with this dish.

Savoury version:

Omit sugar and reduce cream to ½ pint. Add ½ tsp. salt and 3 tbs. chopped chives.

Serve with Bath Oliver biscuits.

COLD LEMON SOUFFLÉ

Serves 6

Ingredients:

3 large eggs
grated rind and strained juice of 2 lemons
6 oz caster sugar
½ oz gelatine
3 or 4 tbs. water
¼ pt. double cream
¼ pt. double cream for decorating
crystallised lemon slices

Method:

1. Separate yolks from whites.
2. Cream yolks and sugar until white.
3. Add lemon rind and juice.
4. Place in a double boiler and whisk over gentle heat until thick and mousse-like.
5. Remove from heat and whisk until cold. (Place the container in a bowl of cold water to accelerate the process.)
6. Add gelatine to a little water and dissolve by heating gently.
7. Add dissolved gelatine to the egg mixture.
8. Whip the whites until soft peaks and fold into the mixture.
9. Whip both lots of cream. Use one half to fold into the mousse.
10. Turn mousse into a glass dish and allow to set.
11. When set, decorate with the rest of the whipped cream, piped, and some crystallized lemon slices.

HOT LEMON SOUFFLÉ
Serves 6

A very impressive end to a meal. Hot soufflés are not so difficult to make, but they will sink quickly if kept waiting.

Ingredients:

2 tbs. butter
2 tbs. cornflour
½ pt. hot milk
pinch of salt
grated rind of 1 lemon
3 tbs. lemon juice
5 egg yolks
6 egg whites

Method:

1. Melt butter and add cornflour. Cook for 2 minutes on low heat.
2. Add hot milk and salt to the cornflour mixture and whisk until smooth.
3. Add rind and juice of lemon.
4. Cool sauce a little.
5. Beat in egg yolks with sugar and add to the sauce.
6. Beat egg whites until they are stiff, but not dry, and fold into the mixture.
7. Prepare a soufflé mould – a round pottery or glass oven dish with straight sides – by spreading it with butter and sprinkling lightly with sugar.
8. Bake at 180° C for 35 to 45 minutes until well risen and golden.
9. Do not open the oven door!

Eat at once, or it might sink!

MALAKOFF TORTE

Serves 8

A rich charlotte russe with chocolate and coffee.

Ingredients:

2 packs sponge fingers
2 tbs. rum or brandy
3 oz plain chocolate
6 oz sugar
6 oz butter
1 egg yolk
3 cups strong coffee – slightly sweetened

For decoration:

¼ pint whipped cream

Method:

1. Oil a pudding basin and line with foil, or use a small rectangular cake tin (it is easier).
2. Place coffee in a bowl and add 1 tbs. of the rum or brandy.
3. Dip sponge fingers lightly into the coffee mixture and line a pudding basin with them, including the base.
4. Put chocolate in a double boiler to melt (or in a microwave).
5. Cream sugar and butter.
6. Add the chocolate and the remaining tablespoon of rum or brandy and the egg yolk to the butter.
7. Put a layer of the butter cream on the bottom layer of biscuits.
8. Add a layer of sponge fingers dipped in the coffee mixture. These lie horizontally in the centre of the cake.
9. Then again a layer of the chocolate mixture.
10. Continue until the chocolate mixture has finished.
11. Cut off any tips of the sponge fingers that protrude above the mixture.
12. Cover with foil and leave overnight in the fridge.
13. Take off the top foil; loosen sides with a knife and very gently invert pudding onto a plate. Peel off the rest of the foil.
14. Decorate with rosettes of whipped cream.

Note:

Serve in small portions.

OLD-FASHIONED CURD TART

Serves 6

Ingredients:

8 oz curd cheese
2 eggs
3 oz caster sugar
1 lemon – peel and juice

For pastry:

3 oz margarine
3 oz lard
6 oz plain flour
pinch of salt

Method:

1. Make pastry by rubbing fats into flour and salt.
2. Add a little very cold water to bind the mixture.
3. Line a 7½" (19cm) tart tin with it.
4. Prick it and bake 'blind' in the oven at 200° C for 15 minutes.
5. To make the filling, mix curd cheese with caster sugar, lemon rind and juice.
6. Whisk eggs together and add them.
7. Fill the cooked case with the mixture and bake at 180° C for about 25 minutes.
8. Serve as a pudding with single cream.

SUMMER PUDDING

Serves 8 to 10

A surprisingly good pudding considering it only contains bread and stewed fruit.

Ingredients:

2 lbs. ripe plums
1 lb. strawberries
1 lb. raspberries
some redcurrants (if available)
½ lb. dark coloured fruit-like blackberries or bilberries
1 pack of medium sliced, white bread
sugar to taste (approx 4 tbsp.)
double cream for pouring

Method:

1. Wash fruit.
2. Hull strawberries.
3. Remove stalks from red or black currants.
4. Chop the larger fruit, leaving the small fruit intact.
5. Put a very small amount of water in a saucepan and add the fruit.
6. Add sugar and bring to the boil.
7. Simmer for about 5 minutes.
8. Test for sweetness.
9. Drain off some of the excess juice but keep it.
10. Remove crusts from bread.
11. Line a 2 pint basin with the bread, bottom and sides, leaving no gaps.
12. Fill with fruit.
13. Place some more bread on top, again leaving no gaps.
14. Place foil on top of the fruit, then a saucer and a weight, e.g. an unopened tin of fruit.
15. Leave in fridge overnight.
16. Turn out just before serving and pour over reserved fruit juice.
17. Cut into wedges for serving.

Note:

The domed pudding may collapse a little but that does not affect the flavour.

Serve caster sugar and cream with it.

PROFITEROLES
(SWEET OR SAVOURY)
Serves 4

Choux pastry:

These little buns can be filled with either a sweet or savoury cream.

Ingredients:

2 oz flour
1 oz butter
pinch of salt
vanilla essence
1 small egg + ½ egg yolk
¼ pint water

Coffee icing:

8 oz icing sugar
1 to 2 tbs. strong instant coffee

Filling:

½ pint cream, whipped and slightly sweetened, for filling buns

Method:

1. Sieve flour and salt.
2. Boil water and butter in a small saucepan.
3. Add flour all at once.
4. Beat well, on the stove, until mixture forms a dough and leaves the sides.
5. Take off the heat.
6. Cool slightly.
7. Add vanilla, then the egg yolk and whole egg, beating well.
8. Fill a piping bag with a large nozzle and pipe small amounts on a dampened baking sheet.
9. Bake at 220° C for 10 minutes.
10. Lower heat to 190° C for a further 20 minutes, until golden.
11. Cool on a wire rack.
12. Cut a slit in the side of each bun while still hot.
13. Whip the cream and add a little sugar.
14. When buns are perfectly cold, pipe a little cream into each bun.
15. Make icing by sifting icing sugar and adding 2 tbs. hot water flavoured with instant coffee gradually into the sugar.
16. Add enough water to make the icing like thick single cream.
17. Brush on the filled buns.

Note:

If you use the buns for savoury cocktail snacks, fill them with blue cheese mixed with cream cheese and lightened with unflavoured whipped cream so that you get an even piping consistency. Omit top glaze.

WINTER FRUIT SALAD

Serves 4

Ingredients:

1 tin plums in syrup (remove stones)
1 apple washed and cubed
one bunch of seedless grapes
3 kiwi fruits
1 orange or pink grapefruit

For the juice:

retain the syrup from the plums
1 glass red wine
2 tbs. sugar

Method:

1. Stone and drain the tinned plums.
2. Place in a bowl.
3. Add apple, washed and halved grapes, kiwi fruit peeled and sliced and orange or grapefruit peeled and sliced. Cut the orange pieces into small segments.
4. Add the wine, sugar and some of the plum juice.
5. Toss together and chill.

BAKING RECIPES

LEMON CAKE

Serves 6

Ingredients:

4 oz butter or margarine
4 oz caster sugar
2 eggs
1 tbs. lemon curd
1 oz ground almonds
rind of a lemon
4 oz self-raising flour

Topping:

2 oz caster sugar
juice of one lemon

Method:

1. Grease a 6" or 7" cake tin.
2. Set oven on 180° C.
3. Cream butter and sugar until light and fluffy.
4. Add beaten eggs gradually.
5. Stir in lemon curd and ground almonds.
6. Add lemon rind and fold in the flour.
7. Pour mixture into baking tin and level off top.
8. Bake for approx. 55 min. until golden.
9. Mix together the caster sugar and the juice of one lemon to make the topping.
10. While still hot pour topping over the cake.
11. Leave to cool.

Delicious!

CHOCOLATE CAKE

Serves 10

Ingredients:

6 eggs
6 oz caster sugar
6 oz soft margarine
6 oz self-raising flour
1 tbs. cocoa mixed with 2 tbs. hot water
1 tbs. milk

Filling:

4 oz butter
6 oz icing sugar
6 oz chocolate
1 tbs. rum or brandy, optional

Covering:

4 oz caster sugar
8 oz plain chocolate

Method to make the sponge:

1. Beat together the sugar and margarine.
2. Add cocoa in water.
3. Add eggs with some flour, one at a time.
4. Add milk and fold in rest of flour.
5. Put into a greased and floured cake tin and bake at 180° C, until well risen and springy on top (about 50 minutes).
6. Leave overnight, if possible, on a cake rack, upside down, to flatten top and cover with foil.

Method to make the Filling:

1. Melt chocolate.
2. Soften butter with icing sugar and beat until fluffy.
3. Add chocolate and spirit if used.
4. Slice the cake in half horizontally.
5. Spread filling over the bottom half and place the top of the cake over it.
6. Prepare covering and spread it over the cake and sides.

Method to make the Chocolate covering:

1. Dissolve sugar in 4 tbs. water.
2. Boil until you get a thick syrup.
3. Cool a little.
4. Melt chocolate in microwave and stir the syrup into it.
5. Add a few drops of oil.

Decorate with chocolate vermicelli, or crumbled Flake bar.

Suitable for a very special occasion.

BANANA CAKE

Serves 6

Ingredients:

5 oz self-raising flour
¼ tsp. bicarbonate of soda
1 ripe banana
2 oz soft margarine
1 egg
5 oz castor sugar
½ tsp. vanilla essence
¼ tsp. salt

Method:

1. Place egg, banana, margarine, sugar, vanilla essence and salt in a liquidizer and blend to a smooth consistency.
2. Sift flour with bicarbonate of soda into a bowl and pour the liquidized mixture over it.
3. Mix well.
4. Place in a greased loaf tin with only the bottom of the tin lined.
5. Bake approximately 40 minutes until well risen and firm, on gas mark 4, 180° C.

VANILLA CAKE (SPONGE)

Serves 6

Ingredients:

2 eggs
1½ cups sugar
2 tbs. vanilla sugar (or 1tsp vanilla essence)
1½ cups flour
2 tsp. baking powder
1 cup boiling water
100g melted butter

Method:

1. Whisk eggs, sugar and vanilla until fluffy.
2. Add melted butter.
3. Mix flour with baking powder.
4. Add to eggs.
5. Carefully fold in the boiling water.
6. Pour batter into a greased and crumbed cake tin.
7. Bake at 175° C for 30 or 40 minutes.

Note:

This cake is very useful as a base for gateaux filled with fruit, cream, jam , crème patissère (thick custard) or butter icing.

SAND CAKE
Serves 8

Ingredients:

200g butter
200g sugar
3 eggs
1 cup flour
1 cup cornflour
1 tsp. baking powder
1 tbs. vinegar

Method:

1. Cream butter and sugar until fluffy.
2. Add one egg at a time.
3. Mix the flour with the cornflour and baking powder.
4. Fold into the egg mixture, add vinegar.
5. Bake in a prepared loaf tin for 45 minutes at 175° C.

Note:

This cake is very delicious and 'short' – not like a usual sponge.

SPICE CAKE
Serves 6

Ingredients:

150g warm butter (i.e. at room temperature, not melted.)
2 cups sugar
3 eggs
2 tsp. mixed spice
3 cups flour
5½ fl oz yoghurt
1 tsp. bicarbonate of soda

Method:

1. Work butter with sugar until fluffy.
2. Add 1 egg at a time.
3. Then the flour mixed with spices and bicarbonate of soda.
4. Finally add the yoghurt.
5. Pour mixture into a prepared cake tin.
6. Bake at 175° C for 45 minutes to 1 hour.
7. Allow cake to cool before turning out.

ELVI'S PASTRY

Serves 8

Very short and delicious.

Ingredients:

1 lb. plain flour
5 oz hard and 5 oz soft margarine
pinch of salt
1 tbs. caster sugar
¼ pint water

Method:

1. Mix the flour, salt and sugar.
2. Cut the hard and soft margarine with a knife into the flour mixture.
3. Pinch lightly with your finger tips until you achieve the texture of breadcrumbs.
4. Add a little water, if necessary, to form a dough.
5. Cover dough with clingfilm and put in the fridge for about an hour before rolling out.

Note:

Elvi is a Finnish friend of mine who always makes beautiful cakes and pastries. This is her recipe for a rich pastry for Fruit pies.

TERHI'S STICKY TEA LOAF
Serves 6

Prepare a moderate oven (180° C) Gas 4.
Grease a 2 lb. loaf tin.

Ingredients:

6 oz granulated sugar
½ pint milk
6 oz mixed dried fruit
8 level tbs. golden syrup OR 6 tbs. black treacle AND 2 tbs. marmalade
12 oz self-raising flour
½ tsp. mixed spice

Method:

1. Place first 3 ingredients in a saucepan over a low heat until sugar is dissolved.
2. Add golden syrup OR black treacle and marmalade and mix well.
3. Add flour and mixed spice.
4. Mix well and pour into the tin.
5. Bake for ¾ to 1 hour. If cooked the loaf should spring back when touched.
6. Leave in tin to cool for at least 5 minutes before turning out.

I usually make double amount and use one whole 1 lb. tin of black treacle.

HEALTHY FRUIT LOAF

Serves 6

Recipe given by Olive Jung.

Use a tin size 8 x 4 x 2½".

Ingredients:

1 heaped cupful Allbran
1 heaped cupful caster sugar
½ cupful of mixed dried fruit
1 cup milk
1 heaped cup of self-raising flour

Method:

1. Place Allbran, sugar and dried fruit in a bowl.
2. Stir in the milk, leave to stand for one hour.
3. Stir in the flour.
4. Pour into greased tin and bake for 1 hour at gas mark 4, (electricity 180° C).

Note:

This recipe does not contain any fat so must be very good for slimmers, especially with all that bran. Also good for constipation, of course!

DATE CRUNCHIES
Serves 12

Recipe given by Margaret.

Ingredients:

8 oz flour
4 oz rolled oats
3 oz sugar
5 oz margarine
12 oz dates
grated rind of 1 lemon
2-3 tbs. water

Method:

1. Put flour, oats and sugar into a basin.
2. Melt the margarine.
3. Add to the dry ingredients and mix well.
4. Chop dates. Put them in a pan with grated lemon rind and water and heat until mixture is soft (10 minutes).
5. Spread half the dry mixture over the bottom of a greased Swiss roll tin.
6. Spread with the date mixture and sprinkle the rest of the dry ingredients on top.
7. Bake in a moderate oven at 180° C for approx. 1 hour.
8. Leave to get cold before cutting into fingers or triangles.

CRISPY BISCUITS

Serves 30 biscuits

Ingredients:

4 oz soft margarine
3 oz sugar
1 tsp. golden syrup
3 tsp. boiling water
1 teacup porridge oats
3 oz self-raising flour
½ tsp. baking powder

Method:

1. Cream margarine, sugar, syrup and boiling water.
2. Then work in dry ingredients.
3. Place teaspoons of the mixture on a greased baking tray.
4. Bake for 15-20 minutes at 180° C.

Makes about 30 biscuits.

GINGER BISCUITS

Serves 12 to 15

Ingredients:

4 oz butter or margarine
1 tbs. golden syrup
6 oz self-raising flour
3 oz caster sugar
1 level tsp. ground ginger
1 pinch bicarbonate of soda

Method:

1. Melt fat and syrup together.
2. Mix well.
3. Add other ingredients.
4. Roll dough into a sausage about 1½" diameter and slice fairly thinly.
5. Put slices on an ungreased baking tray in the oven at 180° C for 12 to 15 minutes.
6. Turn out to cool on a wire rack.

SAND BISCUITS

Serves 15 to 20

These delicious Finnish biscuits are unusual in that they are shaped by a teaspoon, to form little shell-like biscuits.

Ingredients:

200g. (7 oz) butter
250g. (9 oz) caster sugar
1 tsp. vanilla essence
¾ tsp. baking powder
300g. (10 oz) plain flour

Method:

1. Heat the butter until it is light brown, but do not burn it.
2. Leave to cool.
3. Add sugar and vanilla essence.
4. Mix flour with baking powder and add to the mixture.
5. Shape by filling a teaspoon generously with the mixture, pressing it firmly into the spoon.
6. Turn out onto a baking tray.
7. Bake at 350° C for about 15 minutes.

GREEN CAKE – (celebration cake)

Serves 12

This cake is called 'Princess Cake' in Sweden.

Ingredients:

Cake:

4 eggs
4 oz sugar
4 oz flour
6 tbs. water
2 tsp. baking powder
1 tsp. vanilla essence

To decorate the cake:

2 packs marzipan
1 lb. warm jam
green food colouring
icing sugar

Filling:

1 large tin peach slices
½ jar of apricot or other jam
1 pint double cream

Method to make the sponge:

1. Whisk sugar and eggs until very thick.
2. Add boiling water gradually.
3. Add vanilla.
4. Sieve flour with baking powder and fold in the egg mixture.
5. Grease a 9" cake tin with butter and sprinkle with fine breadcrumbs.
6. Pour the cake mixture into the tin and bake at 180° C until done (top feels springy) 35-45 minutes.
7. Leave to cool a few minutes before turning out on a cake rack.
8. When cold slice twice horizontally, so you have three layers. Not so difficult on a cutting board with a serrated knife.

To prepare the marzipan:

1. Knead marzipan with a <u>few</u> drops green food colouring, until a <u>pale</u> green colour is evenly distributed.
2. Put a piece of foil or greaseproof paper on the table.

3. Cover rolling pin and paper with icing sugar and roll out marzipan until slightly thicker than a £1 coin.
4. Roll into a circle.
5. Measure the diameter of the cake and 2 sides (about 13").
6. Cut a circle on the marzipan of this diameter.
7. Leave to one side. (Keep the rest of the marzipan).

To assemble the cake:

1. Heat jam and cover 2 bases and top of cake with jam.
2. Drain peaches.
3. Whip cream.
4. Place the bottom part of the cake on a serving dish.
5. Place half the peach slices on the jam.
6. Place a third of the whipped cream on the peaches.
7. Top with the middle layer of the cake and repeat putting the peaches and cream on top.
8. Top the middle layer with the last layer of cake.
9. Spread with the rest of the cream.
10. Lift up your marzipan circle and cover the cake with it.
11. The marzipan should cover the top and sides and form a pretty green 'skirt' to the cake.
12. Cut out some leaf shapes from the remaining marzipan.
13. Fix these with a little bit of jam, on the top of the cake.
14. Finish off with a layer of sieved icing sugar dusted over the marzipan.

You can add tiny birthday candles stuck into the marzipan, if required.

A great cake or pudding for a celebration.

RYE BREAD (Helen's)

Serves 8 to 12

Ingredients:

2 oz fresh yeast
1½ cups warm water
1 dsp. salt
1 small carton yoghurt
½ cup chopped rye grains
just over 3 cups coarse rye flour
2 cups white flour
1 tbs. sugar

Method:

1. Mix the yeast and warm water – let it froth.
2. Add the other ingredients, except for rye grains, and mix together with a little sugar to form a sticky dough.
3. Set it to rise for 1 hour in a warm place.
4. 'Knock back' the dough and shape into loaves, which are placed in greased loaf tins.
5. Leave them to rise again for 20 minutes.
6. Pierce with a fork and brush with salty water, sprinkle with rye grains.
7. Bake 1 hour at 200° C on lowest oven shelf.

Note:

Makes delicious, solid, black bread. Cut into thin slices and eat with plenty of butter.

MARGARET'S SHORTBREAD

Serves 16 pieces

Makes 2 x 6" flan tins.

Ingredients:

12 oz plain flour
8 oz unsalted butter
4 oz caster sugar + 2 tbs. caster sugar for the top
pinch of salt

Method:

1. Pour flour and salt into a bowl.
2. Cut up butter into little squares and with your hands knead them into the flour, until you have a mixture resembling breadcrumbs.
3. Now add sugar and start kneading as if for dough.
4. Gradually the mass will adhere to form a ball.
5. Press into greased flan tins (½" thick).
6. Smooth top and make stripes with the back of a fork.
7. Bake at 170° C for 40 minutes or until golden.
8. Take out of oven and cool in tin for 2 minutes.
9. Sprinkle with caster sugar, then cut in tin into wedges.
10. Remove when cool.

Note:

Keeps well for weeks in airtight tin.

KARELIAN PASTIES

Serves 12 to 15

This is one of the great dishes of Finland, made with ingredients that you can find on every farm. They are a ubiquitous accompaniment to every meal at weddings and funerals. The farmers' wives used to vie with each other, who could make the finest pasties.

The pastry should be rolled out so thinly that you can see seven church spires through it! The dish is a surprising in the way it shows up the lovely flavours of the rye flour with the contrasting one of the boiled rice and the two are crowned with the wonderful mixture of egg and butter.

Karelia is the eastern part of Finland which the Russians took after the war, and from which the inhabitants all moved to Finland. The half a million people who came, then represented 10% of the population of the country who had to be re-housed and found work. Karelia had inspired much music and literature, including Jean Sibelius's Karelia suite.

Ingredients:

1 cup water
1 tsp. salt
1+⅓ cup of plain flour
1+⅓ cup of rye flour

Filling:

Rice porridge made with 1½ cups pudding rice 1½ cups water and as much milk as it takes to make a thick porridge. Season with ⅓ tsp. salt.

For dipping the pasties:

2 cups boiling water
2 oz butter

Egg butter garnish:

3 hard-boiled eggs roughly chopped and mixed with 2 oz softened butter seasoned with salt and white pepper

Method:

1. Mix water, salt and the 2 kinds of flour until you have a supple dough.
2. Roll out the dough into a long sausage.
3. Cut into 1½" lengths.
4. Roll out each little piece of dough into an oval shape which will be quite large (size of a hand) if the pastry is thin enough. Continue in the same way until the

pastry is used up.

Prepare the porridge:

1. Boil rice in water and gradually add milk and seasoning.
2. Leave to cool slightly.

Prepare the garnish:

1. Hard-boil eggs, chop and work the butter until soft.
2. Add egg to butter and season with salt and pepper.

To assemble pasties:

1. On each piece of oval pastry, place a heaped dessert spoonful of porridge but leave ½" of pastry bare at the edges.
2. Flatten out the porridge to cover neatly.
3. Turn the edge of the pastry over onto the edge of the porridge but not covering it.
4. Pinch the edge all round to make a decorative finish.
5. Bake in a very hot oven, 275° C for 10 minutes.
6. As soon as they are baked – they should have some brown flecks on the rice – take them out with a spatula and dip them in the hot water and butter mixture.
7. Pile the pasties on top of each other and cover with a clean tea cloth.

To serve:

Warm pasties before serving and place a heaped teaspoon of the egg butter on top of each pasty. You normally eat these with a knife and fork on a little side plate though I have served them in cocktail size to be eaten with your fingers.

This is an example of how simple ingredients can be made into something very delicious and popular with most people.

A challenge to make, but worth it!

BEIGNETS – (FRENCH FRITTERS)

Serves 6 to 8 large fritters

My Mother had an Aunt, who lived in a very pretty farmhouse about 10 miles from us. She was an excellent cook, and I have never forgotten her very tasty smoked ham and fried 'buns' as I call them. I used to feel very sick on the bus that took me to her, but survived the journey by thinking of these buns that she served to us with a cup of coffee when we arrived.

Ingredients:

6 tbs. water
1 tbs. butter
6 tbs. flour
4 eggs
1 tsp. vanilla essence
2 tbs. caster sugar
oil for frying

Garnish:

icing sugar

Method:

1. Place the first three ingredients in a pan and boil on low heat for 5 minutes.
2. Add the eggs, one at a time and beat the batter well between each addition.
3. Finally add the vanilla.
4. Heat a large frying pan and pour a layer of oil on the bottom.
5. Pour in the batter, ½ cup at a time.
6. Place them well apart.
7. Cook until one side is brown and then turn over.
8. When golden and puffed up, remove with a spatula onto greaseproof paper.
9. Dust with icing sugar when cool.

Note:

This reminds me of a Dutch delicacy. Some Dutch friends of mine introduced me to a special doughnut shop where they sold 'Pfofferties'. This was a little wooden hut in the middle of a park, where they served these fried doughnuts, smothered with icing sugar. Batter was poured from jugs into round hollows in a large, cast iron slab which was heated on top of a huge stove. The little doughnuts were turned over and cooked very quickly. You were served a dish of these, perhaps ½ dozen on a plate, drenched with icing sugar. It was a *wonderful* treat and such an interesting thing to discover on a Sunday morning!

YOGHURT CAKE
Serves 8

This is a moist plain cake that is very easy to make.

Ingredients:

2 eggs
1¼ cup oil
1½ cups sugar
2 cups mixed, dried fruit
2½ cups self raising flour
vanilla essence
1½ cups plain yoghurt

Method:

1. Mix all ingredients together, putting the dried fruit in last.
2. Add a little milk if the mixture is too stiff.
3. Butter a loose-bottomed cake tin.
4. Fill it with the cake mixture.
5. Bake at 180° C for about 1 hour or until the cake begins to leave the sides of the tin.
6. Leave to cool on a rack.

Given to me by a South-African doctor. It is a very good, everyday cake and good for picnics.

DRINKS, PARTY SNACKS & DIPS
(ENTERTAINING)

COLD CANAPÉS
FOR A LARGE PARTY
Serves 50 to 80 people

Savoury eats:

Triple decker sandwiches, filled with egg, cream cheese and sardines.
Asparagus rolls.
Eggs, stuffed, curry flavour, or anchovies.
Vol-au-vents with prawn mayonnaise flavoured with dill.
Canapés with blue cheese and egg butter, decorated with red grapes.
Triple cheese quiche.
Crostini with chicken liver, onion and sage.
Crostini with egg mayonnaise, capers and gherkins.
Cold frikadeller (meat balls) served with mustard.

Sweet things:

Cream-filled choux buns with coffee icing.
Strawberries dipped in chocolate.
Green marzipan birthday cake, if appropriate.
Fresh dates, stone removed, filled with cream cheese or blue cheese.
Dried dates, stone removed, filled with Danish Blue or Marzipan.

Please note that not everybody has everything, and some people are happy with 4-5
pieces, others clear the decks!

HOT & COLD CANAPÉS
FOR A GARDEN PARTY

COCKTAIL FOOD

I like to leave a few things ready on the table as the guests arrive; then bring the rest of the eats in over a period serving the cold dishes before the hot ones and finishing off with something sweet.

This menu is suitable for a garden party in the summer.

On the table:

A tray of:

- Stuffed Greek olives
- Sliced cervelat sausage (like salami)
- Cubes of fetta cheese in olive oil. Serve with cocktail sticks

Another tray with:

- Crisps
- Pistachio nuts
- Home-baked almonds

THREE DIPS surrounded by crudités (sticks of celery, carrot and florets of cauliflower) or crisps

- Avocado dip
- Cream cheese dip with garlic
- Houmous dip (Chickpeas)

Cold canapés:

- Halved small hard boiled eggs stuffed with curry flavoured filling
- Small triple-decker sandwiches filled with egg mayonnaise, mashed sardine and cream cheese.
- Smoked salmon on brown bread canapés
- Spiced herring on black bread canapés
- Sliced French Sticks with German liver sausage and gherkins
- Sliced French Sticks with roasted peppers in olive oil garlic and herbs.

Hot canapés:

- Spicy meatballs with tomato sauce (served separately)
- Small cabbage pasties

<u>Suggested sweets</u>:

- A dish of small melon slices and hulled strawberries.

<u>Suggested drinks</u>:

- Pimms
- Fruit cup
- Wines

TRIPLE-DECKER SANDWICHES
FOR COCKTAIL PARTIES
Makes 24 mini sandwiches

<u>**Ingredients**</u>:

8 slices of white bread, thinly cut from a large loaf
8 slices of brown bread, thinly cut from a large loaf (this makes four packs of
sandwiches – each pack contains 4 slices of bread)
3 tins of sardines in tomato sauce (most of the sauce removed)
4 hard boiled eggs, chopped
4 tbs. mayonnaise
6 oz cream cheese
butter

<u>**Garnish**</u>:

mustard and cress and cherry tomatoes

<u>**Method**</u>:

1. Butter the bread cutting the top and bottom crusts off only.
2. Mix chopped eggs with mayonnaise and season.
3. Mash sardines in a bowl.
4. Soften cream cheese slightly with a wooden spoon.

Serve on a plate, decorated with mustard and cress and cherry tomatoes.

Suitable for vegetarians who eat fish.

Note:

This is a complicated recipe to make, but not at all difficult once you remember that you use 2 white and 2 brown slices for each pack which you then cut into 6 little sandwiches and that you try to alternate the colour of the bread. The fillings can be made the day before, and so can the sandwiches.

Figure 1.

Brown Bread
Sardine filling
White Bread
Egg Filling
Brown Bread
Cream Cheese
White Bread

Figure 2. To cut the filled stack of bread. You will get six triple-decker cocktail sandwiches.

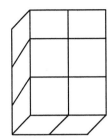

CABBAGE PASTIES

Serves 2 large pasties or 30 small ones

Ingredients:

short-crust pastry, buy ready-made (2 packs of 500g)

Filling ingredients:

1½ lbs. white cabbage
4 oz butter or margarine
1 pint water or stock
salt
1 dsp. brown sugar
1 dsp. white wine vinegar

Method:

1. Melt the butter in a large saucepan.
2. Chop the cabbage finely, removing the core.
3. Combine with the butter and add water, a little bit at a time, with the sugar and the seasoning and vinegar (if used).
4. The cabbage should change colour slightly, without really browning, and become quite tender. This generally takes about 1 hour, on low heat.
5. Allow to cool.
6. Roll out the short crust pastry to fit a 2 x 10" tart tin.
7. Fill them with the cabbage and bake for 40 minutes at 180° C.

Alternatively:

1. You can make small individual pasties, by rolling out small pieces of pastry into rounds.
2. Place some cabbage on one half of the pastry and turn the other half of the pastry over so that you have a half-moon shaped pasty.
3. Brush these with egg and milk wash before baking.

Serve warm with drinks.
A surprisingly delicious pastry dish. They were once specially ordered by the Finnish Tourist Office for their Christmas party.
Also an example of how delicious food can be made with very cheap ingredients.

CROSTINI

Serves 20

These Italian canapés taste even better on thick, white, country bread fried as suggested. They are rustic so need not look too neat and uniform.

CROSTINI WITH CHICKEN LIVERS

The bread (Thin bread stick):

1 day old thin baguettes, sliced obliquely into 20 slices and fried lightly in olive oil

For the topping:

3 oz softened butter
1 lb. frozen chicken livers
2 onions, finely chopped
2 cloves garlic, crushed
some rosemary and a bay leaf
2 glasses of red wine
seasoning

For decoration:

2 tomatoes, thinly sliced

Method:

1. De-frost chicken livers, trim and halve them.
2. Fry 5 to 8 minutes in a frying pan, a few at a time, until golden and still pink inside.
3. Add some oil to the pan and fry the chopped onion and garlic.
4. When slightly brown add the chicken livers, the wine, herbs and seasoning.
5. Cook for 10 minutes. Remove bay leaf.
6. Drain the juice off and mash liver etc. with a fork, returning a little bit of the juice to make a moist mixture.
7. Add softened butter.
8. Taste for seasoning.
9. Spread a spoonful of this liver mixture on each crostini.
10. Decorate with a tiny slice of tomato.

Note:

This filling can be made the day before.

CROSTINI WITH EGG

Serves 20

Ingredients for the bread:

1 day old thin baguette (bread stick), sliced obliquely into 20 slices and fried lightly in olive oil for frying

For the topping:

1½ cups thick, preferably home-made mayonnaise, slightly flavoured with garlic
8 hard boiled eggs
1 tbs. capers
2 tbs. chopped parsley
3 tbs. chopped gherkins
1 tbs. finely chopped onion
seasoning

Method:

1. Peel and chop the eggs fairly finely in a blender.
2. Mix mayonnaise with the rest of the ingredients.
3. Fold in the chopped egg.
4. Test for seasoning.
5. Spread a spoonful of this mixture on each piece of fried bread.

CROSTINI WITH ROAST PEPPERS

Serves 20

Ingredients for the bread:

1 day old thin baguettes, sliced obliquely into 20 slices and fried lightly in olive oil

For the topping:

3 large yellow peppers
3 large red peppers
olive oil
3 cloves of garlic, crushed
1 tbs. mixed herbs
seasoning

Method:

1. Halve peppers, take out seeds and inner membrane, slice into long strips.
2. Place on an oven dish, generously brushed with olive oil.
3. Scatter with mixed herbs, garlic and seasoning.
4. Sprinkle liberally with olive oil.
5. Cook at 200° C for about 20 minutes.
6. Place some yellow and red peppers on each piece of fried bread and serve.

THREE CHEESE QUICHE
Serves 10 to 12

A firm quiche that cuts well into small portions for finger food. Ideal for cocktail parties.

Ingredients:

Pastry:

4 oz flour, pinch of salt
2 oz butter + 2 oz lard
2 oz cream cheese

Filling:

5 oz cottage cheese
4 oz grated mature cheddar
2 eggs
1 cup milk
seasoning, including 1 tsp. mustard

Garnish:

slices of tomato

Method:

Pastry:

1. Magimix flour and salt with fats.
2. Lastly add cream cheese.
3. Form into a ball. Roll out to fit tin.
4. Press into a 7½" flan tin.
5. Prick and bake 'blind' for 15 minutes at 200° C until pastry looks cooked.

Filling:

1. Mix filling together.
2. Put in the quiche base.
3. Bake about 30-35 minutes on 180° C or until risen and brown.
4. Leave to cool and cut into small wedges.
5. Decorate with tiny slices of tomato.

ASPARAGUS ROLLS

Serves about 20

Ingredients:

1 small loaf of fresh brown bread (not sliced)
1 tin green asparagus spears
butter, softened

Method:

1. Slice bread thinly, butter lightly and remove crust (do NOT use margarine).
2. Drain asparagus.
3. Roll each spear tightly in a piece of bread.
4. Cut off any surplus bread.
5. Cut each roll into 2 or 3 pieces.
6. Arrange the rolls, the opening facing down, into a plastic box.
7. Pack the rolls in tightly, so that they do not open.
8. Place greaseproof paper between the layers.
9. Close box with a tightly fitting lid.
10. Can be made the day before and kept in the fridge. Arrange on a platter with other canapés.

Note:

I was told that a slightly dampened sheet of kitchen paper on top of the rolls keeps them nice and fresh. This really works.

STUFFED EGGS

Serves 20

These savoury eggs can be flavoured in various ways. Here I suggest curry flavouring or anchovy flavouring.

Ingredients:

10 medium eggs, hard-boiled and cold
3-4 tbs. mayonnaise
1 heaped tsp. mango chutney (remove lumps)
1 tsp. hot curry powder
salt and pepper

Garnish:

chopped parsley

Method:

1. Halve the eggs, remove the yolks.
2. Mash yolks and blend with mayonnaise, curry powder, chutney and seasoning.
3. Re-fill the halved egg whites.
4. Decorate with chopped parsley.

Alternative filling:

Add a little very finely chopped onion and 2 anchovy fillets into the mayonnaise, and mixed with the yolks, fill the whites. Decorate with capers or a sliver of olive, or small piece of anchovy.

You cannot use a piping bag as lumps will block the flow.

SMOKED SALMON CANAPÉS

Serves 12

Ingredients:

8 oz smoked salmon, sliced and a good red colour
1 small brown Hovis loaf, sliced
4 oz butter, softened

For decoration:

1 lemon
fennel or dill fronds, otherwise parsley as decoration on the tray

Method:

1. Butter bread.
2. Cut off crusts.
3. Place salmon on each slice to cover completely.
4. Cut off any surplus salmon.
5. With a sharp knife (NOT serrated) cut each slice into 4, diagonally, so you get 4 triangular pieces. (Place a buttered slice of bread on top if you want to make salmon sandwiches.
6. Continue until salmon is used up.
7. Slice lemon thinly, with the peel on. Cut each slice into 8 tiny triangles.
8. Place salmon canapés slightly overlapping, on a plate.
9. Place a triangle of lemon on each slice. (One can eat the lemon decoration).
10. Decorate with fennel, dill or parsely.
11. Cover with clingfilm and refrigerate until ready for use. (Best made same day as the party.)

HERRING CANAPÉS
Serves 12 to 15

Though unfamiliar to some, marinated herrings are very tasty and generally liked at parties. You can buy the herrings in a supermarket in jars or loose. They originate in Denmark. The flavours are:

Herring with onion, or spiced herring, Dill herring, Wine herring, Tomato herring, Mustard herring.

Ingredients:

1 jar marinated herring, ready cut in small pieces
1 pack sliced German rye bread OR
1 loaf black Russian rye bread (Waitrose sell it)
butter

Decoration: (optional)

dill fronds
cherry tomatoes

Method:

1. Butter each slice of bread generously, right to the edge. (This is very important) If you use Russian bread slice it fairly thinly and butter it.
2. Cut each slice horizontally and 3 times vertically so each slice gives you 8 small pieces.
3. Place a piece of herring on each small piece of bread.
4. Arrange neatly on a plate.
5. Decorate plate with dill or fennel fronds and perhaps cherry tomatoes, halved (optional).

I find it hard to grow dill, but fennel, which is so similar though different in flavour, is almost a weed in my garden. Tender fennel fronds make an attractive decoration for fishy canapés.

EGG & BLUE CHEESE CANAPÉS

Serves 6 to 8

This recipe was given to me by a very nice Jewish lady, my landlady in Finland when I was a student.

Ingredients:

2 oz Danish blue cheese
3 oz softened butter
4 eggs, hard-boiled and finely chopped
salt and pepper

Method:

1. Mash the blue cheese and combine with softened butter.
2. Chop hard-boiled eggs in blender. This will only take 1 or 2 seconds.
3. Season eggs and mix well with the cheese and butter paste.
4. Use as a topping for crackers.

CHEESE & HERB STUFFING FOR SMOKED SALMON ROULADES

Serves 4 to 6 as a starter but makes approximately 12 cocktail canapés

Ingredients:

½ lb. of sliced smoked salmon
1 small tub of cottage cheese
¼ lb. of cream cheese
¼ pint tub of crême fraiche or sour cream
2 tsp. finely minced onions
2 tbs. finely chopped parsley
1 tsp. dried dill
juice of ½ a lemon
a few drops of Tabasco
salt and pepper

Method for stuffing:

1. Mix cottage cheese and creme cheese.
2. Add the rest of the ingredients except the salmon.
3. Check seasoning.
4. Cut the salmon into smaller slices.
5. Wrap each piece of salmon around a teaspoon of stuffing to form a roll.
6. Serve on a bed of lettuce as a starter.

Note:

If you use these rolls for cocktails: place each roll on a small piece of buttered pumpernickel bread.

Garnish:

Slivers of black olive may be attached to the salmon with some cream cheese, looks very good!

HOME SALTED ALMONDS
Serves 15

You can get blanched almonds where the skin has been removed but you can easily do it yourself as you see below.

Ingredients:

8 oz almonds
oil
salt

Method:

1. If your almonds have not been skinned, cover them with boiling water and leave for 2 to 3 minutes when it will be easy to rub off the skins, especially if you cut them slightly with a sharp knife.
2. When the almonds have been prepared, grease an oven tray with vegetable oil and scatter the almonds on the top.
3. Turn the almonds around so that they are coated with oil.
4. Sprinkle liberally with salt.
5. Roast in a medium oven, about 180° C.
6. It takes about 10 minutes before the almonds *begin* to brown and a *little bit* longer to turn coffee coloured. They burn very easily so do watch them.
7. Allow to cool.

Note:

One can detect by the smell of the almonds when they are browning. When cool, keep in a screwtop jar. They are much nicer than bought almonds.

CHICKPEA PÂTÉ – (HOUMUS)

Serves 6 as a starter or 12 as a dip

This is a Middle Eastern dish.

Ingredients:

2 x 14 oz tins of chickpeas, drained
3 cloves of garlic, squeezed
2 tbs. lemon juice
1 small cup olive oil OR
4 oz Tahini paste (bought in delicatessens)
a few drops of Tabasco sauce
salt and pepper

Garnish:

black olives
a few mint leaves
a drizzle of olive oil

Method:

1. Blend chickpeas with garlic but leave slightly grainy.
2. Slowly add the oil, lemon juice and seasoning and taste for flavour.
3. Pour into a pottery serving bowl.
4. Garnish.

The home made version of houmus (chickpea paste) is more interesting than the bought variety and not so rich. Good on warm pitta bread for cocktails or starters.

DIPS

A very good base for dips is Philadelphia cream cheese and plain yoghurt. The right texture is important, also the way you stir the mixture, which must be by hand with a wooden spoon, then you can control the consistency.

BASIC GARLIC DIP
Serves 12

Ingredients:

8 oz Philadelphia cream cheese (or other full fat cream cheese)
1 small tub plain yoghurt
1-2 cloves of garlic, squeezed
2 tbs. chopped parsley or chives
salt and white pepper
a few drops of Tabasco

Method:

1. Slowly work the yoghurt into the cream cheese.
2. Add rest of the ingredients.
3. Put into a bowl surrounded by raw vegetable fingers – of cucumber, carrots, celery, cauliflower, peppers etc., or crisps.

Note:

See following pages for recipes for variations to the basic dip recipe.

CREAM CHEESE DIP

Serves 12 for cocktails

Ingredients:

8 oz full fat cream cheese
1 small carton plain yogurt
2 tbs. parsley or chives
salt and white pepper
a few drops of Tabasco or chilli powder

Crudités:

Choose 4 kinds from the following list:
fleshy part of chinese leaves
organic carrots
celery heart
fennel
yellow or orange peppers
cauliflower

Method:

1. Slowly work the yogurt into the cream cheese by hand.
2. Add parsley, salt and pepper.
3. Put into a bowl surrounded by raw vegetable sticks – see crudités above.
Note:

You must not mix cream cheese in a blender or freeze it because it can curdle.

VARIATIONS TO THE BASIC DIP RECIPE

BLUE CHEESE DIP
Serves 12

1. Add 2 oz Danish Blue cheese to some yoghurt and work until smooth. Then add the cream cheese and more yoghurt to make a soft dip. Taste for flavour. Add salt and pepper and more blue cheese if liked.

SPRING ONION & PARSLEY DIP
Serves 12

2. Omit the garlic from the basic recipe and add 3 chopped spring onions and 3 tbs. of finely chopped parsley.

CRAB DIP
Serves 10 to 12

3.
Ingredients:

1 lb. white crabmeat (frozen will do)
1 lb. cream cheese
¼ cup dry sherry
¼ pt. mayonnaise
2 tsp. French mustard
1 tsp. salt
1 tsp. white ground pepper
1 tbs. very finely chopped onion
8 drops Tabasco
2 tbs. lemon juice

Method:

1. Defrost crab and drain.
2. Mix cream cheese with other ingredients.
3. Taste for flavour.
4. Gently stir in the broken crab meat.
5. Check seasoning.

Serve with corn chips, plain white biscuits or Melba toast.

HORSERADISH DIP

Serves 6 to 8

Ingredients:

4 oz cream cheese
1 tub sour cream
1 tsp. lemon juice
1 tbs. horseradish sauce
1 tsp. english mustard

Method:

1. Mix all ingredients together, but do not stir too much as this will make the dip thinner.
2. Serve as a dip with vegetable sticks or crisps, or in small rolls of rare beef (fixed with a toothpick).

GREEN PEPPER DIP

Serves 8

Ingredients:

2 tbs. green peppercorns.
4 oz cream cheese
1 small tub plain yoghurt
1 clove garlic
1 dsp. chopped parsley
salt and pepper

Method:

1. Mash 1 tbs. peppercorns, leaving the rest whole.
2. Stir chopped parsley, squeezed garlic and herbs into cream cheese.
3. Add yoghurt, gradually until you have a soft dip.
4. Add seasoning and the rest of the peppercorns.
5. Check for flavouring.
6. Serve with plain crisps or pieces of Grissini – Italian bread sticks cut into short lengths.

HOW TO SERVE A DIP

With drinks or as part of a buffet. Place a small bowl of dip in the middle of a large plate. Surround the dip with plain crisps, which you dunk into the dip. Or surround with small sticks of fresh vegetables such as carrots, celery, cauliflower, peppers and turnip, and use to scoop up the dip.

The vegetables are much appreciated by slimmers!